Myth a...

Myth and archive

A theory of Latin American narrative

ROBERTO GONZÁLEZ ECHEVARRÍA

Duke University Press   Durham and London

1998

© 1990 Cambridge University Press
This edition © 1998 Duke University Press
Printed in the United States of America on acid-free paper ∞
Library of Congress Cataloging-in-Publication Data appear
on the last printed page of this book.

A la memoria de
Carlos F. Díaz Alejandro

Contents

Preface to the Duke Edition

I wrote *Myth and Archive* spurred by the intemperate ambition to explain to Latin American novelists what they were doing and why. By writing a critical construct about theirs, I hoped to pry away the layers of deceit and self-deceit accumulated over years of pontificating about their own works. I wanted to create a role for the critic's voice in Latin American literature distinct from those of the writers, an urge incited not only by the intellectual challenge, but also by a historical condition known to all but largely unspoken because of the many vested interests involved: the complicity between literature and criticism in Latin America.

Latin American writers all too often fashion themselves as critics, while precious few are the critics who have resisted the temptation to commit a novel, a spate of short stories, or a little book of poems. The results are sometimes ghastly but mostly just tedious and justifiably forgotten. A criticism that is the accomplice of literature is prone to mimicry rather than inquiry and tends to be collusive or self-serving in its value judgments. Literature by critics often reads like a laboratory experiment, poetry or fiction by formula, cast in language that cannot altogether rid itself of academic propriety and retains a penchant for abstraction. There is also the issue of respect. How can a critic who is also only a minor writer claim the authority to judge his superiors? Fortunately obscurity and oblivion are stern judges. Who today reads Angel Rama's collection of stories (*Tierra sin mapa*, 1961) or Mario Vargas Llosa's study of Gabriel García Márquez (*Historia de un deicidio*, 1971)?

There are some exceptions, to be sure. We cannot do without Octavio Paz's brilliant critical essays, but his poetry suffered from his practice of criticism and his ideological *caudillismo:* his lesser poems tend to be somewhat pedagogical, and his allegiance to this or that school of thought left a trail of poetic trash even in his best poems. García Márquez is another exception but in a different sense, for he has never pretended to be a critic. Emir Rodríguez Monegal was yet another because he abstained from literary creation in the conventional manner.

The challenge stemmed from the polymorphous nature of the novel as genre, a discourse without sharp boundaries outside of which to remain clear. In writing *Myth and Archive* this uncertainty was like a Circe call to literature in conflict with the resistance raised by the historical condition mentioned. Could one write only that part of a novel that reflects on its own nature paying its dues to previous practices and conventions? Could the pattern on the back of the tapestry itself be worthy of being the picture? This is the sense in which the book took for me the form of a critical fiction. But the challenge was all the more daunting because of the novel's malleability, which seemed to me chameleon-like in its ability to blend in with other discourses. This process of textual simulation became the plot of my own narrative, the story of my search for the etiology of novelistic forms in Latin America since the colonial period. Given the strategic anti-aestheticism of the novel, this exploration took me into the realms of the law, scientific travel writing, and anthropology. But how could my own discourse not be absorbed by the last of these, precisely because of my effort not to write literature? How can one be meta-discursive without falling back into the novel?

Deep into the quest, which I cannot resist imagining like that of the protagonist in Alejo Carpentier's *The Lost Steps* (1956), I discovered that my own initial interest centered on the link between writing and the law, or more precisely between printing and punishment. This, in turn, revealed that the subplot of *Myth and Archive* was one of escape from mediation, an unattainable dream, transformed into all the tales of flight that novels often tell. These are like the remembered (surface) anecdotes of that elusive dream of flight. How much the writings of Michel Foucault influenced this passion of mine I cannot say for sure beyond what I acknowledge in the book. I tend to believe—or delude myself into believing—that I learned more about literature from Cervantes, Hawthorne, Kafka, and Conrad than from any critic or theorist. Circe's call again? It does not matter. Who can be delusional enough to believe that he has invented something *ex nihilo?* However, I do at least *feel* that I absorb more from the sweetness of literature than from the usefulness of theory, to echo Horace.

Re-reading *The Scarlet Letter* recently I was again struck by the disturbing relationship between writing and punishment in novels: that cabalistic "A" attached to Hester Prynne's body becomes her identity, as though she were indistinguishable from her punishment. In Spanish picaresque novels of the sixteenth century, as well, the narrating self that emerges is entangled with the written law that oppresses it. The pícaro is not a self caught in a cage, he is the bars of the cage. Hence I could not avoid seeing a link between the development of a modern state run by a patrimonial bureaucracy and the appearance of picaresque fiction, in particular Cervantes's work and with it the modern novel. In *Don Quixote,* once the knight and his squire set the galley-slaves free (I, 22), they become fugitives from justice, having committed a grave crime against the Crown. The rest of the novel is—among many other things, to be sure—their flight from prosecution and punishment. Sancho, because his social background makes him more vulnerable, is more aware of the reach of the Santa Hermandad, the vigilante force created by the Crown to persecute lawbreakers through regional jurisdictions. The persistence of the theme of persecution, prosecution, and punishment in the novel since then is conspicuous, from Hugo to Hawthorne, from Dostoyevsky to Kafka, from Faulkner to García Márquez, Fuentes, and Vargas Llosa. In Latin America, Manuel Puig's *Kiss of the Spiderwoman* is yet another re-enactment, perhaps the most brilliant and profound narrative that engages this topic.

Vows, covenants, and all other promises conventionally acquire binding power through writing. (I say "conventionally" because, unless backed up by the threat of violence, such acts are ineffectual—except psychologically—and limited by time and space.) While the instillment of fear is not the exclusive domain of writing, writing does expand its region of influence. Once writing was endowed with an exponentially longer reach by printing, the capacity of language to organize a polity through the submission of great numbers of people over vast territories became possible. This first occurred in Spain and its far-flung empire in the sixteenth century. With the advent of printing, the kingdom was no longer restricted to the realm of the ruler's voice, or that of his mouthpieces. The King's signature ("Yo el rey") could endure and travel far in its written manifestations, and the vehicles that carried his commands were furnished by the notarial arts. Legal rhetoric became the state's verbal arena of power. The *letrados* had to devise a language that would magnify the implicit threats and so constructed a body of texts that pledged to maim, constrain, or annihilate the body of the disobedient subject.

My central contention in *Myth and Archive* is that this is the (dangerous) textual environment in which the novel emerged and evolved. It could very well also be a reflection of the book's own emergence in relation to the archival fictions out of which it presumes to arise. If that is the case, then I have fallen into my own trap and become one with my object of study, which has swallowed me to neutralize my discourse and involve me in the kind of collusive affair from which I fervently wished to escape.

I wrote *Myth and Archive* at the same time as my dear, departed friend Severo Sarduy wrote his novel *Cocuyo*. Both books were published in 1990. I read the novel in manuscript, as I did nearly all of Sarduy's work, suggesting stylistic changes here and there, and gave him my own text to work through (his English was not very good). I remember well how we both laughed and slapped our foreheads in wonder at the unforeseen and totally unplanned coincidences in the two books. Sarduy's autobiographical protagonist works as a young man for a law firm, sleeping in the office at night amidst reams of legal documents. In this portrait of the artist as a young man, the writer arises from the archive. Sarduy was the object (protagonist?) of my *La ruta de Severo Sarduy* (1987), dedicated to me one of his most beautiful novels (*Colibrí* [1984]), and integrated me more than once into his fictional world as a character or an allusion. The opportunities for collusion and the collapse of critical and fictional discourses into each other were certainly many. But whenever Severo tried to influence what I wrote about him, I would protest that Help and Mercy, the dioscuri of his *De donde son los cantantes* (1967), were still separate characters. We had to at least feign the distinct voices of our roles, if only for the sake of discipline.

Just before *Myth and Archive* appeared, García Márquez published what I take to be a new variation of the "archival fiction": *El general en su laberinto* (1989). Along with Carlos Fuentes's *La campaña* (1993), García Márquez's novel about Simón Bolívar's last journey swerves away from the colonial chronicles as origin and toward the post–Independence period in Latin America. Here, instead of the variegated texts of discoverers and conquistadors we have the more premeditated constitutions of the new nations and their redactors closely considered. Bolívar, writer of thousands of letters that make up a voluminous archive, author of the most famous letter in Latin American history (the "Jamaica Letter," 1815), and principal framer of several constitutions, is the spent spark of a second Big Bang: Independence and the creation of the modern Latin American nations. In dealing with one of the untouchables of the Latin American patriotic pantheon, García Márquez may have opened the way for a searing and polemic reevaluation of Latin America's modern history and politics, a project with much more currency and potential for conflict than shaking the foundations of the colonial archive. But, like *La campaña, El general* evolved, not diverged, from previous texts such as *One Hundred Years of Solitude* and *Terra nostra.**

At the end of *Myth and Archive* I speculated about what would come after archival fictions. Six years is not a long enough period to make any final pronouncements; literary history, even today, moves slowly. Still I can discern that in what is being proclaimed as the "postmodern era," a kind of text not animated by anxieties of origin, devoid of identity longings, and innocent of history is touted as the new Latin American writing. Seamless, undifferentiated texts that blend elements of both criticism and fiction are offered as the fresh norm of some hybrid form that is no longer literature. I fail to see the novelty. Besides, there has yet to emerge one such work that commands the kind of attention that archival fictions did. If the Boom was like a golden age, it seems that we are now, at best, in an iron age, to judge by the quality of what is published.

I would be dishonest not to confess that I was very pleased by the reception of *Myth and Archive*, particularly the two prizes that it received. I want to express my deepest gratitude to the juries that bestowed those awards. I was greatly satisfied as well when a Harvard Law School student wrote to me that she had used my book to write her thesis about how, as late as the eighteenth century, the descendants of the natives of Mexico took recourse to the archive to regain some of their privileges (as Garcilaso de la Vega, el Inca, had tried to do before). I have also been amused and even honored by the rumor that, because of the cost of the first edition, illegal xeroxed copies of *Myth and Archive* abounded in graduate and undergraduate courses. I have learned from all the reviews and taken no offense at the disagreements. I am a firm believer in Alfonso Reyes's famous dictum that "entre todos lo sabemos todo" (among us all we know all there is to know), which I suspect has its origin in Vico, one of my favorite philosophers.

I am especially grateful to Reynolds Smith of Duke University Press, whose idea it was to bring out this second edition of *Myth and Archive*, which I thought was destined to become nothing but a myth, and doomed to remain forever in the archive. He is not responsible for

---

* See my "Archival Fictions: García Márquez's Bolívar File," in *Critical Theory, Cultural Politics, and Latin American Narrative*, eds. Steven M. Bell, Albert H. LeMay, and Leonard Orr (Notre Dame: University of Notre Dame Press, 1993), pp. 183–207. Another piece relevant to *Myth and Archive*, dealing with a colonial archivist, perhaps the first, is my "Pedro Mártir de Anglería y el segundo descubrimiento de América," *La Torre* (Universidad de Puerto Rico), nueva época, año 9, no. 33 (1995), pp. 29–52. *The Yale Review* will soon publish an English version.

whatever new blemishes a second look at the book will no doubt expose. From a distance of six years since its publication—which, added to the six it took me to write it, makes an even dozen since its premises first occurred to me—I see the book, like the last Buendía in Melquíades's manuscript in *One Hundred Years of Solitude,* as a single entity that is independent of me, yet somehow contains me. Does this make me an unwitting postmodern?

Roberto González Echevarría
Northford, Connecticut
May 1997

Preface

What I recall as the original idea for this book occurred to me while teaching Cervantes' "exemplary novels" at Cornell around 1975. It seemed to me that in *El casamiento engañoso* and *El coloquio de los perros* Cervantes was probing, as usual, for the origins of fiction, but with a peculiar twist: he made the frame tale a reading scene in which the reader is a lawyer. I thought it was significant that Cervantes should make the reader someone trained in interpreting texts and determining their validity and truthfulness. The story Licentiate Peralta read and could not easily dismiss was, of course, quite fanciful, and herein lies the usual Cervantine irony, but there had to be more to it than an elegant joke. I thought (or so it seems now) that Cervantes was actually unveiling the origins of picaresque fiction, not only by alluding to the notorious climate of delinquency prevailing in those works which calls for the presence of the law in various guises, but more technically to the actual model for the picaresque text: a deposition or confession by a criminal that is addressed to someone in authority. A look back at *La vida de Lazarillo de Tormes* confirmed my intuition. This discovery led me to ponder the origins of the modern novel, and its relation to the law. Many factors contributed to this. One being that I was at the time also reading colonial Latin American texts and contemporary novels by Alejo Carpentier, Carlos Fuentes, Gabriel García Márquez, Severo Sarduy, and others. There appeared to be much about the law in both kinds of texts, and in novels in general outside the Hispanic field. Another that, like most members of my generation, I was concerned with the theory of the novel, which at the time meant Erich Auerbach, Northrop Frye, Wayne Booth, Georg Lukács, Mikhail Bakhtin, and the French structuralists and post-structuralists. It is clearly out of this combination of interests that this book evolved.

I was enormously impressed by all the theory, but it struck me that most of it ignored the Spanish Picaresque, and that all of it insisted on associating the novel with a previous literary form, such as the epic or the Menipean satire. Yet I thought that the Picaresque and Latin American novels could only be made to fit such a genealogical scheme through a good deal of distortion. This dissatisfaction brought me to the theory and history that I expound here, which focuses on the novel's persistent disclaimer of literary origins and its imitation of other kinds of discourse. I perceived vestiges of those non-literary texts in novels such as Carpentier's *Los pasos perdidos*, which takes, at times, the form of a travel journal, and in the preoccupation of Latin American novels with myth in a way that recalled not so much literature as anthropology and even myth-criticism. My persistent, perhaps obsessive, reading of that novel of Carpentier's finally led me to the history that I propose here, with no small measure of help from the theories of Michel Foucault, and some of the work being done today on colonialism and literature.

I consider this book an essay, though I have labored to furnish it with as much corroborative material as possible, and have adhered as best I can to the established norms of academic discourse. But I cannot claim to be an expert on all the areas of Latin American narrative that it covers, and much less in fields such as colonial law, nineteenth-century science or modern anthropology. I bring to these areas an outsider's boldness, which I am afraid is often based on ignorance, but has the advantage, I hope, of freshness of outlook. I also hope to bring to my project an enthusiasm for blurring the frontiers of academic disciplines which has enriched contemporary criticism in the past twenty years or so. However, I would be the first to acknowledge a certain amateurishness in the fields mentioned that would probably take a lifetime to overcome, and it is for that reason that I confess the book to be above all an essay, in the sense of its being an experiment, a deal struck with time, knowledge and my own limitations.

My point of departure is that I do not think it is satisfactory to treat the narrative as if it were a self-contained form of discourse, nor a raw reflection of socio-political conditions. In my view the relationships that the narrative establishes with non-literary forms of discourse are much more productive and determining than those it has with its own tradition, with other forms of literature, or with the brute factuality of history. Narrative and poetry do not follow the same historical path, nor do they change at the same rhythm, hence

I think it is a mistake to write literary history as if it all moved together in the same direction like a vast river. Narrative is too profoundly affected by non-literary forms to constitute a neat historical unit, in the way that perhaps the lyric can. Conventional literary history, following a philological model, masks what I take as the true history of narrative prose. Sarmiento and Euclides da Cunha are more important in that history than José Mármol or Jorge Isaacs. Only by applying mechanically a model of literary history, drawn from European sources, can *Amalia* and *María* play a significant role in the history of Latin American narrative.

This book merely offers a hypothesis about how the Latin American narrative tradition works. But it does not reject others, such as the philological one that aligns novels with novels and sets up genealogies of literary texts, even though it points out what I perceive as their deficiencies. I have learned from all of them, and will continue to do so. My effort has been to expand the field of literary criticism, not to reduce it.

There is a certain serendipity at play when an academic strays from his or her field of expertise. It was my good fortune to meet at Yale's Whitney Humanities Center colleagues from other disciplines such as Clifford Geertz and Nathalie Zemon Davis who unknowingly led me to books and ideas that I would never have encountered among my fellow literati. Even among these I was fortunate to have coincided at the School of Criticism and Theory with Edward Said, from whom I have learned much, and at the Whitney Humanities Center with Christopher Miller, whose work on Africa is so illuminating for Latinamericanists. Yale itself, with its pleiad of critical luminaries, has been an inspiration. I have learned more than they know from my dear friends Harold Bloom, Peter Brooks, J. Hillis Miller and Geoffrey Hartman, who heard or read parts of the book, and from my colleagues at the *Yale Journal of Criticism*, who published part of a chapter.

Bloom sharpened an apprehension with which all who write surely struggle: that whatever method they elaborate or follow is merely a mask for their own self, that perhaps all criticism is a form of autobiography. Although I have consciously attempted to repress this, I have no doubt that there is much in my displaced condition and intellectual career that attracts me to Garcilaso de la Vega, el Inca, and Carpentier's *Los pasos perdidos*. I am certain that even the choice of English, a further effort on behalf of method, brings me closer to the problematic in that novel and in other books discussed in this one. Is my stance ethnographically advantageous because of my expatriate condition? But is not expatriation, real, metaphorical or strategic, the stance of all members of the intelligentsia, as defined by Toynbee in his prologue to the *Comentarios reales*? Mine is perhaps a necessary or enabling fiction about the Latin American imagination or mind, hopefully true to it because of the distance and literary mediations. Whichever the filter may be, personal or communal, my conviction is that, even while attempting to assert its uniqueness (which has not, at least not consciously, been the case here), the self is always subsumed by discourse. My desire has been to be archival, in the sense that the word is used in this book.

Acknowledgments

I have many friends and institutions to thank for their help with this book, so many, in fact, that I am afraid that I will forget some. But I will do my best to name them at the risk of offending those whom I forget. I would like to express my gratitude first to the National Endowment for the Humanities, which funded a year-long seminar for college teachers in which I first tried out some of the hypotheses of the book. The participants in the seminar were patient and encouraging, and I profited much from the dialogue they provided. I should like to name Gwen Kirkpatrick, Ricardo Diez, Alicia Andreu, John Incledon and Ray Green for their friendship and collegiality. The Guggenheim Foundation provided a fellowship that allowed me to travel to Spain to work on and in archives. In Madrid I was given generous help by my friend and publisher José Porrúa, a great bibliophile, and by two colleagues at the University of Madrid: Rafael Núñez Lagos, professor emeritus specializing in notarial documents, and José Manuel Pérez Prendes, currently professor of law.

I should like to thank my longtime friend Peter Brooks, director of the Whitney Humanities Center, where I was a fellow for three unforgettable years during which I wrote most of the book.

Frederick Luciani and Claire Martin assisted me in my research with ability and tact. César Salgado and Sandra Ferdman were teaching assistants in a lecture course for Yale's Literature Major on which I used some of the ideas contained here. Their suggestions have been invaluable. Andrew Bush sent me books from Spain and pictures of pillories from Mexico; Adriana Méndez also sent me materials from Mexico; Leopoldo Bernucci brought me others from Brazil; Stephanie Merrim translated into English portions of chapter 2 that I have incorporated into the text; Gertrui van Acker sent me an article on reading in the colonial period when she was working at the John Carter Brown Library; Carlos J. Alonso lent me his manuscript on the *novela de la tierra* and discussed with me many of the ideas in the book; Vera Kutzinski helped pare down chapter 2 and made innumerable suggestions concerning content and style; Antonio Benítez Rojo enriched my knowledge of history and fiction in Latin America; Silvia Molloy, Nicholas Shumway and María Rosa Menocal, colleagues in the Department of Spanish and Portuguese at Yale, provided much encouragement and many insightful comments. Carlos J. Alonso, Leo Bernucci, Cathy L. Jrade and Jay Williams were generous enough to read the entire manuscript. I cannot express the measure of my gratitude to them for their many valuable corrections and recommendations. Special thanks to John and Carol Merriman, who make Branford College at Yale a haven for scholarship and good fellowship, and to Amy Segal, computer wizard.

This book was written during my six year tenure as chairman of the Department of Spanish and Portuguese at Yale, which also coincided with three as chairman of the Latin American Studies Program. Without the generosity and loyalty of my assistants Mrs. Sandra Guardo and Mrs. Mary Faust, I would never have had the time and peace of mind to finish the book. My debt to them can never be repaid.

Isabel, with her usual forbearance, endured my obsession with this project, and the large and small pains associated with its accomplishment.

Finally, I would like to thank Enrique Pupo-Walker, friend, colleague and editor, for all of his help, encouragement, good humor, and hospitality. Many special thanks also to Betty for untold kindnesses and warmth.

Work on this book really began around 1975, with an article on Ramón Pané. I have made use of ideas from several of my publications, including that article, which go back to those years. These are indicated in the footnotes. But portions of the following articles have been incorporated into the book, sometimes verbatim, at others in revised form (including translation when the piece was originally written in Spanish). I wish to thank the editors of the various journals first for publishing my work, and secondly for allowing me to use the material in this book. The articles, which are naturally not mentioned in the notes, are the following: "*One Hundred Years of Solitude*: The Novel as Myth and Archive," *Modern*

Language Notes, 99, no. 2 (1984), pp. 358–80; "Humanism and Rhetoric in *Comentarios reales* and *El carnero*" in *In Retrospect: Essays on Latin American Literature (In Memory of Willis Knapp Jones)*, edited by Elizabeth S. Rogers and Timothy J. Rogers (York, South Carolina, Spanish Literature Publications Company, 1987), pp. 8–23; "Carpentier y Colón: *El arpa y la sombra*," *Dispositio*, 10, nos. 28–9 (1987), pp. 1–5; "The Law of the Letter: Garcilaso's *Commentaries* and the Origins of Latin American Narrative," *The Yale Journal of Criticism*, 1, no. 1 (1987), pp. 107–32; "Redescubrimiento del mundo perdido: el *Facundo* de Sarmiento," *Revista Iberoamericana*, Special Issue on Sarmiento, no. 143 (1988), pp. 385–406; "Colón, Carpentier y los orígenes de la ficción latinoamericana," *La Torre* (Universidad de Puerto Rico), nueva época, año 2, no. 7 (1988), pp. 439–52.

A clearing in the jungle: from Santa Mónica to Macondo

> The Roman legalistic tradition is one of the
> strongest components in Latin American culture:
> from Cortés to Zapata, we only believe in what is
> written down and codified.
>
> Carlos Fuentes[1]

I

After a painful journey away from the modern world, the protagonist of Alejo Carpentier's *Los pasos perdidos* (1953) reaches Santa Mónica de los Venados, the town founded by the Adelantado, one of his traveling companions.[2] Santa Mónica is but a clearing in the South American jungle on which a few huts have been built.[3] The nameless protagonist has arrived, or so he wishes to believe, at the Valley-Where-Time-Has-Stopped, a place outside the flow of history. Here, purged of civilization, he hopes to rekindle his creative energies, to return to his earlier life as a composer; in short, to be true to himself. The narrator-protagonist plans to write a threnody, a musical poem based on the text of the *Odyssey*. Musical ideas rush to his mind, as if he had been able at last to tap a deep well of creativity within him. He asks the Adelantado, or Founder of Cities, for paper to write all this down. The latter, reluctantly, for he needs them to set down the laws of his new society, gives him a notebook. The narrator fills it very quickly in a frenzy of creativity and begs for another. Annoyed, the Adelantado gives it to him with the admonition that it will be the last one. He is forced to write very small, packing every available space, even creating a kind of personal shorthand, to be able to continue his work. Later, feeling sorry for him, the Adelantado relinquishes yet another notebook, but the narrator-protagonist is still reduced to erasing and rewriting what he has composed, for he lacks the space to move forward. Writing, erasing, rewriting, the narrator-protagonist's belabored manuscript already prefigures the economy of gain and loss of the Archive, the origin unveiled, the mode of current Latin American fiction made possible by Carpentier's novel. Many other such manuscripts will appear in the works of Gabriel García Márquez, Carlos Fuentes and Mario Vargas Llosa as emblems of the very text of the Latin American novel.

When the narrator decides to go back to civilization temporarily, he does so with the intention of procuring enough paper and ink to continue his composition once he returns to Santa Mónica. He does neither. Instead of finishing his threnody, the narrator-protagonist writes a series of articles about his adventures, which he tries to sell off to various publications. These may be, within the fiction, the fragments that lead up to the writing of the text we read, *Los pasos perdidos* (as in other modern novels, an unfinished manuscript represents, within the fiction, the novel in which it appears). The return to Santa Mónica is never accomplished either, for the rising waters of the river cover the inscription on the trunk of a tree that marked the channel to the town. There is writing everywhere in the jungle, but it is as unintelligible as that of the city from which he wishes to escape. The protagonist is caught between two cities, in one of which he must live. What he cannot do is live outside the city, outside of writing.

Two events, related to the need for paper, occur at the same time that the narrator-protagonist is pestering the Adelantado for notebooks. The first is when Fray Pedro, another traveling companion, insists that the protagonist marry Rosario, the native woman with whom he has paired off during his journey upriver. The second is the execution of Nicasio, the leper who raped a girl in the town. The narrator, who has a wife back in the modern world, does not want to subject Rosario to a hollow ceremony and cannot bear the thought of her treasuring a piece of paper from one of the notebooks that he so desires, on which the marriage certificate would no doubt be written. But Rosario, it turns out, has no urge to seal their union according to laws that would tie her down and make her subservient to him. Nicasio, killed by Marcos when the narrator-protagonist is unable to pull the trigger, is said to suffer from the leprosy of Leviticus, that is to say, from the malady that led nomadic tribes to draw up laws excluding those infected with the disease as they settled down in a given place. Marriage and the execution of Nicasio are events that stand at the beginning of the need to write, like the creative impulse of the narrator-protagonist. All three will find their way into the notebooks hoarded by the founder of cities. Writing begins in the city with the need to order society and to discipline in the punitive sense. The narrator-protagonist recognizes that the clearing he seeks is already occupied by civilization:

No sólo ha fundado una ciudad el Adelantado, sino que, sin sospecharlo, está creando, día a día, una *polis*, que acabará por apoyarse en un código asentado solemnemente en el *Cuaderno de ... Perteneciente a ...* Y un momento llegará en que tenga que castigar severamente a quien mate la bestia vedada, y bien veo que entonces ese hombrecito de hablar pausado, que nunca alza la voz, no vacilará en condenar al culpable a ser expulsado de la comunidad y a morir de hambre en la selva ... (p. 268)

Not only had the Adelantado founded a city, but, without realizing it, he was creating day by day a *polis* that would eventually rest on a code of laws solemnly entered in *Notebook ... Property of ...* And the moment would come when severe punishment would have to be imposed on anyone killing an animal in the closed season, and it was apparent that this little, soft-spoken man would not hesitate to sentence the violator to being driven from the community to die of hunger in the forest ... (p. 209)

Writing is bound to the founding of cities and to punishment.[4] The origin of the modern novel is to be found in this relationship, thematic traces of which appear throughout its history, from *Lazarillo* and *El coloquio de los perros* to *Les Misérables*, *Der Prozess*, and *El beso de la mujer araña*.

The reader of contemporary Latin American fiction will no doubt recognize in Santa Mónica de los Venados and the story about the unfinished manuscript – both of the threnody and the novel – prefigurations of Macondo and of Melquíades' writings in *Cien años de soledad* (1967). Carpentier's *Los pasos perdidos* is a turning point in the history of Latin American narrative, the founding archival fiction. It is a book in which all the important narrative modalities in Latin America, up to the time when it was published, are contained and analyzed as in a kind of active memory; it is a repository of narrative possibilities, some obsolete, others leading up to García Márquez. *Los pasos perdidos* is an archive of stories and a storehouse of the master-stories produced to narrate from Latin America. Just as the narrator-protagonist of the novel discovers that he is unable to wipe the slate clean to make a fresh start, so the book, in searching for a new, original narrative, must contain all previous ones, and in becoming an Archive return to the most original of those modalities. *Los pasos perdidos* brings us back to the beginnings of writing, looking for an empty present wherein to make a first inscription. What is found instead is a variety of beginnings at the origin, the most powerful being the language of the law. Thus *Los pasos perdidos* dismantles the central enabling delusion of Latin American writing: the notion that in the New World a new start can be made, unfettered by history. The new start is always already history; writing in the city. Because of his anxiety about origins, the narrator-protagonist's is the quintessential Latin American story and its critical undoing; hence its foundational quality both in terms of Latin American history and the history of the novel. By foundational I mean that it is a story about the prolegomena of telling a Latin American story. For instead of being relieved of history's freight, the narrator-protagonist discovers that he is burdened by the memory of the repeated attempts to discover or found the newness of the New World.[5] *Los pasos perdidos* is the story of this defeat that turns into a victory. In loosening the central constitutive idealization of Latin American narrative from its moorings, Carpentier's novel opens up the possibility of a critical reading of the Latin American tradition; one that would make manifest the stories, including the one of which the narrator is the protagonist, that constitute the Latin American narrative imagination. It is in the process of baring the consciousness of his narrator-protagonist that Carpentier lays out the ruins of that construct as a map for his fresh narrative project. But what are the fragments, the analecta in those ruins, and what do they have to do with the notebooks that the narrator-protagonist seeks from the Adelantado in Santa Mónica de los Venados?

The answer, as a kind of counterpoint, is found in García Márquez' *Cien años de soledad*, a text in which those master-stories are again told and the vestiges of the origin found by Carpentier examined in greater detail. *Cien años de soledad* contains, as in a blow-up, a map of the narrative possibilities or potentialities of Latin American fiction. If Carpentier's novel is the founding archival fiction, García Marquez' is the archetypical one. This is the reason why the Archive as myth constitutes its core.

2

This man had in his possession a leaden box which, so he said, he had found among the ruined foundations of an ancient hermitage, that was being rebuilt. In this box he had found some parchments written in the Gothic script but in Castilian verse, which contained many of the knight's exploits and dwelt upon the beauty of Dulcinea del Toboso, the shape of Rocinante, the fidelity of Sancho Panza, and the burial of this same Don Quixote, together with various epitaphs and eulogies of his life and habits. Such of these as could be read and understood the trustworthy author of this original and matchless history has set down here, and he asks no recompense from his readers for the immense labours it has cost him to search and ransack all the archives of La Mancha in order to drag it into the light.   *Don Quijote*, I, 52[6]

To most readers, the Latin American novel must appear to be obsessed with Latin American history and myth. Carlos Fuentes' *Terra Nostra* (1976), for instance, retells much of sixteenth-century Spanish history, including the conquest of Mexico, while also incorporating pre-Columbian myths prophesying that momentous event. Carpentier's *El siglo de las luces* (1962) narrates Latin America's transition from the eighteenth century to the nineteenth, focusing on the impact of the French Revolution in the Caribbean. Carpentier also delves into Afro-Cuban lore to show how Blacks interpreted the changes brought about by these political upheavals. Mario Vargas Llosa's monumental *La guerra del fin del mundo* (1980) tells again the history of Canudos, the rebellion of religous fanatics in the backlands of Brazil, which had already been the subject of Euclides da Cunha's classic *Os Sertões* (1902). Vargas Llosa's ambitious work also examines in painstaking detail the recreation of a Christian mythology in the New World. The list of Latin American novels dealing with Latin American history and myth is very long indeed, and it includes the work of many lesser known, younger writers. Abel Posse's *Daimón* (1978) retells the story of Lope de Aguirre, the sixteenth-century rebel who declared himself free from the Spanish Crown and founded his own independent country in South America. As the title of the book suggests, Posse's fiction centers on the myth of the Devil and his reputed preference for the New World as residence and field of operations, a theme that had been important in two earlier Latin American masterpieces,

Carpentier's *El reino de este mundo* (1949) and João Guimarães Rosa's *Grande sertão: veredas* (1956).

Given that myths are stories whose main concern is with origins, the interest of Latin American fiction in Latin American history and myth are understandable. On the one hand, Latin American history has always held the promise of being not only new but different, of being, as it were, the only *new* history, preserving the force of the oxymoron. On the other hand, the novel, which appears to have emerged in the sixteenth century at the same time as Latin American history, is the only modern genre, the only literary form that is modern not only in the chronological sense, but also because it has persisted for centuries without a poetics, always in defiance of the very notion of genre. Is it possible, then, to make of Latin American history a story as enduring as the old myths? Can Latin American history be as resilient and as useful a hermeneutical tool for probing human nature as the classical myths, and can the novel be the vehicle for the transmission of these new myths? Is it at all conceivable, in the modern, post-oral period, to create myths? Are the coeval births of the novel and the history of Latin America related beyond chronology? Can a new myth make the New World intelligible? More importantly for our purposes, can a novelistic myth be inscribed in the clearing that the narrator of *Los pasos perdidos* seeks, and is such a myth the archival fiction this novel and others following it turn out to be? Because it is the repository of stories about the beginnings of modern Latin America, history is crucial in the creation of this myth. Latin American history is to the Latin American narrative what the epic themes are to Spanish literature: a constant whose mode of appearance may vary, but which is rarely absent. A book like Ramón Menéndez Pidal's *La epopeya castellana a través de la literatura española*[7] could be written about the presence of Latin American history in the Latin American narrative. The question is, of course, how can myth and history coexist in the novel? How can founding stories be told in this most ironic and self-reflexive of genres? The enormous and deserved success of García Márquez' masterpiece *Cien años de soledad* is due to the unrelenting way in which these forms of storytelling are interwoven in the novel, which thereby unveils the past of the narrative process in Latin America and leads to a consideration of the novel as genre.

It is an uncritical reflex of philologically inspired literary history to think of the evolution of the novel in the same terms as that of other literary genres. This is a vestige of a kind of primitive historicism that is modeled on the natural sciences and which, in the case of the history of conventional literary forms, has yielded impressive results. I do not think that the same can be said of studies on the novel. I am not convinced by theories that attempt to make the novel evolve solely or even chiefly from the epic, or any other literary form. The most persistent characteristic of books that have been called novels in the modern era is that they always pretend not to be literature. The desire not to be literary, to break with *belles-lettres*, is the most tenacious element in the novel. *Don Quijote* is supposed to be the translation of a history written in Arabic, or of documents extracted from the archives of La Mancha; *La vida de Lazarillo de Tormes* is a deposition written for a judge, *The Pickwick Papers* are *The Posthumous Papers of the Pickwick Club, Being a Faithful record of the Perambulations, Perils, Travels, Adventures, and Sporting transactions of the Corresponding Members: Edited by Boz*. Other novels are or pretend to be autobiographies, a series of letters, a manuscript found in a trunk, and so forth. Carpentier once exclaimed that most modern novels were received by criticism with the complaint that they were not novels at all, making it seem that, to be successful, the novel must fulfill its desire not to be literature.[8] He cited as examples *A la recherche du temps perdu* and *Ulysses*. A number of years ago Ralph Freedman made a useful suggestion concerning the origins of the novel:

Instead of separating genres or subgenres artificially and then accounting for exceptions by stipulating mixtures and compounds, it is simpler to view all of prose fiction as a unity and to trace particular strands to different origins, strands which would include not only the English novel of manners, or the post-medieval romance, or the Gothic novel, but also medieval allegory, the German *Bildungsroman*, or the picaresque. Some of these strands may be close to folk material or to classical epics, others may have modeled themselves on travelogues and journalistic descriptions of events, and others again suggest drawing-room comedies and even lyrical prose poetry, yet all, to varying degrees, seem to mirror life in aesthetically defined worlds (life as myth, as structure of reality, as worlds of feeling or quotidian reality) . . .[9]

I wish to retain from Freedman the notion of multiple origins and add that the origin of the novel is repeated, over and over again, only retaining the mimetic act *vis-à-vis* a nonliterary form, not directly as a mirror of life. The novel's origin is not only multiple in space but also in time. Its history is not, however, a linear succession or evolution, but a series of new starts in different places. The only common denominator is the novel's mimetic quality, not of a given reality, but of a given discourse that has already "mirrored" reality.

It is my hypothesis that the novel, having no fixed form of its own, often assumes that of a given kind of document endowed with truth-bearing power by society at specific moments in time. The novel, or what is called the novel at various points in history, mimics such documents to show their conventionality, their subjection to strategies of textual engenderment similar to those governing litera-ture, which in turn reflect those of language itself. It is through this simulacrum of legitimacy that the novel makes its contradictory and veiled claim to literariness. The power to endow a text with the capacity to bear the truth is shown to lie outside the text by narratives that we call novelistic; it is an exogenous agent that bestows authority upon a certain kind of document owing to the ideological power structure of the period, not to any inherent quality of the document or even of the outside agent. The novel, therefore, is part of the discursive totality of a given epoch, occupying a place opposite its ideologically authoritative core. Its conception is itself a story about an escape from authority, which is often its subplot. Needless to say this flight to a form of freedom is imaginary, a simulacrum predicated on textual mimetism that appears to be embedded in narrativity itself, as if it were the *Ur*-story, the irreducible masterstory underlying all storytelling. This is perhaps the reason why the law figures prominently in the first of the masterstories the novel tells through texts like *La vida de Lazarillo de Tormes*, Cervantes' *novelas ejemplares*, and the *crónicas de Indias*. The novel will retain from this origin its relation to punishment and the control of the State, which determines its mimetic penchant from then on. When the modern Latin American novel returns to that origin, it does so through the figure of the Archive, the legal repository of knowledge and power from which it sprung, as we observed in *Los pasos perdidos*.

Although I have learned a good deal from the theories of Mikhail Bakhtin, as should be obvious, my approach here differs consider-ably from his. In the first place, because I like to see the novel as part of the textual economy of a given epoch, not simply or even primarily that part considered literary. In the second, I place more emphasis on texts that are part of official culture in the formation of the novel. In addition, I will include in my purview texts such as *Facundo* which are not considered novels in the conventional sense. My departure from Bakhtin may be due to the nature of my object of study – the Latin American narrative – which is created under circumstances that are considerably different from the European novel that interests him. I believe that Bakhtin dismisses too easily the role of official texts, which to my mind are fundamental in the formation of the modern novel. Bakhtin writes that "Carnival is the people's second life, organized on the basis of laughter. It is a festive life. Festivity is a peculiar quality of all comic rituals and spectacles of the Middle Ages."[10] He also writes: "This is why the tone of the official feast was monolithically serious and why the element of laughter was alien to it" (p. 9). Bakhtin conceives of the official as something alien to society, as if officialdom were something extra-terrestrial, imposed on humanity by some foreign invader. But what he calls official is as much a part of society as laughter and carnival; in fact, one could not exist without the other.

Having said this, however, I should make clear that I do share certain assumptions with Bakhtin. For instance, that humankind is a producer of texts, that these texts never exist individually, but in relation to others, and that there is no possible metatext, but always an intertext.[11] That is to say, that I believe that my text is part of the economy of texts that it attempts to describe and classify, that my book is necessarily also an archival fiction. To my mind, the problem with Bakhtin is that he is still within the sphere of influence of classical anthropology, in the sense that he feels that the folk are some sort of privileged element of humankind, as the non-Europeans were to anthropologists, where something true, that can be betrayed by another part of humankind, survives. This is why he has trouble with the written. Writing is precisely part and parcel of officialdom. Here is where I choose to follow Michel Foucault. For Foucault, mediation is the very process of constraining, denying, limiting, invented by humanity itself; these hegemonic discourses which oppress, watch, control, and furnish the models parodied later, models without which parody itself could not exist. Cutting, slicing, locking up, writing, authority, is as much a contrivance of humankind as its antidotes. This is what I do not see present in Bakhtin's theories, and this is why he idealizes the folk. Intertextuality is not a quiet dialogue of texts – a pluralistic utopia perhaps born of the monolithic hell Bakhtin lived through – but a clash of texts, an imbalance among texts, some of which have a *molding and modeling* power over others.

The object of my study, then, is not simply the Latin American novel, but more broadly the Latin American narrative, and within that narrative an evolving core whose chief concern, particularly since the nineteenth century, is with the issue of the uniqueness of Latin America as a cultural, social and political space from which to narrate. The search for uniqueness and identity is the form the question of legitimacy takes after the colonial period. The very first narrative of Latin America is determined by the issue of legitimacy as granted by the documents through which the first modern state – Habsburg Spain – dealt with the issue of enfranchisement.

In sixteenth-century Spain, the documents imitated by the incipient novel were legal ones. (I use incipient only to signal a beginning, not to suggest that as the structure was established it first yielded a kernel; the whole structure is assumed to have been present in *Lazarillo*, the very "first" novel.) The form assumed by the Picaresque was that of a *relación* (report, deposition, letter bearing witness to something), because this kind of written report belonged to the huge imperial bureaucracy through which power was administered in Spain and its possessions. The early history of Latin America, as well as the first fictions of and about Latin America, are told in the rhetorical molds furnished by the notarial arts. These *cartas de relación* were not simply letters or maps, but were also *charters* of the newly discovered territories. Both the writer and the territory were enfranchised through the power of this document which, like Lazarillo's text, is addressed to a higher authority, as in the case of Hernán Cortés, who wrote to Emperor Charles V. The pervasiveness of legal rhetoric in early American historiography can hardly be exaggerated. Officially appointed historians (with the title of *Cronista Mayor de Indias*) were assigned a set of rules by the Crown and the Royal Council of the Indies which included ways of subsuming these *relaciones* into their compendious works. Latin American history and fiction, the narrative of Latin America, were first created within the language of the law, a secular totality that guaranteed truth and made its circulation possible. It is within this totality that Garcilaso de la Vega, el Inca, wrote his *Comentarios reales de los incas* (1609), for, as will be seen in greater detail, the mestizo's book is an appeal to exonerate his father. Like Lázaro,

Garcilaso addresses a letter to a higher autority to gain enfranchisement.

Since the eighteenth century, all forms of narrative, but particularly the novel, have had to compete with those created or adapted first by the natural and later by the social sciences. These were the true stories. Balzac, Galdós, and Dickens were the social analysts and theoreticians of their time, as was, even more forthrightly, Zola. A study of the relationship of the European novel to scientific forms of hegemonic discourse has yet to be written, as far as I know. Our study is concerned with the strand of the narrative that takes us to Latin America, where the mediating force of science was such that the most significant narratives did not even pretend to be novels, but various kinds of scientific reportage. Consequently, in Latin America, in the nineteenth century (until the teens of our century) the narrative assumes the form of a new hegemonic discourse: science, and more specifically the scientific consciousness that expresses itself in the language of travelers who journeyed across the Continent, writing about its nature and about themselves. Scientific exploration brought about the second European discovery of America, and the traveling naturalists were the new chroniclers. Traces of their writings are present in the journey the narrator-protagonist undertakes in *Los pasos perdidos* (the diary form of parts of the novel is also derived from this kind of writing) and in those by Melquíades in *Cien años de soledad*. Comparatively little attention has been paid to this vast process of exploration and reportage, whose dimensions can be glimpsed by looking at the recent *Travel Accounts and Descriptions of Latin America and the Caribbean 1800–1920: A Selected Bibliography*, compiled by Thomas L. Welch and Myriam Figueras, and published by the Organization of American States (1982).[12] Though selective, this volume contains nearly three hundred pages of tightly packed entries. The names of these scientific travelers are quite impressive, ranging from Alexander von Humboldt to Charles Darwin, and including the likes of Robert and Richard Schomburgk, Charles-Marie de la Condamine, Captain Richard Burton, and many others. Their fictional counterpart is Professor Challenger in Sir Arthur Conan Doyle's *The Lost World* (1912), whose voyage to the origins of nature takes him to South America.

A consciousness that expresses itself in the language of the scientific travelogue mediates the writing of Latin American narratives in the nineteenth century. I am aware that the canon of Latin American literary history places conventional novels such as *Amalia* and *María* at the centre of the evolution of Latin American narrative. This is an uncritical copy of European literary history which veils the fact that the most significant narratives, the ones that had a powerful impact on those that followed in the twentieth century, were not novels copied from European models, as Mármol's and Isaacs' texts were, but issue from the relationship with the hegemonic discourse of the period, which was not literary, but scientific. This is so, even, of course, in the case of some conventional Latin American novels, such as Cirilo Villaverde's *Cecilia Valdés* (Cuba, 1880), which owed much to reports on slavery in Cuba that were cast in a sicentific mold. Domingo Faustino Sarmiento's *Facundo* (1845), Anselmo Suárez y Romero's *Francisco* (1880), and Euclides da Cunha's *Os Sertões* (1902) describe Latin American nature and society through the conceptual grid of nineteenth-century science. Like the chronicles of the discovery and conquest, which were often legal documents, these are books whose original role lies outside of literature. *Francisco* was originally part of a report sent to the British authorities documenting the horrors of slavery in Cuba. Latin America's history and the stories of adventurers, who sought to discover the innermost secrets of the New World, that is to say, its newness and difference, are narrated through the mind of a writer qualified by science to search for the truth. That truth is found in an evolutionary conception of nature that profoundly affects all narratives about the New World. Both the self and science that make this conception possible are reflections of the power of the new European commercial empires. The capacity to find the truth is due not so much to the cogency of the scientific method, as to the ideological construct that supports them, a construct whose source of strength lies outside the text. The "mind" that analyzes and classifies is made present through the rhetorical conventions of the travelogue. Sarmiento ranges over the Argentine landscape in a process of self-discovery and self-affirmation. In his book he dons the mask of the traveling savant, distanced from the reality he interprets and classifies according to the intervening tenets of scientific inquiry.

This particular mediation prevails until the crisis of the 1920s and the so-called *novela de la tierra* or telluric novels.[13] This modern novel avails itself of a different kind of mediation: anthropology. Now the promise of knowledge is to be found in a scientific discourse whose object is not nature but essentially language and myth. The truth-bearing document the novel imitates is the anthropological or ethnographic report. The object of such studies is to discover the origin and source of a culture's own version of its values, beliefs, and history through a culling and retelling of its myths. Readers of anthropology are aware that in order to understand another culture, the anthropologist has to know his own to the point where he can distance himself from it, and in a sense disappear in the discourse of method. Distancing, a process whose counterpart can only be found in modern literature, involves a kind of self-effacement. This dramatic process has been beautifully expounded by Lévi-Strauss in *Tristes tropiques*, a book in which he devotes a good deal of space to his stay in Brazil. John Freccero and Eduardo González have studied how much this book has in common with Carpentier's *Los pasos perdidos*, and today Clifford Geertz and others are studying, from the point of view of anthropology, the relationship between the discourse of anthropology and that of literature in a way that is prefigured in the Latin American novels that I shall be dealing with here.[14]

Anthropology is the mediating element in the modern Latin American narrative because of the place this discipline occupies in the articulation of founding myths by Latin American states. But, of course, anthropology assumes such mediating power also because of the role anthropology plays in Western thought and the place Latin America occupies in the history of that discipline. Anthropology is a way through which Western culture indirectly affixes its own cultural identity. This identity, which the anthropologist struggles to shed, is one that masters non-historical cultures through knowledge, by making them the object of its study. Anthropology translates into the language of the West the cultures of the others and in the process establishes its own form of self-knowledge through a kind of annihilation of the self. Existential philosophy, as in Heidegger, Ortega y Gasset and Sartre, is akin to this process, because it is only through an awareness of the other that Western thought can pretend to wind back to the origin of being. The natives, that is to say, Latin Americans or in general those who could be politely called the inhabitants of the post-colonial world, provide the model for this reduction and beginning. The native has timeless stories to explain his changeless society. These stories, these myths, are like those of the West in the distant past, before they became a

mythology instead of a theogony. Freud, Frazer, Jung, and Heidegger sketch a return to, or a retention of, these origins. Anthropology finds them in the contemporary world of the native. The
modern Latin American novel is written through the model of such
anthropological studies. In the same way that the nineteenth-
century novel turned Latin America into the object of scientific
study, the modern Latin American novel transforms Latin
American history into an originary myth in order to see itself as
other. The theogonic Buendía family in *Cien años de soledad* owes its
organization to this phenomenon, as does the very concept of
Macondo, which recalls the village-studies common in ethnography.

The historical data behind my hypothesis concerning the modern
novel and its relation to an anthropological model are extensive and
I shall return to it in the last chapter. Suffice it to say that Miguel
Angel Asturias studied ethnology in Paris under Georges Raynaud,
an experience that produced in 1930 his influential *Leyendas de
Guatemala*. One of the Asturias' classmates at the Sorbonne was none
other than Alejo Carpentier, who was then writing *¡Ecué-Yamba-O!*
(1933), a novel which is, in many ways, an ethnological study of
Cuban Blacks. Carpentier's interest in anthropology never abated.
For instance, at the time he was writing *Los pasos perdidos* in the late
1940s, he followed the Griaule expedition closely as well as the
activities and writings of the group of anthropologists who took
refuge in New York during World War II.[15] Another Cuban writer
was also preparing herself in Paris in those years: Lydia Cabrera,
whose pioneering studies of Afro-Cuban lore would culminate in her
classic *El monte* (1954). In more recent times, Severo Sarduy has
been a student of Roger Bastide, and his *De donde son los cantantes*
(1967) is, amongst several other things, an anthropological study of
Cuban culture, seen as the synthesis of the three main ethnic groups
inhabiting the island: the Spanish, the African and the Chinese.
Borges' 1933 essay "El arte narrativo y la magia," where the art of
storytelling is compared to two kinds of primitive cures outlined in
The Golden Bough, is but one indication of the widespread impact of
Frazer on Latin America. Traces of this influence are visible in
Octavio Paz, Carpentier, Carlos Fuentes, as well as in many others.

Lydia Cabrera is perhaps the most significant author here
because she stands for a very important kind of Latin American
writer who sits astride both literature and anthropology. Cabrera is

a first-rate short-story writer, just as she is a first-rate anthropologist. Her teacher, Fernando Ortiz, was also claimed by literature and his influence on modern Cuban letters is vast. Examples of writers straddling literature and anthropology are plentiful. The most notorious in recent years is Miguel Barnet, whose *Biografía de un cimarrón* (1966) not only contains all the perplexing dualities and contradictions of that relationship, but is also the perfect example of a book whose form is given by anthropology yet winds up in the field of the novel. The Peruvian José María Arguedas is without a doubt the most poignant figure among these anthropologist-writers: a novelist and anthropologist, Arguedas was brought up by Indians and his first language was Quechua not Spanish. He felt within himself the contradictions and the tragedy inherent in the relationship between anthropology and literature with an intensity that in 1969 led him to choose suicide.

Arguedas' extreme solution is a literal version of the reduction of the self inherent in the process of rewriting Latin American history in the context of the anthropological mediation. Method, discourse, writing, take the place of life. Arguedas' gesture has its literary counterpart in *Los pasos perdidos* and *Cien años de soledad*. Arguedas' radical effacement of self, like the one practiced by Barnet as he turns, or pretends to turn, himself into Esteban Montejo, is part of the "unwriting" involved in the modern Latin American narrative. For the most recent Latin American narrative is an "unwriting" as much as it is a rewriting of Latin American history from the anthropological perspective mentioned. The previous writings of history are undone as the new one is attempted; this is why the chronicles and the nineteenth-century scientific travelogues are present in what I call the Archive in modern fiction, the mode beyond anthropology, inaugurated by *Los pasos perdidos*. The new narrative unwinds the history told in the old chronicles by showing that history was made up of a series of conventional topics, whose coherence and authority depend on the codified beliefs of a period whose ideological structure is no longer current. Those codified beliefs of the origin were literally the law. Like the Spanish galleon crumbling in the jungle in *Cien años de soledad*, the legal discourse in the chronicles is a voided presence. Likewise, modern novels disassemble the powerful scientific construct through which nineteenth-century Latin America was narrated by demonstrating the relativity of its most cherished concepts or by rendering literal the metaphors on which such knowledge is based. The power of genealogy is literalized in *Cien años de soledad* by, among other devices, the stream of blood that flows from José Arcadio's wound to Ursula. The presence of the European naturalists Robertson and Bonplant in Augusto Roa Bastos' *Yo el Supremo* attests to this second voided presence, as do the obsolete and partially magical scientific instruments that Melquíades brings to Macondo, soon to be replaced by the machinery of the banana company which comes to exploit the area.

But the paradigmatic text among these unwritings is Carpentier's *Los pasos perdidos*. This is no accident. Carpentier was associated from the beginning of his career with avant-garde artists, particularly the surrealists, who were intimately associated with anthropological pursuits. It is clear that in Caracas, when he was writing *Los pasos perdidos*, he kept a close eye on developments in anthropology, especially French anthropology. I have already mentioned Carpentier's interest in the group of anthropologists (among them Lévi-Strauss and Leiris), who took refuge in New York during the war, and suggested that the musicologist Schaeffner may have been the model for the narrator-protagonist of the novel, but there were others, who were in Venezuela at the time actually journeying to the sources of the Orinoco.[16] Essentially, the journey the narrator-protagonist makes is that of an anthropologist, and the whole novel is so much like *Tristes tropiques* because it could very well be taken as the personal account of an anthropologist formed in the avant-garde years surveying the state of his discipline and of himself at a time when ethnography was going through a crisis which severely undermined its discourse. But what he brings back is an archaeology of Latin American narrative forms.

As the narrator-protagonist of the novel travels upriver – clearly the river in which Melquíades dies many years later – he writes about his voyage as if it were a journey back not only through time but through recorded history. Hence he passes through various epochs, the two most significant of which are: the nineteenth century with its traveling European scientists, who provide him with a way of interpreting nature and time; and the colonial period of Latin American history, characterized by activities such as the founding of cities; in short, the beginning of history in the New World as set down by the charters of those institutions – the *cartas de relación*. There are other epochs, reaching all the way back to prehistoric times, but the above are the most important ones, because they are present not only thematically or allusively, but through mediating texts themselves, through the very substantiality of their voided forms. The era of the petroglyphs, for instance, is narrated in the language of the naturalists and the founding of cities in that of the legalist chronicles. At various points in the novel the narrator-protagonist plays the roles of conquistador, naturalist, and also anthropological expert in myth, comparing stories he hears in the jungle to those of classical times, looking, in short, for the founding structure of storytelling. He plays these roles because none is current any longer, none provides him with the ideological underpinning to reach a truth, a beginning, an origin. His own story is the only one that he can authenticate, that is, his story about looking for stories, telling past stories, repeating their form. The narrator-protagonist's text is organized according to a set of rhetorical conventions – hollowed out, obsolete, extinct – that reveal themselves as such in the process of reading. In the fiction of the novel, the narrator-protagonist cannot remain in what he termed the Valley-Where-Time-Has-Stopped, the origin of time and history, for, as we saw, he needs to secure enough paper to set down the music he has begun to compose. In the fiction, the quest for that degree zero of time and history on which to inscribe a rewriting of Latin American history has not been found; the protagonist escapes from one city to find another city. But in the writing of the novel a clearing has been reached, a metafictional space, a razing that becomes a starting point for the new Latin American narrative; the clearing for the building of Comala, Macondo, Coronel Vallejos, for the founding of the imaginary city containing all previous forms of Latin American narrative as well as the origins of the novel; a space for the Archive.

That razing involves the various mediations through which Latin America was narrated, the systems from which fiction borrowed the truth-bearing forms, erased to assume the new mediation that requires this level-ground of self and history. This clearing is the point at which *Cien años de soledad* begins, and the reason why the world is so recent "que muchas cosas carecían de nombre, y para mencionarlas había que señalarlas con el dedo" (p. 71); ("that many things lacked names, and in order to indicate them it was necessary to point" [p. 1]).[17] It is also the place that the last Aureliano seeks at the very end when he discovers how to translate Melquíades' manuscripts. He reads in a frenzy "descubriendo los primeros indicios de su ser, en un abuelo concupiscente que se dejaba arrastrar por la frivolidad a través de un páramo alucinado, en busca de una mujer hermosa a quien no haría feliz" (p. 492); ("discovering the first indications of his own being in a lascivious grandfather who let himself be frivolously dragged across a halluci- nated plateau in search of a beautiful woman whom he would not make happy" [p. 421]).[18] What is left for the novel after *Los pasos perdidos* and *Cien años de soledad?* Clearly, only fiction. But novels are never content with fiction; they must pretend to deal with the truth, a truth that lies behind the discourse of the ideology that gives them form. So, paradoxically enough, the truth with which they deal is fiction itself. That is to say, the fictions Latin American culture has created to understand itself. What is left is the opening up of the Archive or perhaps only the story about the opening of the Archive – the story I hope to be telling in this book.

The Archive is a modern myth based on an old form, a form of the beginning. The modern myth unveils the relationship between knowledge and power as contained in all previous fictions about Latin America, the ideological construct that props up the legiti- macy of power from the chronicles to the current novels. This is why a kind of archive, usually containing an unfinished manuscript and an archivist-writer, appears with such frequency in modern novels. The Archive keeps, culls, retains, accumulates, and classifies, like its institutional counterpart. It mounts up, amounts to the law, the law of fiction. Fictions are contained in an enclosure, a prisonhouse of narrative that is at the same time the origin of the novel. It is not by chance that Cervantes began to write the *Quijote* in jail, nor that the narrator-author of *Historia de Mayta* (1984) should seek the ultimate truth about his character in a prison. The Archive goes back to the origins of Latin American narrative because it returns to the language of the law, the language that the protagonist of *Los pasos perdidos* will find in the innermost recesses of the jungle, where a city awaits him. That city, which the Adelantado had called Santa Mónica de los Venados, becomes Macondo, the story of which is the myth of the Archive. Let us read in detail the contradictory origin and nature of that myth in *Cien años de soledad*, the archetypal archival fiction.

3

The importance of myth in *Cien años de soledad* was noticed by the first commentators of the novel, and later studies have again taken up the topic.[19] It seems clear that myth appears in the novel in the following guises: (1) there are stories that resemble classical or biblical myths, most notably the Flood, but also Paradise, the Seven Plagues, the Apocalypse, and the proliferation of the family, which with its complicated genealogy, has an Old Testament ring to it; (2) there are characters who are reminiscent of mythical heroes: José Arcadio Buendía, who is a sort of Moses; Rebeca, who is like a female Perseus; Remedios, who ascends in a flutter of white sheets in a scene that is suggestive not just of the Ascension of the Virgin, but more specifically of the popular renditions of that event in religious prints; (3) certain stories have a general mythic character in that they contain supernatural elements, as in the case just mentioned, and also when José Arcadio's blood returns to Ursula; (4) the beginning of the whole story which is found, as in myth, in a tale of violence and incest. All four, of course, commingle, and because *Cien años de soledad* tells a story of foundations or origins, the entire novel has a mythic air about it. No single myth or mythology prevails. Instead, the various ways in which myth appears give the novel a mythical character without it being a distinct version of any one myth in particular.

At the same time, there is lurking in the background of the story the overall pattern of Latin American history, both as a general design made up of various key events and eras, and in the presence of specific characters and incidents that seem to refer to real people and happenings. Thus there is a period of discovery and conquest when José Arcadio and the original families settle Macondo. There is in this part of the book little sense that Macondo belongs to a larger political unit, but such isolation was in fact typical of Latin American towns in the colonial period. Even the viceroyalties lived in virtual isolation from the metropolitan government. The sense of beginning one has when reading about Macondo was shared by some of the conquistadors, who, for instance, when encouraging Gonzalo Pizarro to rebel against the Crown, urged him to declare himself king of Peru, thinking that the deeds he had accomplished with his brothers were of the kind to merit the establishment of a new monarchy. The appearance in Macondo of Apolinar Moscoso and his barefoot soldiers is the beginning of the republican era, which is immediately followed by the outbreak of the civil wars in which Colonel Aureliano Buendía distinguishes himself. Though Colombia is the most obvious model for this period, nearly the entire continent suffered from civil strife during the nineteenth century, a process that led to the emergence of *caudillos*. Argentina, with Facundo Quiroga and Juan Manuel Rosas, could just as well be the model for this era in Macondo's history. This period is followed by the era of neocolonial domination by the United States and the struggles against it in most Latin American countries. These culminate in the novel with the general strike and the massacre of the workers. There are, unfortunately, countless models for this last, clearly defined period in the novel. After the flood, there is a time of decay before the apocalyptic wind razes the town at the end. The liberal priest and the various military types who surround Colonel Aureliano Buendía are among the characters with counterparts in Latin American history. Lucila I. Mena has already demonstrated that some of the historical incidents in the novel can be documented, and a sedulous critic with time and the proper library can probably document many others.[20] But to carry this sort of research much further than Mena has would be a rather gratuitous critical exercise. Set against the global, totalizing thrust of the novel are these historical details which, without being specific, are nonetheless true in a general sense. Each of the above-mentioned epochs is evoked not only through major historical events but also through allusions to specific minor incidents and characters. For instance, early Macondo is inhabited by a *de jure* aristocracy made up of the founding families, which is analogous to towns in colonial Latin America where the first conquistadors and their descendants enjoyed certain privileges and exemptions, a situation which, in some measure, provoked the civil wars of Peru.

The blend of mythic elements and Latin American history in *Cien años de soledad* reveals a desire to found a Latin American myth as well as the voiding of the anthropological mediation. Latin American history is set on the same level as mythic stories; therefore, it too becomes a sort of myth. The lack of specificity of the various incidents, which appear to represent several related or similar events, points in that direction. The Latin American myth is this story of foundation, articulated through independence, civil war, struggle against United States imperialism, all cast within a genealogical line that weaves in and out, repeating names and characters. There is a Whitmanesque thrust to the brash declaration of the existence of a literary language that underlies this mixture of historical fact and mythic story in *Cien años de soledad*. The novel is in fact intimately related to similar efforts in poetry, such as the ones by Neruda in his *Canto general*, Nicolás Guillén in his *El diario que a diario* and Octavio Paz in his *Piedra de sol*. *Canto general* in particular is one of the most important sources of García Márquez' novel. Framed by Genesis and Apocalypse, fraught with incest and violence, the story of the Buendía family thus stands as Latin American history cast in the language of myth, an unresolved mixture that both beckons and bewilders the reader. Latin America's irreducible historicity – its discovery creates an awareness of transitoriness and change that propels Western consciousness into modernity, self-questioning and relativity – constantly undermines the language of myth.

This duality – history/myth – is present throughout *Cien años de soledad*, separating the world of writing from the atemporal world of myth. But the play of contradictions issuing from this duality reaches a precarious synthesis that is perhaps the most important feature of the novel. Myth represents the origin. Latin American history is narrated in the language of myth because it is always conceived as the history of the other, a history fraught with incest, taboo, and the founding act of naming. Latin American history must be like myth to comply with this conception, which issues from the authority of the anthropological mediation. The novel's persistent preoccupation with genealogy and supernatural acts performed by various characters belongs to this mythic realm.[21] History, on the other hand, is critical, temporal, and dwells in a special place: Melquíades' room in the Buendía house, which I have chosen to call the Archive. The room is full of books and manuscripts and has a time of its own. It is here that a succession of characters attempt to decipher Melquíades' parchments, and the last Aureliano, in an epiphanic inspiration, orally translates nearly the whole manuscript and dies. What occurs here, the text of the novel suggests, is unrepeatable. In the fiction of the novel, on the other hand, there are many repetitions. Ursula, for instance, twice feels that time is going around in circles and that members of the family follow one or two patterns of behavior indicated by their names. Time is circular in the fiction but not in Melquíades' room. The Archive appears to be successive and teleological, while the plot of the novel itself is repetitive and mythical. *Cien años de soledad* is made up of two main stories: one has to do with the family and culminates in the birth of the child with the pig's tail, while the other is concerned with the interpretation of Melquíades' manuscript, a linear suspense story that culminates in Aureliano's final discovery of the key to the translation of the parchments. The product of incest and revelation is the same: Does it stand for truth? And if the truth of the novel is like the child with the pig's tail, what are we to conclude about the nature of novelistic discourse?

That there should be a special abode for manuscripts and books in *Cien años de soledad* should come as no surprise to readers of modern Latin American fiction. There are analogous enclosures in *Aura, Yo el Supremo, El arpa y la sombra, Crónica de una muerte anunciada* and *Oppiano Licario*, to mention a few of the novels in which the figure plays a prominent role. One could also say that this enclosure is prefigured in the box where the narrator-protagonist of *Los pasos perdidos* keeps the manuscript of his threnody. What is characteristic of the Archive is: (1) the presence not only of history but of previous mediating elements through which it was narrated, be it the legal documents of colonial times or the scientific ones of the nineteenth century; (2) the existence of an inner historian who reads the texts, interprets and writes them; and finally (3) the presence of an unfinished manuscript that the inner historian is trying to complete. In *Cien años de soledad* the most tenuous presence is that of the legal texts, but one can infer it from the allusions to the chronicles that were in fact *relaciones*, and particularly in the founding of Macondo, for the founding of cities, primordial activity of conquistadors, was closely connected to the writing of history. The vagueness of this presence is only so in relation to the others, for at least two critics have convincingly argued in favor of the overwhelming influence of the chronicles in *Cien años de soledad*.[22] The presence of nineteenth-century travel books is evident in the descriptions of the jungle and at a crucial moment when José Arcadio Segundo hears Melquíades mumble something in his room. José Arcadio leans over and hears the gypsy mention the name of none other than Alexander von Humboldt and the word *equinoccio*, which comes from the title of the latter's book, which in Spanish is *Viaje a las regiones equinocciales del Nuevo Continente*. In Macondo's Archive, there are in addition two key works: the so-called *English Encyclopedia* and *The Thousand and One*

Nights. These two books play an important role in Melquíades'
writing, and the *Encyclopedia* is instrumental in the decoding of his
manuscripts. The existence in Melquíades' fiction of precisely these
two books adds a peculiar twist to the Archive, one that points to its
own literary lineage.

I do not think it would be too farfetched to say that *The Thousand
and One Nights* and the so-called *English Encyclopedia* together are
allusions to that master of fictions: Borges. In fact, Melquíades is a
figure of the Argentine writer. Old beyond age, enigmatic, blind,
entirely devoted to writing, Melquíades stands for Borges, the
librarian and keeper of the Archive. There is something whimsical
in García Márquez' inclusion of such a figure in the novel, but there
is a good deal more. It is not difficult to fathom what this Borgesian
figure means. Planted in the middle of the special abode of books
and manuscripts, a reader of one of the oldest and most influential
collections of stories in the history of literature, Melquíades and his
Archive stand for literature; more specifically, for Borges' kind of
literature: ironic, critical, a demolisher of all delusions, the sort of
thing encountered at the end of the novel when Aureliano finishes
translating Melquíades' manuscript. There are in that ending
further allusions to several stories by Borges: to "Tlön, Uqbar,
Orbis Tertius," for Macondo is a verbal construct; to "El milagro
secreto," in that Aureliano, like the condemned poet, perishes the
moment he finishes his work; to "El Aleph," for Aureliano Babilonia's glimpse of the history of Macondo is instantaneous and
all-encompassing; and particularly to "La muerte y la brújula," for
the moment of anagnorisis is linked to death. Like Lönnrot,
Aureliano only understands the workings of his fate at the moment
of his death.

The Archive, then, is like Borges' study. It stands for writing, for
literature, for an accumulation of texts that is no mere heap, but an
arché, a relentless memory that disassembles the fictions of myth,
literature and even history. The masterbooks in the Archive are, as
indicated, the *Encyclopedia* and *The Thousand and One Nights.* The
Encyclopedia, which Aureliano has read, according to the narrator,
from A to Z as if it were a novel, is in itself a figure of the totality of
knowledge as conceived by the West. But how is it knowledge, and
how has Aureliano read it? The moment we consider the order of
knowledge in the *Encyclopedia* and the way in which Aureliano reads
it, we realize the paradoxes inherent in the Archive as repository of

history. The *Encyclopedia* is organized, of course, in alphabetical order, without the order of the entries being affected by any chronological or evaluative consideration: Napoleon appears before Zeus and Charles V before God. The beginning is provided arbitrarily by the alphabet as well as by the sequence: apocalypse must appear in the first volume. *The Thousand and One Nights*, on the other hand, stands for a beginning in fiction, or beginning as fiction, as well as for a series of individual, disconnected stories linked only by the narrator's fear of death. Aureliano is like Scheherazade, who tells her stories on the verge of death. Neither book seems to have a priority over the other. Both have a prominent place within the Archive, providing their own form of pastness, of documentary, textual material. The order that prevails in the Archive, then, is not that of mere chronology, but that of writing; the rigorous process of inscribing and decoding to which Melquíades and the last Aureliano give themselves over, a linear process of cancellations and substitutions, of gaps.

Writing and reading have an order of their own, which is preserved within the Archive. It might be remembered that in Melquíades' room it is always Monday and March for some characters, while for others his study is the room of the chamberpots, where decay and temporality have their own end embodied in the essence of eschatology. The combination of feces and writing in the Archive is significant enough. Writing appears as an eschatological activity in that it deals with the end. Yet, writing is also the beginning insofar as nothing is in the text until it is written. Hence the prevalence of Monday and March in the secret abode of Melquíades, the beginning of the week and of spring respectively (March, not April, is the "cruelest month" in García Márquez). Melquíades is both young and old, depending, of course, on whether or not he wears his dentures; he presides over the beginning and the end. The Archive, then, is not so much an accumulation of texts as the process whereby texts are written; a process of repeated combinations, of shufflings and reshufflings ruled by heterogeneity and difference. It is not strictly linear, as both continuity and discontinuity are held together in uneasy allegiance. This fictional archive, of course, is a turning inside out of the Archive in its political manifestation, a turn that unveils the inner workings of the accumulation of power; accumulation and power are a rhetorical effect in this archive of archives. This is the reason why the previous mediations through which Latin Americans narrated are contained in the Archive as voided presences. They are both erased and, at the same time, a memory of their own demise. They are keys to filing systems now abandoned, but they retain their archival quality, their power to differentiate, to space. They are not archetypes, but an *arché* of types.

This process is manifest in the way in which Melquíades' manuscript is written and translated. Throughout the novel we are told that Melquíades writes indecipherable manuscripts, that his handwriting produces something that looks more like musical notation than script, that his writing resembles clothes hung on a line. Eventually José Arcadio Segundo discovers, with the aid of the *Encyclopedia*, that the writing is in Sanskrit. When Aureliano begins to translate from the Sanskrit, he comes up with coded Spanish verses. These verses have different codes, depending on whether they are even or odd numbered. Aureliano is finally illuminated when he sees the dead newborn being carried away by the ants and remembers the epigraph of the manuscript, which is supposed to read: *"El primero de la estirpe está amarrado en un árbol y al último se lo están comiendo las hormigas"* (p. 490); (*"The first of the line is tied to a tree and the last is being eaten by the ants"* [p. 420]) (emphasis in the original). He realizes then that the manuscript contains the story of his family and hurries on to translate it to discover his own fate and the date and circumstances of his death. I shall return to the significance of all this, but not before I complete the description of the manuscript and its translation, for it is very easy to leap to false conclusions about Melquíades' writing.

Aureliano begins to translate the text out loud, jumping ahead twice to arrive at the present faster. Once he reaches the present he has a second illumination: that he would die in the room where the manuscript is kept once he finished translating the last line of poetry ("el último verso"). Is this the text of Melquíades' version of the history of Macondo, and is this version *Cien años de soledad*? Even if in fact it is Aureliano's translation that we read, then some changes have been made. The text is neither finished nor definitive, like that of the narrator-protagonist of *Los pasos perdidos*. To begin with, the epigraph has been omitted. In addition, Aureliano's leaps to get to the present have either not been accounted for in this version or the holes they left have been restored. But when and by whom? The only solution to this enigma is to say that our reading – that each reading

– of the text is the text, that is to say, yet another version added to the Archive. Each of these readings corrects the others, and each is unrepeatable insofar as it is a distinct act caught in the reader's own temporality. In this sense, we, like Aureliano, read the instant we live, cognizant that it may very well be our last. This is the eschatological sense announced in various ways by the Archive: the chronicle of a death foretold.

The radical historicity to which the Archive condemns us belies its apparent atemporality and the bizarre order that the master-books within it have. It is a historicity that is very much like the one to which the narrator-protagonist of *Los pasos perdidos* is condemned at the end of that novel. In fact, Aureliano's reading of the manuscript in search of his origins and of an understanding of his being in the present is analogous to the reading performed by Carpentier's character in search of the origins of history and of his own beginnings. Such dearly achieved historicity in spite of the circularity and repetition of the family's history is somewhat ironic, given the sense of ahistoricalness with which many readers, intoxicated by the similarity of names and by Ursula's notion that time is going round and round, leave the novel. Such historicity, however, is needed to represent, within the anthropological mediation posited, the "lucid" consciousness of the West, able to understand itself by posturing as the other, but unable to abandon the sense of history to which writing sentences it. This is a sentence from which we can gain acquittal by means of a willful act of delusion, but one that *Cien años de soledad*, for all its fictive force, does not allow the reader.

There is a significant fact that few readers of *Cien años de soledad* remark upon: Even though the novel begins with Colonel Aureliano Buendía facing the firing squad, the one who dies at the end is not Aureliano the soldier, but Aureliano the reader. This displacement, plus the fact that Aureliano's moments of vision are flashes of insight parallel to the rebel's, seem to suggest a most significant connection between the realms of history and myth, one that constitutes a common denominator of the repetitions of the family history and the disassembling mechanisms of the Archive. In the Archive, the presence of Melquíades and Aureliano (and in *Aura*, Felipe Montero, in *Yo el Supremo*, Patiño, etc.) is an insurance that the individual consciousness of a historian/writer will filter the ahistorical pretense of myth by subjecting events to the temporality of writing. But in *Cien años de soledad* the death of these figures is indicative of a mythic power that lurks within the realm of writing, a story that makes the Archive possible. In *Yo el Supremo* this is clearly indicated by Patiño's being a "swollen foot," that is an Oedipus who pays a high price for his knowledge. In *Cien años de soledad* Aureliano suffers a similar fate. He commits incest with his aunt, engenders a monster with her and dies the moment he has a glimpse of his fate. Aureliano is the propitiatory victim necessary for us to be able to read the text, for us to acquire the arcane knowledge we need to decode it. He (we) is/are no Oedipus but more likely the Minotaur, which brings us back to Borges (and also to Cortázar). The ritualistic death – which prefigures *Crónica de una muerte anunciada* – is necessary because of the incest committed both at the genealogical and the textual level. In both cases, what has been gained is a forbidden knowledge of the other as oneself, or vice versa.

The most salient characteristic of the text we read is its heterogeneity. However, this heterogeneity is made up of differences within similarity. The various versions of the story are all related, yet differ in each instance. Their difference as well as their relation is akin – *valga la palabra* – to the relationship between the incestuous characters and the broader confrontation between writer and a primitive other who produces myth. Put differently, the self-reflexiveness of the novel is implicitly compared to incest, a self-knowledge that somehow lies beyond knowledge. A plausible argument can be made that the endresults of both are similar, in the most tangible sense, or at least related. When the ants carry away the carcass of the monstrous child engendered by Amaranta Ursula and Aureliano, its skin is described in terms that are very reminiscent of Melquíades' parchments. The English translation blurs that similarity. It reads: "And then he saw the child. It was a dry and bloated bag of skin that all the ants in the world were dragging . . ." (p. 420). The Spanish reads: "Era un pellejo [it was a skin] hinchado y reseco, que todas las hormigas del mundo iban arrastrando . . ." (p. 349). I need not go into the etymological and historical kinship uniting skin and parchment because the novel itself provides that link. The parchments are once described as "parecían fabricados en una materia árida que se resquebrajaba como hojaldres" (p. 68), and the books in the Archive are bound "en una materia acartonada y pálida como la piel humana curtida" (p. 160). The English reads: "The parchments that he had brought with him and that seemed to have been made out of some dry material that crumpled like puff paste" (p. 73), and "the books were bound in a cardboard-like material, pale, like tanned human skin" (p. 188).

The monster and the manuscript, the monster and the text, are the product of the turning in on oneself implicit in incest and self-reflexivity. Both are heterogeneous within a given set of characteristics, the most conspicuous of which is their supplementarity: the pig's tail, which exceeds the normal contours of the human body, and the text, whose mode of being is each added reading and interpretation. The plot line that narrates the decipherment of the manuscripts underscores our falling into this trap. Like Aureliano, we follow along in search of the meaning of the manuscripts, constantly teased by scenes where Melquíades appears scratching his incomprehensible handwriting onto rough parchment, by scenes where José Arcadio Segundo or Aureliano make preliminary discoveries that eventually lead them to unravel the mystery. But like Lönnrot in "La muerte y la brújula," and like Aureliano himself, we do not discover until the very end what the manuscripts contain. Our own anagnorisis as readers is saved for the last page, when the novel concludes and we close the book to cease being as readers, to be, as it were, slain in that role. We are placed back at the beginning, a beginning that is also already the end, a discontinuous, independent instant where everything commingles without any possibility of extending the insight, an intimation of death. This independent instant is not the novel; it is the point to which the novel has led us. By means of an unreading, the text has reduced us, like Aureliano, to a ground zero, where death and birth are joined as correlative moments of incommunicable plenitude. The text is that which is added to this moment. Archive and myth are conjoined as instances of discontinuity rather than continuity; knowledge and death are given equivalent value. Death, as we shall see, is the trope for the Archive's structuring principle.

It is a commonplace, almost an uncritical fetish, to say that the novel always includes the story of how it is written, that it is a self-reflexive genre. The question is why and how it is so at specific moments. Clearly, *Cien años de soledad* is self-reflexive not merely to provoke laughter or to declare itself literary and thus disconnected from reality or history. In García Márquez, and I dare say in all major Latin American novelists, self-reflexivity is a way of disassembling the mediation through which Latin America is narrated, a mediation that constitutes a pre-text of the novel itself. It is also a way of showing that the act of writing is caught up in a deeply rooted mythic struggle that constantly denies it the authority to generate and contain knowledge about the other without, at the same time, generating a perilous sort of knowledge about itself and about one's mortality and capacity to know oneself.

What do we learn about Latin American history in *Cien años de soledad*? We learn that while its writing may be mired in myth, it cannot be turned into myth, that its newness makes it impervious to timelessness, circularity, or any such delusion. New and therefore historical, what occurs in Latin America is marked by change, it is change. García Márquez has expressed this by tantalizing the reader with various forms of history as writing, of history as Archive. He has also achieved it by making Borges the keeper of the Archive, for the figure of the Argentine ensures that no delusions about literature be entertained. In a sense, what García Márquez has done is to punch through the anthropological mediation and substitute the anthropologist for a historian, and to turn the object of attention away from myth as an expression of so-called primitive cultures to the myths of modern society: the book, writing, reading, instruments of a quest for self-knowledge that lie beyond the solace mythic interpretations of the world usually afford. We can always use *Cien años de soledad* to escape temporality, but only if we willfully misread it to blind ourselves of its warnings against that. Latin American history can only become myth enmeshed in this very modern problematic that so enriches its most enduring fictions.

It is not toward a high-pitched rationality that *Cien años de soledad* moves, but toward a vision of its own creation dominated by the forces that generate myth. This is perhaps most evident if we consider that the Archive may very well be the most powerful of cultural retentions and the origin of the novel. The Archive is, first of all, a repository for the legal documents wherein the origins of Latin American history are contained, as well as a specifically Hispanic institution created at the same time as the New World was being settled. As is known, the great archive at Simancas, begun by Charles V but finished by the King Bureaucrat Philip II, is the first and possibly the most voluminous of such storehouses in Europe. The same Herrera who designed the Escorial had a hand in planning the archive, that is to say, in turning a castle that was originally a prison into the archive. Simancas became the Archive in

1539; *La vida de Lazarillo de Tormes, y de sus fortunas y adversidades* was published in 1554. The Archive and the novel appear at the same time and are part of the same discourse of the modern state. Latin America became a historical entity as a result of the development of the printing press, not merely by being "discovered" by Columbus. Latin America, like the novel, was created in the Archive. It may very well have been Carlos Fuentes in his *Terra Nostra* who most clearly saw the connection, making Cervantes the inner historian in that novel. In terms of the novel's ability to retain and pass on cultural values, the message contained in books such as Fuentes' and *Cien años de soledad* is indeed disturbing, for they tell us that it is impossible to create new myths, yet bring us back to that moment where our desire for meaning can only be satisfied by myth.

4

Ferdinand and Isabella, Charles I and Philip II can truly be called – all four, not only the last one – papermonger kings, for they all indeed were, each in his or her own way. And the most seasoned fruit of their tenacious and intelligent archival policies was the world-famous Simancas Archive, near Valladolid, which was then a true capital … Philip II's shrewd foresight, aided by Juan de Herrera's solid technical knowledge, turned a fifteenth-century castle into the first fire-proof Archive known to Europe, and crowning the efforts of his predecessors, he managed to gather there the central Archive of the State.

José María de la Peña y Cámara, *Archivo General de Indias de Sevilla. Guía del Visitante.*[23]

And the temple of God was opened in heaven, and there was seen in his temple the ark of his testament; and there were lightnings, and voices, and thunderings, and an earthquake, and a great hail.   *Revelation*, 11, 19

I am interested in the cluster of connections between secrecy (or privacy of knowledge), origin and power encrypted in the concept of Archive. This is so, perhaps, because like the modern novel, my own discourse tends to mythify the Archive, to use it as a heuristic device to investigate, conjure, or invent its own foundations. By heuristic device I mean, in the best of cases, that the Archive is a hypostasis for method, for my method in this book; in the worst, it is a wild card or joker around which to build a system to read the history of the Latin American narrative and the origins of the novel. If my apprehensions about the contamination of my discourse by that of the novel turn out to be justified, then Archive is a sort of liturgical object that I invest with the faculty of calling forth the innermost secrets of the narratives – the hidden, secret origin. Whichever of these it is, the term is derived from the reading of *Los pasos perdidos* and *Cien años de soledad* offered above. Though my theoretical debts should be obvious, I fancy to read this new history of the Latin American narrative, and its origin, by activating a self-interpreting discourse latent within it. That is, I wish to legitimize my theory by drawing it from within my very field of study. I am conscious of the circularity of this approach, but circling around a point (like the plane that comes to rescue the protagonist of *Los pasos perdidos*) may be revealing, may allow one to see, or at least make one think he or she sees it from many perspectives. The reader will decide on the usefulness of my approach, and whether by circling I am not really spiraling into the ground, or mistaking dizziness for insight.

Etymologically, "archive" has a suggestive background that supports, I hope, the work that it is made to perform here. Corominas writes: "*Archivo*, 1490, Tomado del latín tardío *archivum*, y éste del griego *archeion* 'residencia de los magistrados,' 'archivo,' derivado de *arkhe* 'mando,' 'magistratura'." ("Taken from late Latin *archivum*, and this from the Greek *archeion*, 'residence of the magistrates,' 'archive,' derived from *arkhe* 'command,' 'magistracy.')"[24] The dictionary of the Spanish Academy reads: "*Archivo* (Del lat. *archivum*, y éste del griego [...] principio, origen) m. Local en que se custodian documentos públicos o particulares. 2. Conjunto de estos documentos. 3. fig. Persona en quien se confía un secreto o recónditas intimidades y sabe guardarlas./fig. Persona que posee en grado sumo una perfección o conjunto de perfecciones. *Archivo* de cortesía, de la lealtad." (From the Latin *archivum*, and this from the Greek [...] beginnings or origin.) Masculine. Building in which public or private documents are placed for safekeeping. 2. The sum total of these documents. 3. Figurative. A person to whom is entrusted a secret or very private knowledge and knows how to guard them/ Figurative. A person who is endowed with the highest degree of perfection or sum of perfections. To be an *archive* of courtesy or of loyalty.") Power, secrecy and law stand at the origin of the Archive; it was, in its most concrete form, the structure that actually housed the dispensers of the law, its readers, the magistrates; it was the building that encrypted the power to command. In Philosophy *arche* is the primordial stuff in the beginning, the first principle. In Anaximander and the earlier Greek philosophers it was a substance or primal element, with later philosophers, especially Aristotle, an actuating principle, a cause. It is this word *arche* which appears in the first verse of the Fourth Gospel: "In the *beginning* was the word." All observable regularities were viewed as reflections of the *arché*'s enduring presence in the cosmos.[25] So *arch*, as in *monarch*, denotes power, to rule, but also the beginning, that which is chief, eminent, greatest, principal; it denotes primitive, original. Through the *arche*, in addition, *archive* is related to arcane, to arcanum (*Webster*, "*arcanum*, A secret, a mystery, esp. one of the great secrets that the alchemists sought to discover; hence, a sovereign remedy"). So *Archive* suggests not only that something is kept, but that which is secret, encrypted, enclosed, and also the common, though old-fashioned Spanish word for chest, for safe, for trunk, like the trunk found in *Lazarillo de Tormes* and *Aura*.[26] Trunk, *arca*, according to the Academy: "Caja, comunmente sin forrar y con una tapa llana que aseguran varios goznes o bisagras por uno de los lados, y uno o más candados o cerraduras por el opuesto. Especie de nave o embarcación (Noé). Ant. sepulcro o ataúd." ("Box, commonly without a lining, which has a flat lid secured by several hinges on one side and one or more locks on the other. A kind of ship or boat (Noah). Old Spanish, sepulcher, tomb."). Power encrypts knowledge of the origin, the principles, kept in a building or enclosure that safeguards the law, the beginning of writing; it also kept the body after death, like a relic of life, possessor still of its darkest secrets, abandoned abode of the soul. It is no accident that the word *archivo*, according to Corominas, appears to have entered Spanish in 1490, during the reign of the Catholic Kings, two years before the discovery of America; it was in that period that modern archival practices began, organized by the new state created by Ferdinand and Isabella. The mystery of the object, its prestige, is made a functional part in the foundation of the modern state, and a key figure in the narratives therein generated.

Like the Archive, the novel hoards knowledge. Like the Archive's, that knowledge is of the origin, meaning that it is about the link of its own writing with the power that makes it possible, hence with the possibility of knowledge. In the beginning that power was the law, but later, other origins replaced it, though preserving the seal of that initial pact between power and writing. The modern novel retains those origins and the structure that made them possible. While the knowledge kept there is difficult to plumb, hence its secretiveness, it is not private, but on the contrary common property. It can be read, and it is indeed read. The very act of reading and sharing that knowledge assumes the form of ritual, of celebrating the common knowledge, the transpersonal history. Archives keep the secrets of the state; novels keep the secrets of culture, and the secret of those secrets.

It should be evident that the archaeology of narrative forms that I seek to describe owes much to Foucault's theories about discursive regularities and their relation to power in society. I am interested in the place of narrative within discursive practices overdetermined by power structures that either base or project their authority through them. The novel's contamination with non-literary forms of discourse justifies the association I propose here with the language of the law, that of natural science, and with anthropology. But, most of all, at the point of departure and arrival of the project, it is the Archive that seeks our attention. I am also inspired by Foucault's version of the Archive, though mine has somewhat different characteristics because, in spite of the novel's pull away from literature, it is ultimately in that ambiguous and shifting space called literature that my Archive is lodged. I wish to retain from Foucault, above all, the negative, proscriptive element of his Archive, because interdiction, that is negation, is at the beginning of the law, hence of writing and of the novel. Foucault writes in *The Archaeology of Knowledge*:

The Archive is first the law of what can be said, the system that governs the appearance of statements and unique events. But the Archive is also that which determines that all these things said do not accumulate endlessly in an amorphous mass, nor are they inscribed in an unbroken linearity, nor do they disappear at the mercy of chance external accidents; but they are grouped together in distinct figures, composed together in accordance with specific regularities; that which determines that they do not withdraw at the same pace in time, but shine, as it were, like stars, some that seem close to us are already growing pale. The Archive is not that which, despite its immediate escape, safeguards the event of the statement, and preserves, for future memories, its status as escapee; it is that which, at the very root of the statement-event, and in that which embodies it, defines at the outset *the system of enunciability* [. . .] far from being only that which ensures that we exist in the midst of preserved discourse, it is that which differentiates discourses in their multiple existence and specifies them in their own duration.[27]

Narrative in general, the novel in particular, may be the way in which the statement's status as escapee is preserved, the Counter-

Archive for the ephemeral and wayward. The novel endows the negativity of the Archive, the proscription of the Archive with a phantasmagoric form of being, embodying only, particularly in the modern period, the Archive's very power to differentiate. The following, from Foucault again, would be an apt description of the modern novel, one that, as we shall see, has already taken shape in another text by Carpentier, though these lines could also be about Melquíades' room in *Cien años de soledad*:

The description of the Archive deploys its possibilities (and the mastery of its possibilities) on the basis of the very discourses that have just ceased to be ours; its threshold of existence is established by the discontinuity that separates us from what we can no longer say, and from that which falls outside our discursive practices; it begins with the outside of our own language (*langage*); its locus is the gap between our own discursive practices [...] it deprives us of our continuities; it dissipates that temporal identity in which we are pleased to look at ourselves when we wish to exorcise the discontinuities of history; it snaps the thread of transcendental teleologies; and where anthropological thought once questioned man's being or subjectivity, it now bursts open the other and the outside. In this sense, the diagnosis does not establish the fact of our identity by the play of distinctions. It establishes that we are difference, that our reason is the difference of discourses, our history the difference of times, our selves the difference of masks. That difference, far from being the forgotten and discovered origin, is this dispersion that we are and make.[28]

The dispersive quality of this Archive is found in the modern novel's apparent grab-bag approach to history, its endemic power to negate previous narrative forms from which it takes texts rather than continuities; the power, in short, to question received knowledge and its ideological coagulations as identity, culture, educational institutions, even language, or perhaps better, ultimately, language itself. By letting loose the arcana, by breaking open the safe, the novel-Archive unleashes a ghostly procession of figures of negation, inhabitants of the fissures and cracks which hover around the covenant of writing and the law.

Carpentier's last novel, *El arpa y la sombra* (1979), deployed and displayed the inner workings of this Archive in a way that is most instructive. The protagonist of Carpentier's novel is Columbus; not Columbus in his role as discoverer of the New World as much as Columbus the first writer of the New World, Columbus as origin of the Latin American narrative record. In one strand of the narrative the Discoverer appears on his deathbed in Valladolid. He is reviewing his life to prepare for the visit of the priest who will confess him and administer extreme unction. Technically, as he remembers his life, Columbus is performing an act of contrition, a sort of inner narrative atonement. He is also rereading and commenting upon some of the texts that he wrote about his most famous deed, the ones that we all read in the opening chapter of all anthologies of Latin American literature. Carpentier finished *El arpa y la sombra* when he knew that he had terminal cancer, in a sense also on his deathbed and as a kind of final audit of his life as novelist. Since Carpentier's texts often, almost obsessively, deal with the origin of Latin American history, with the beginning of the Latin American narrative tradition, Carpentier's identification in his role as writer with Columbus is evident. In the conventional scheme of Latin American literary history Columbus' texts constitute the origin, the beginning of the narrative tradition, the foundational writing. Columbus was the first to name things in the New World, like Blake's Adam, a gesture that in Carpentier's Neo-Romantic ideology signals the start of Latin American literature.

But Columbus is not the only projection of Carpentier in *El arpa y la sombra*: there is also Mastai Ferreti, that is to say, Pope Pius IX, who is described, in the opening scene of the novel, with his pen suspended over a sheet of paper, hesitating whether he should sign the documents that will set in motion Columbus' beatification process. This would constitute the first step toward an eventual canonization of the Admiral of the Ocean Sea. Like Columbus and Carpentier, Mastai is both a reader and a writer: he has gathered as many documents as possible about the Discoverer to prepare the dossier that must be presented at the trial in which, once read and examined in detail, sentence will be passed in the case. Columbus' authority as narrator, of course, rests on his being at the beginning: his is the prestige of the origin. Mastai's authority rests on his erudition, and needless to say, on his office. Carpentier's identification with Pius IX is clear and ironic. Like Carpentier Mastai was a man of two worlds: Europe and Latin America. Having once gone on a mission to Latin America, he identified with the New World, where he became an avid reader of Latin American and Spanish texts. Mastai is the Compiler of the Dossier, the Researcher for Facts and Documents, the Curator of the File, the Archivist *par excellence*. By means of that signature that he delays in scribbling, his sacred presence will endow with authority the texts that he has gathered: Mastai creator of the canon, canonizer of the Latin American narrative tradition from Columbus to Carpentier, Alfa and Omega. Columbus, because he occupies the origin, and Mastai, because of his investiture, are capable of making the texts sacred; they are texts outside the flow of history, hence possessors of an irreducible truth about history, texts containing a story of mythic proportions, the stories that make possible all other stories. They are the key to the Archive.

Mastai and Columbus are figures of the Archive, hoarders of secrets, owners of the first, most *arch*aic rule, emblems of authority and power. Columbus jealously keeps his texts under the pillow, from where he pulls them out to read and reread them. He later hides them under the bed. The Archive keeps and hides, it guards the secrets, which is the first law. Mastai keeps his papers in a portfolio which, one assumes, is part of the Vatican Archive. This Archive is evoked in the novel through yet another repository: the Vatican's stockpile of saints' bones, the *ostea sacra* kept and classified to be distributed around the world to constitute the relics each church requires. This is the *lipsanateca*. The Archive safeguards, retains, orders dissemination, both commands it and organizes its regularities as a discourse. The Archive keeps the arcanum, the secret. It keeps the secret of Columbus' texts, their foundational arch-texture, from which, like the bones in the Vatican dispensing sacredness, issue the Latin American texts; origin as death, as cut, as void, as proscription, as negation. The secret is the negation, the prohibition, the origin of law. It is the proscriptions that Fray Pedro will have to write in the notebooks that the narrator wants in *Los pasos perdidos*. Columbus, his texts, is the modern myth that Mastai wishes to sacralize, compiling the documents at the origin and of the origin, submitting those documents to the Archive's *arche*.

Mastai signs the document and sets in motion the judicial process.

The judgment goes against Columbus. He is not beatified, hence he cannot be canonized. The canon that the Keeper of the Archive seeks to establish is not sanctioned. This Archive's origin is not a library, volumes here float unbound, without pagination; this is its true secret, the negation in the origin. The Archive contains essentially nothing. This is the contradictory force that constitutes the Archive, the cut, the loss, whose image is the eschatology of

Melquíades' abode, the bones signifying death in Carpentier's. Death's dark perimeter encircles the Archive and at the same time inhabits its center. This secret is also revealed in the part of *El arpa y la sombra* where Columbus the reader comments on his own texts and declares them to be false, a tissue of lies:

> Y la constancia de tales trampas está aquí, en estos borradores de mis relaciones de viajes, que tengo bajo la almohada, y que ahora saco con mano temblorosa – asustada de sí misma – para releer lo que, en estos postreros momentos, tengo por un Vasto Repertorio de Embustes.

> And the proof of such tricks is here, in these drafts of my travel accounts that I keep under my pillow, and that I now pull out with a trembling hand, afraid of itself, to reread what in these final moments I consider a Vast Repertory of Lies.[29]

The Archive does not canonize, because the first law of the Archive is a denial, a cut that organizes and disperses. This negation is represented by the phantasmic figure of Columbus, present as a ghost at his own trial; present and absent at the very moment when his sacralization is denied. That afterlife of Columbus' is the escape from the Archive, the thrust to freedom forever present in the narrative, only that it is a fictive supplement, a fake afterlife. This is the profound statement made by Carpentier about the novel, himself on the verge of death; that it is that cut, one of whose representations is extinction itself, that rules the Archive, and constitutes the ultimate form of knowledge. The truth of the Archive, the secret of its secret, is that it contains no truth but that "dispersion that we are and make," as Foucault put it, the image of which in *El arpa y la sombra* is the *lipsanateca*, the collection of bones to be disseminated throughout the world, relics of an order that only exists in the dissembling memory of the Archive, or in our desire to project our fictive capacity upon it.

It is this dissembling quality, this empty space where the novel's capacity for retention and loss balance out, that leads to the series of breaks in history, breaks where the novel's mimetic desire leads it to choose a different form in reaction to changes in the textual field in which it is inscribed. A new non-literary document will acquire the legitimating powers lost by the previous model, and the novel will follow that form as it had done originally in relation to the legal documents of the Archive. This mimetic displacement is more important than superficial, aesthetic changes, such as those that

novels outside of the core of the tradition will undergo. Texts like
that will not be remembered except in conventional literary histories; they will be forgotten, and this is what is important, by the new
novels that will look always outside of literature to implement a
radical change. This is why the history of the Latin American novel
proves to be so deficient, except when told by the internal process of
reading and rewriting that I have been sketching here. That is to
say, when that history is told by the Latin American novel itself.

The history of the Latin American novel has been variously told.
For the most part, however, no matter what method the historian
employs, the blueprint of evolution and change continues to be that
of European literary or artistic historiography. Whether he or she be
a thematic historian of the novel or of Latin American literature in
general, or one whose approach purports to be socio-political and
hence Marxist inspired, ordinary categories like romanticism,
naturalism, realism, the avant-garde, surface sooner or later. If it is
questionable that this historiographic grid is applicable to European literature, it is even more so regarding the literature of Latin
America. What undermines this approach is, to begin with, the
inclusion of the narrative within the broader concept of literature, or
belles-lettres. As I have suggested, what is most significant about the
novel, or even about prose narrative in general, is that its point of
departure is to deny that it is literature. The novel, as we have seen,
continues to exist without a poetics because the main tenet of its
poetics is to have none. The novel dons a disguise to appear as
something else; the novel is always something else. That something
else includes a desire to preserve secrets about the origin and history
of a culture, and in this it may be related to the epic (as Lukács
suggested, and others, like Bakhtin, continued to accept),[30] but also
its Protean ability to change and to disavow the knowledge/power
equation lodged in those secrets. For reasons about which one can
only speculate, this phenomenon seems to be particularly prevalent
in Latin America, where the greatest narratives are not novels (but
appear to be so), or are novels pretending to be something else. I
have in mind, of course, Columbus' diaries and letters about the
discovery, Sarmiento's *Facundo*, Euclides da Cunha's *Os Sertões*,
Lydia Cabrera's *El monte*, Martín Luis Guzmán's *El águila y la
serpiente*, Miguel Barnet's *Biografía de un cimarrón*, and many others.
This is the reason for including in my discussion books such as
Facundo and *Os Sertões*, which do not claim to be novels, but in not

doing so, appeal to the most basic conceit of novelistic discourse; not to be literature. It is a hopeless task to force texts such as these into a conventional history of the Latin American novel, and a blatant error to leave them out. It is clear that they are the very core of that tradition.

I seek to produce a history of the Latin American narrative that goes beyond the surface differences determined by artistic trends, looking for the subtext determined by the phoenix-like quality of novelistic discourse, a subtext that takes into account the synchronicity between the Picaresque and the first narratives of and about Latin America, and delves into the relationship between novelistic discourse and nonliterary forms of hegemonic discourse. The novel razes all previous constructs to create itself anew in the image of another text, a text which, as I suggest, is endowed with specific power to bear the truth at a given moment in history, owing to a given set of socio-economic circumstances. That truth, in the case of the narratives being discussed here, is about Latin America itself as a cultural entity, as a context or archive from which to narrate. The first issue is, precisely, one of legitimation, as the trial to decide upon the canonization of Columbus clearly reminds us. Archival fictions like *El arpa y la sombra* bear the indelible imprint of the law, the form of writing that was generated by the initial political circumstances that made Latin American narrative possible.

The first and defining set of circumstances that determined the emergence of such narrative was the development in Spain and its colonies of a modern state, and the fashioning of a legal system to sustain it by controlling individuals. The evolution of narrative prose prior to 1554, when *Lazarillo* is published, is of interest, but of minor relevance when compared to the importance of the state bureaucracy and the emergence of texts, based on models provided by the bureaucracy, to allow individuals, often criminals or otherwise marginal people, to obtain exculpation or enfranchisement. There are fabliaux, oral and written tales, Petronius, Boccaccio, Don Juan Manuel, Chaucer, *Il Novellino*, Juan Ruiz and the novelistic elements of Dante's *Commedia*, but all these are absorbed into a large quilt with a radically new pattern when Lazarillo "writes": "Pues sepa Vuestra Merced que a mí llaman Lázaro de Tormes . . ." ("May Your Worship know that I am called Lázaro de Tormes . . .") A different mimetic contract is established by that enunciation, which has the form of a legal act. The object of that mimetic contract will be violated, as the novel or the narrative takes on different forms, but not its basic structure.

This version of the history of the Latin American narrative wishes, then, to find, analyze and describe those breaks and renewals, believing that the central strand in that narrative obeys such an underlying structure and tells the same story about constraint, mimesis, and escape. I do not believe, of course, that every Latin American narrative within a given period is dependent on each of the models offered here; but I do argue that the major ones are, and that is the structure that defines the tradition, the canon, or the key to the canon, as it were. Hence I do not maintain that the psychological novels of Eduardo Barrios, for instance, are as crucial as *La vorágine*, or that any servile imitation of *Paul et Virginie* can compare with *Facundo*, or that the last echo of the *nouveau roman* stands next to *Biografía de un cimarrón*. What determines the centrality of these works is their rewriting or their being rewritten. *Terra Nostra* takes up Cervantes, the chronicles of the conquest of Mexico, *Cien años de soledad*, *Tres tristes tigres*, but not *María*, or *Santa*. Novels like these last two do fit in the conventional European historiographic scheme, precisely because they are mere echoes. It is important to determine if Gamboa's novel is naturalistic or not, and how romantic Isaacs was. Not so with narratives at the core of the tradition, which are redeployed violently as they insert the new form assumed by the narrative. Hence the chronicles of the exploration accounts are turned into part of the new Archive, or passed off as mythic, foundational stories.

In the chapters that follow I plan to analyze the main forms that the Latin American narrative has assumed in relation to three kinds of hegemonic discourse, the first of which is foundational both for the novel and for the Latin American narrative in general: legal discourse during the colonial period; the scientific, during the nineteenth century until the crisis of the 1920s; the anthropological, during the twentieth century, up to *Los pasos perdidos* and *Cien años de soledad*. I will then return to the Archive, to the current mode, perhaps beyond the anthropological mediation, the locus on which my own text is situated. It would be aseptically formalistic not to recognize that the law, nineteenth-century science and anthropology are powerful *cultural*, not merely narrative, constructs. Latin America continues to be a culture of lawyers, as well as one whose beliefs about itself are strongly colored by science and anthropology;

the absorbing preoccupation with the issue of cultural identity, the ever-present belief in the uniqueness of Latin American nature and its influence on everything. It is because of the weight of these forms of discourse within the culture that I believe them to play such an important role in the narrative, not the other way around. There is no doubt, either, that both anthropology and science, as they existed then, were present in Latin American narratives since the colonial period. Ramón Pané, and many of the friars and missionaries that followed him, embarked on activities and wrote reports that were precursors of modern anthropology. The same can be said of science. From Columbus on, and particularly in writers like Fernández de Oviedo and José de Acosta, there was a curiosity about American reality and an effort at description and classification. But neither anthropology nor science became disciplines *per se* until later, nor did they acquire, until much later, a hegemonic position in relation to the discovery and dissemination of the truth. No matter. Their embryonic presence surely facilitated their acquiring such a status in Latin American culture and narratives, as well as the possibility of remaining as strong memories in modern narratives such as those by Carpentier and García Márquez.

By hegemonic discourse I mean one backed by a discipline, or embodying a system, that offers the most commonly accepted description of humanity and accounts for the most widely held beliefs of the intelligentsia. Within such a discourse, the individual finds stories about himself and the world that he or she finds acceptable, and in some ways obeys. Prestige and socio-political power give these forms of discourse currency. When they are abandoned, they are merely stories or myths, voided of power in the present, the way in which we read about Melquíades' scientific prowess in the early chapters of *Cien años de soledad*. It does not escape me that the hegemonic discourse described here comes from "outside" Latin America; therefore Latin America appears to be constantly explaining itself in "foreign" terms, to be the helpless victim of a colonialist's language and image-making. There is a level at which this is true and deplorable. However, in Latin America, in every realm, from the economic to the intellectual, the outside is also always inside; García Márquez and Vargas Llosa hardly think like *llaneros* or *campesinos*. This duality, which is for the most part a stance, or in the worst of cases, a posture, is present from the start, for instance, in Garcilaso de la Vega, el Inca. Latin America is part of the Western world, not a colonized other, except in founding fictions and constitutive idealizations. In addition the internalization of these forms of discourse is not a passive process, nor a celebration, but a dialectical struggle with no victor and no satisfactory synthesis, save through fiction; if our individual subconscious is not made up of nice stories about mommy and daddy, neither is our history composed of epic tales leading to independence and cultural identity, yet both are irreducibly ours, and part of our stories. The Latin American narrative, both in the stories it tells, and in the structure of those stories, reflects a struggle to free the imagination of all mediation, to reach a knowledge of self and collectivity that is liberating and easily shared; a clearing in the current jungle of discourses of power, emblematized in the one the narrator of *Los pasos perdidos* seeks, or in the remote and foundational Macondo created by the Buendías. But since this foundation has not yet occurred in reality, and is unlikely to occur in the foreseeable future, the stories told here, which I think are masterstories, are about a process toward liberation, not the story of its accomplishment. Nor is one naively to suppose that similar stories culled from the European tradition could be substantially closer to such a desideratum. Pollyanna only exists in Eleanor Porter's novel, and in the naive doctrines of dull ideologues and bad novelists.

I have chosen the most representative works, at the risk of covering territories better charted by others. I begin with the law and shall end with a return to the law in the Archive.

The law of the letter: Garcilaso's *Comentarios*

It's a nice thing for you to try and persuade me
that all these fine books say is nonsense and lies,
when they are printed by license of the Lords of
the Royal Council – as if they were people who
would allow a pack of lies to be published . . .
Miguel de Cervantes, *Don Quijote*, I, 32[1]

I

No event prior to it, and few since, has been written about as much
as the discovery and conquest of America. It is commonplace to say
that America was "discovered" by the printing press that made the
news available to many throughout the Western World. Columbus'
letter to Luis de Santángel, written in February of 1493, was quickly
printed and distributed in Latin translation as well as in versions
in vernacular languages. Soon, by 1500, Peter Martyr d'Anghiera
had written his first set of "decades," which already attempted to
incorporate Columbus' deed into history.[2] Other distinguished
historians, with or without the official approval of the Spanish
Crown, set out to write the history of America: Gonzalo Fernández
de Oviedo, Francisco López de Gómara, Bartolomé de las Casas,
Francisco de Herrera y Tordesillas, José de Acosta, are among
many others. Writing the history of America, of course, was no
ordinary task. The discovery and conquest pushed these historians'
skills and received ideas to the limit. How could this new story be
told in a language burdened by old stories? How did this event affect
the idea of history held until then? How did America fit in the
scheme of sacred and secular history? Where was America in the
Holy Scriptures, where in the classical tradition? Why had the
Church Fathers not written about this land teeming with people
whose origin was difficult to establish?

Writing in the Middle Ages and the Renaissance was not conceived as an activity whereby a naked consciousness, faced with a
fresh empirical or spiritual phenomenon, expresses its reaction *ex
nihilo*. Writing was then an activity that took place within a grid of
strict rules and formulae which comprised what could loosely be
called rhetoric. Therefore, writing the story of America had to take
place through such a network, which had connections to broader
systems that regulated social activity. The narrator-protagonist of
Los pasos perdidos wished to void himself of all prior mediations in the
clearing at Santa Mónica. Even the most recalcitrant renegades of
the sixteenth century – Lope de Aguirre, for instance – felt that to
write they had to do so according to a prescribed set of norms.
Aguirre's seditious letter to Philip II, one of the more outlandish
texts of the period, was still a letter written and sent to the Emperor
according to the rules of the Empire, one of which granted all
subjects the right to communicate in writing directly with the King,
thus bypassing the bureaucracy of the State. Aguirre's letter, like the
letter the *pícaro* writes in *Lazarillo de Tormes*, is an act of defiance as
well as one of compliance. Felipe Guamán Poma de Ayala's history
of the New World, particularly of Peru, was written from the
outraged perspective of a victim, to denounce the conquest. His
command of Spanish was (perhaps defiantly) precarious, nevertheless Guamán Poma complied, sometimes excessively so, with the
rhetorical norms of the day, as in his numerous prologues. When
America was discovered and conquered, writing was a tightly
regulated activity through which the individual manifested his or
her belonging to a body politic. Justina's convoluted meditations on
writing, at the beginning of the picaresque novel bearing her name
(*La pícara Justina*, 1605), is the most remarkable example of this
phenomenon.

One of the truisms about Garcilaso de la Vega, el Inca, is that he
wrote well. No matter what we make of the *Comentarios reales de los
Incas*, the fact remains that, by any standards – whether of his time
or ours – Garcilaso was indeed a great stylist.[3] He had a penchant
for using just the right word, his sentences have a measured
cadence, an inner rhythm leading toward a logical resolution, and
there is, more often than not, an elegant touch of irony. Only
Cervantes, Garcilaso's contemporary, with whom he shared a
crepuscular humanism, was a better prose writer in Spanish at the
end of the sixteenth and the beginning of the seventeenth century.

Why did Garcilaso write so well? Why did this mestizo son of a
Spanish conqueror and an Inca noblewoman endeavor to produce
such polished prose as he wrote his vast history of the New World?
Garcilaso, it might be remembered, not only wrote a history of
pre-Hispanic Peru, but what amounts to an entire history of
America, from pre-Incaic times to about 1580, when the last Inca
rebel was defeated. Such a vast span of time encompassed quite a
varied array of subject-matter: from the succession of Inca emperors, whom he viewed with a deference usually reserved in the
Renaissance for their Roman counterparts, to the daily life of the
Spanish conquistadors in Peru; from noblemen vying for political
power, to the riff-raff who rushed to the New World in search of
money and social advancement. The *Comentarios* and the *Historia
general del Perú* also included Garcilaso's own compelling autobiography, filled with the drama of his father's participation in the
conquest and government of Peru, and the tragedy of his mother's
life; his father's failure to make her his wife, the defeat of her people;
and most poignantly the demise of her family, which was that of the
last ruling Inca.[4] What sustained Garcilaso's prose style through
such a broad and varied undertaking? Why and under what
circumstances did this illegitimate mestizo learn to write so well?
Answering this question will allow me to posit and describe the first
mediation through which the story of Latin America was narrated,
as well as to speculate about the relationship between writing the
history of the New World and the parallel emergence of the
Picaresque, that is to say, of the novel.

In the sixteenth century writing was subservient to the law. One
of the most significant changes in Spain, as the Peninsula was
unified and became the center of an Empire, was the legal system,
which redefined the relationship between the individual and the
body politic and held a tight rein on writing. Narrative, both
fictional and historical, thus issued from the forms and constraints of
legal writing. Legal writing was the predominant form of discourse
in the Spanish Golden Age. It permeated the writing of history,
sustained the idea of Empire, and was instrumental in the creation
of the Picaresque. The way the Inca wrote, and the reason why he
and other chroniclers wrote, has a great deal to do with the
development of notarial rhetoric that resulted from the evolution
and expansion of the Spanish State. To write was a form of
enfranchisement, of legitimation. The *pícaro*, the chronicler, and in

a sense the whole New World, seek enfranchisement and a validation of their existence through the writing of their stories.

By the time Garcilaso wrote his masterpiece, the history of
America had been told and retold by numerous historians,
explorers, and discoverers, so that what the Inca undertook was, of
necessity, a revisionist task. But, while the freshness of the story he
told may have been lost, that of Garcilaso's perspective as a writer
was not. Writing from his dual point of view as Indian and
European, Garcilaso offered a dramatic account of the history of
America that not only told the story but also reflected upon the
telling. This quality is of the utmost importance to understanding
how Latin American history became a story that could be told; how
it could be added to that of the West as it was known then; and how
an individual with roots in the New World could tell his or her own
story. Garcilaso's writings were produced within a complex process
in which various rhetorical possibilities offered themselves as means
of expression and vied with each other for hegemony. This process
involves notarial rhetoric as well as Renaissance historiography, the
origins of the picaresque novel as much as those of *Don Quijote*.

2

In rhetoric, more than in anything else, the continuity of the old European
tradition was embodied.   C. S. Lewis[5]

America existed as a legal document before it was physically
discovered. In the *Capitulaciones de Santa Fe*, the Catholic Kings drew
up a contract with Columbus, before he set out, outlining in
considerable detail his, and the Crown's, rights over any discovered
territories. The papal bull *Inter Caetera* of 1493 was also a legal title
by which the Spanish Kings were declared proprietors of the new
realms. Francis I, who was none too happy with these claims, raged
that he wished to see the will in which Adam had bequeathed such
vast territories to Spain. Columbus' claims soon became the object
of bitter disputes with the Crown. The Admiral and his heirs sued
for many years, referring back to the *Capitulaciones*, and though the
honorific side of the claim was granted, their proprietary plea was
not.[6] The Crown had soon realized that Columbus' family wished to
acquire precisely the sort of power that the State was trying to wrest
from the Castilian aristocracy.[7] The importance of Columbus'

demands was such that even the official history of the discovery and conquest was affected. America was not only a legal document before it was discovered, but soon thereafter became the object of continued legal jousting. The sixteenth century is marked not only by the protracted cases involving Columbus' heirs, but also by equally lengthy litigation involving Cortés, Pizarro, Cabeza de Vaca and other conquistadors, not to mention the thousands of cases provoked by the issuance of the New Laws (1542) partially revoking the *encomienda* system, and the disputes concerning the rights of the native population.[8] In 1544, a weary Hernán Cortés, exasperated by judicial battles that would rage for over a century after his death, wrote to Emperor Charles V: "más me cuesta defenderme del fiscal de vuestra Magestad que ganar la tierra de mis enemigos" ("I find it more difficult to defend myself from your prosecutor than to conquer the lands of my enemies").[9] Columbus' legal entanglements brought about the foundation of the Audiencia of Santo Domingo in 1512, the first of what was soon to become one of the most important institutions in the New World, one that would eventually define the territorial boundaries of many of today's Latin American republics.[10] The founding of the first Audiencia as a result of Columbus' contested rights is a clear example of what was at stake socially and politically in the process of conquering the New World. To gain wealth, power, a title, and vassals was the aspiration of Spaniards for whom a sense of worth meant a sense of being.[11] A clash with the Crown was all but inevitable. The discoverers and conquerors were soon followed by the *letrados*, the lawyers who "reconquered" the new territories for the Crown. Basking in the reflected power of the State that they represented, the *letrados* clipped the wings of the conquistadors' aspirations. Military action was followed by legal action. As Malagón Barceló put it:

The lawyer or *letrado* is found in every advance of the conquest and colonization. At the discovery of the Pacific, an *escribano* accompanied Balboa. Every city had the official act of its birth drawn up by the scribe who accompanied the founding expedition. In my opinion there is nothing equal in history to the act of founding drawn up by the Spanish scribe. It gave the geographical situation of the new urban nucleus, the name of the founder, how it was established, and how the lands were divided, etc. Above all, it detailed how the *picota*, formerly of seigneurial power, now acquired the significance of royal sovereignty.[12]

The legalistic, bureaucratic character of Spanish administration pervaded the Empire. Haring, in his authoritative history, goes so far as to say that the Spaniards, "like the Romans [...] were pre-eminently creators of laws and builders of institutions. Of all the colonizing peoples of modern times, the Spaniards were the most legal-minded. In the new empire they speedily developed a meticu-lously organized administrative system such as the world had rarely seen."[13] Legal papers covered the New World, charting it and binding it to the Old through the written language. The generators of these papers were the *letrados* and their minions: *escribanos, notarios*, and other members of the state bureaucracy charged with drawing up, copying, and filing documents. Just as in Spain, where the *letrados* formed a class that would eventually dislodge the aristocracy from positions of power, in the New World they eroded the power of the conquistadors. Garcilaso's father belonged to this latter class, and Garcilaso to that of the *letrados*.[14]

Though medieval in many ways, the new political system created by the Spanish was modern because individuals defined their relationship to it in legal, not genealogical terms. J. H. Parry writes in his *The Spanish Theory of Empire in the Sixteenth Century*:

The deliberate, self-conscious purpose which was so characteristic of the imperialism of the Spaniards and so conspicuously lacking in that of the Portuguese, and later that of the British, reflected the immense influence and importance of the Spanish legal profession. Sixteenth-century Spain led the rest of Europe not only in the practice of law and government, but also in the abstract field of jurisprudence. The Spanish jurists, before the middle of the century, evolved a theory of sovereignty distinct equally from the narrow kinship of the Middle Ages and from the unbridled absolutism pictured by Hobbes and his followers. It was, in fact, a theory of a constitutional state, possessed of the right of legislation and unrestricted in its sphere of action, but restricted in its exercise of power by the man-made laws and customs of its subjects.[15]

If the most significant characteristic of the new State was its legalistic make-up, the most visible feature was the pervasive meticulousness of its organization and the entanglement of the individual in a complex set of relationships with the central power. The system was so thorough that it sought to regulate not only individuals, but also its own codes: for instance, by creating the position of *cronista mayor*, a person officially appointed to write the State's version of history. An equally prominent characteristic, one

that bespeaks its modernity, was the urban-oriented organization of
the Spanish Empire. The first thing Cortés did upon setting foot on
the Continent was to found the city of Vera Cruz, an act that
enabled him to communicate directly with the Crown through
letters drawn up by the city's municipal government.[16] The Castilian state as reproduced in America was urban; the citizenship of
individuals was civic, of the city. Celestina and Lazarillo are
eminently urban characters. The serf was linked to the feudal lord
by "natural codes," or better, by codes whose tropological coherence was conveyed through nature metaphors of strong referential
appeal: the land, kinship, in short, tradition. In the Spanish
settlements the very grid of the city reflects the political mediations
that stand between the citizen and the State. This is particularly
evident in American cities, whose layout was dictated by the central
government. No sooner had a town been founded than its plan was
deployed according to the model stipulated by the Crown, a plan in
which the symbols of the powers of the State were prominently
placed at the very center – the *plaza mayor*, with its church, town hall,
and the most characteristic symbol of all, the *picota* or whipping post.

Any reader of Garcilaso's *Historia general del Perú* will soon discover
that the pillory was no ornament, and that very famous heads
wound up on it with frightening frequency. The *picota* symbolized
the law; it was a reminder of the individual's subservience to the
State. The evolution of this most phallic symbol of seigneurial power
is indicative of the evolution of the Spanish State.[17] Before the
unification of the Peninsula, each town's pillory displayed the coat
of arms of the local lord, under whose authority punishment was
meted out. After the accession to power of the Catholic Kings,
pillories bore the Castilian coat of arms. At the pillory, the citizens of
the domain were whipped, tortured, shamed, their severed organs
put on public display. The pillory is predominantly urban in that it
presupposes that the culprit be seen by others as he is being
humiliated. The punishment becomes a spectacle of the city as well
as a display of the machinery of the State at work. Urban justice
involves public shame, a public acknowledgment that breaking the
law of the State is not only an offense against a paternal figure but
against an organic set of interdictions. Lazarillo and Celestina are
likely candidates for a turn at the pillory. Guzmán "writes" as a
galley-slave.[18] Writing, like the whipping post, involved a relationship with a code of interdictions set up by the State; that is to say,

the relationship was not merely legal but more specifically penal. The history of America and the incipient novel are mediated by such a relationship. Guzmán, the protagonist of the quintessential picaresque novel, writes as a prisoner, Lazarillo as someone who has been accused. The importance of such a penal relationship of the individual with the state is reflected in the evolution of pillories in Latin America. With the passage of time they became even more elaborate. Some of them are ornate baroque constructions that parallel similar developments in sculpture and architecture.

If America existed first as a legal document, the proliferation of laws and edicts that accompanied its conquest was stupendous, as if a paroxysmal dissemination of the printed word were needed to preserve its being. Thousands of laws were promulgated before the famous *Recopilación* of 1681 – according to one expert, almost a law per day, excluding Sundays.[19] This proliferation of legal writing was due to the meticulousness of the Spanish State and to the casuistry of the Spanish legal system. The production of so many documents led to the construction of the great archive at Simancas. The building itself – medieval castle, later prison, finally archive – is an emblem both of the evolution of the Spanish monarchy and of the nature of the documents it sheltered and classified. As J. H. Elliott writes: "Anyone who spends any length of time in the great state archive of Simancas cannot fail to be impressed by the overwhelming mass of documentation generated by the Spanish administrative machine in the sixteenth and seventeenth centuries. Habsburg Spain was a pioneer of the modern state, and the presence of the state can be felt at every turn in the history of Spain and its overseas possessions, at once influencing and being influenced by the societies it seeks to control."[20] Like the Escorial, the archive at Simancas was a kind of mausoleum, a tomb for myriads of texts containing the lives and deeds of individuals throughout the vast Spanish Empire, set in its very center, next to the seat of power. Later, in the eighteenth century, the Archivo de Indias was built in Seville to keep the documents related to Spain's possessions in the New World. It is a treasure-house of information that has not been exhausted by generations of zealous scholars.[21] The millions of legal papers that it contains still have the allure of offering total knowledge about American origins. It contains in its vaults – appropriately built in the city that was the capital of picaresque life – the writings of hundreds of Lazarillos, Bernal Diaz's, and others who wrote about their lives to the central authority.

It is no accident, then, that Fernando de Rojas, the author of *La Celestina*, was a lawyer: the law saturates the Spanish literature of the Golden Age and is a determining factor in the origins of the novel. Not a few among the great Spanish authors of the sixteenth and seventeenth centuries spent time in prison. Garcilaso de la Vega (the poet), Fray Luis de León, San Juan de la Cruz, Mateo Alemán, Miguel de Cervantes, Francisco de Quevedo and Calderón de la Barca were all incarcerated at one point or another, while Lope de Vega and Luis de Góngora barely kept one step ahead of the law. The great playwright was exiled from the capital because of his scandalous love life, and Góngora narrowly escaped being implicated in a murder. Spanish Golden Age literature, particularly the novel and the theater, is filled with allusions to the law. Lawyers, together with officers from all echelons of the imperial bureaucracy, populate plays and stories, both as protagonists and in secondary roles (the most famous being perhaps Cervantes' Glass Licenciate).[22] The *pícaro* is a creature conceived in the web of the law, while many a *comedia* (not to mention the *entremeses*) contains a scene in which a judge or a lesser official sets up on stage his writing paraphernalia to pass sentence or record an event (Cervantes' *El juez de los divorcios* is a case in point). There are many well-known plays in which the legal authority and jurisdiction of *alcaldes* and *comendadores* is at the core of the conflict, and the so-called honor dramas often involve a legal dispute concerning the rights of the outraged husband. But it is particularly in the plays that pit officials of various ranks against one another that the legal and administrative upheavals of Spain under the Habsburgs are best reflected. *El alcalde de Zalamea*, in the versions by Lope and Calderón, and, of course, *Fuenteovejuna*, are the outstanding examples. Cervantes, himself a member of the state bureaucracy, filled his works with *alguaciles*, *oidores*, *licenciados*, and other officers. The *Quijote* is full of these characters, and one of the many memorable scenes in the book is the one involving the galley-slaves who tell the mad hero the crimes for which they have been sentenced. The scene enacts the typical picaresque situation of the criminal telling his story to someone in higher authority (the fact that authority is vested in a madman is a typical Cervantean debunking of power).[23] *Guzmán de Alfarache*, *El Buscón*, and *La pícara Justina* are teeming with characters who are either representatives or victims of the law. To Quevedo, lawyers and other officers of the Spanish legal system were, together with deceived husbands, the favourite target of his corrosive humor. Lawyers were as much an obsession with him as doctors were with Molière. The reason for this, as Lía Schwartz Lerner has written, is very much in keeping with the entire process of bureaucratization that withdrew power from the aristocracy to place it in the hands of government functionaries.[24]

A brief consideration of the Spanish legal system is in order to explain how the centralization of the Spanish State bears upon the writing of the story of America and the origins of the Picaresque. Haring, Ots Capdequí, Schafer, Elliott and others have more than adequately described how this centralized state functioned.[25] I need not repeat their work here, except to say that Spain was governed through a conciliar system, with each council having under its jurisdiction an area of the empire (be it geographical or administrative). The significance of this kind of organization lies in the fact that, though these deliberate bodies had a practical impact on decision-making, as well as a duty to voice their opinions, theoretically, final authority remained with the Crown which could and did exercise it. This model, consisting of a deliberative body answering to a higher authority, is repeated in lower echelons. In the case of the Peninsula, during the reign of the Catholic Kings, and even before the discovery of America, two institutions have to be taken into account as forerunners of the Imperial State, both of which, impervious to local rights, policed the people: the paramilitary Santa Hermandad (so feared by Sancho) and the Holy Office of the Inquisition. Haring states:

The government of Castile in the fifteenth and sixteenth centuries [...] was rapidly becoming an absolute, patrimonial monarchy. Like other growing nation-states of Europe as they were consolidated in the age of the Renaissance, it escaped from the medieval limitations of Empire and Church and the feudal rights of the nobility – also from the acquired rights of municipal autonomy represented in Spain by the *fueros* of its principal cities. The superiority of the state over all long-standing customs, local privileges, and private jurisdictions was more and more accepted.[26]

Ots Capdequí and other legal historians have remarked in passing how fruitful it would be to think of the Spanish State in terms of Max Weber's well-known categories to which Haring alludes, and Magali Sarfatti has carried out precisely such an analysis in her well-documented *Spanish Bureaucratic Patrimonialism in America*.[27] But it was Richard Morse, in an influential essay, who laid the groundwork for an interpretation of the Spanish State that would take into account the ideology that supported it as well as the way in which it functioned.[28] Morse maintains that Latin American society was founded on (and continues to be guided by) certain principles prevalent in sixteenth-century political theory, as propounded by Francisco Suárez, the eminent Jesuit exponent of Thomist political philosophy in Spain: "Francisco Suárez (1548–1617) is generally recognized as the thinker who most fully recapitulated Thomist political thought in Spain's age of *Barock scholastik* [...] His fresh marshalling of scholastic doctrines, under powerful influences of time and place, encapsulated certain assumptions about political Man and certain political dilemmas that pervade Hispanic political life to this day."[29] Morse believes that Neo-Thomism offered a justification for a set of socio-political realities in Spain and her Empire. It is ironic and revealing that what is no doubt a modern feature of the Spanish Empire should be sustained by a political ideology whose sources are so thoroughly medieval. Sarfatti, following Morse, concludes:

For more than three centuries, the American territories were subjected to a structure of government and administration which can be defined as patrimonial and bureaucratic. This structure, legitimized by a tradition expressed in the Thomist and neo-scholastic doctrines, was already apparent in Spain at the time of the Conquest. Later in the sixteenth century, when the Crown no longer had to reckon at home with the challenge posed by the nobility or the urban bourgeoisies, this model of government – expressed in the economic sphere by the mercantilist theory – was even more forcefully brought to bear upon the New World.[30]

In what way did this patrimonial bureaucracy affect the writing of Latin American history and the origins of the novel? And what does patrimonial bureaucracy really mean in terms of the functioning of the Spanish State?

The patrimonial state, according to Weber's theory, is one which "grows out of the narrow sphere of domestic power (that is, generally, land-based lordship) by an extension of the patriarchal bonds that linked the lord to his kin, retainers and serfs."[31] In other words, the patrimonial state is a symbolic extension of the domestic structure of power, whose source and center is the paternal figure of the lord. Legitimation is granted within this structure of power by

adherence to tradition, rather than to law, and the locus of functionality is the land, the fiefdom within which such power was
operational, hence the pillories bearing the lord's coat of arms.

The bureaucratic state, on the other hand, is organized on the
basis of the functional rationality of the system, whose authority and
legitimacy are inherent in its operational validity. Consequently,
functionaries within this organization are chosen according to their
ability to operate in the bureaucratic machinery; ideally, they do not
owe their position to a favor granted by the lord or monarch. The
Spanish State was a patrimonial bureaucracy insofar as power was
lodged in the seigneurial authority of the Crown. But at the same
time, and increasingly so after the sixteenth century, the bureaucracy became a self-enclosed, self-regulating, machine whose grist
was paper and which was oiled with ink. The *encomienda* system, for
all it appeared to be feudalistic, exemplified this power structure.[32]
By undermining or removing its hereditary character and subjecting conquistadors to the rules set forth by the Crown, the *encomienda*
was an extension of the patrimonial bureaucratic state. The scholastic origin of the duality present in the patrimonial bureaucratic
system is clear. Morse summarizes Suárez' doctrine in the following
manner:

Natural law is a general rule; conscience is a practical application of it to
specific cases. Natural law is never mistaken; conscience may be. Society
and the body politic are therefore seen as properly ordered by objective and
external natural-law precepts rather than by consensus sprung from the
promptings of private consciences [...] God is the author of civil power,
but He created it as a property emanating from nature so that no society
would lack the power necessary for preservation. A proposition of this sort
allowed the view that most of the pre-Columbian Indians were not savages
but lived in societies ordered by natural law [...] The people do not
delegate *but alienate their sovereignty* to their prince.[33]

The casuistry of the Spanish law, which made for the writing of so
many documents, is a direct result of this view of the State, for "to
adjudicate is to determine whether a given case affects all of society
or whether it can be dispatched by an ad hoc decision."[34] Here lies
precisely the bridge, so to speak, from the patrimonial to the
patrimonial bureaucratic state. Increasingly, paternal authority
becomes an entelechy against which to adjudicate in a manner that,
rather than being *ad hoc*, answers to an internal, systemic, bureaucratic structure. In other words, in the patrimonial bureaucracy

legitimation is granted through the alienated political codes that have become a simulacrum of seigneurial power. The individual conscience, which can and does err, writes to the embodiment of natural law (Lázaro to Your Lordship, Cortés to Charles V) to exculpate and recapture his or her legitimacy (Cortés, it might be well to remember, had taken actions of more than questionable legality at the start of his enterprise). This is the beginning of the Picaresque, and of the novel: the story of a new, civil individual, who writes on his own, subject to no myths and to no tradition.

Politics is the mediating code of frozen casuistry. The symbolic relationships of the patrimonial state are replaced with the codified signs of the bureaucratic one. The symbolic relationships of the family are replaced by the graphic signs of the city: the pillory bearing the arms of Castile; writing, and the overwhelmingly ornate architecture of churches and viceregal courts. The viceroys stand in for the King, but will also be cogs in the machinery of the State. The history of America as well as the emerging novel will be the letter the individual writes to this absent father, whose presence is felt only through the codes, like writing, that denote his absence. In his *Summa dictaminis*, Guido Faba, one of the great Bolognese *dictatores* (masters of rhetoric), calls the letter a *libellus*, technically a legal petition sent to someone who is absent.[35] The letter he writes is the *pícaro*'s *carte d'identité*, and the letters that conquerors, such as Cortés, write are not only *cartas*, both in the sense of letters and maps, but *charters* of the New World.

3

The truth is that many do not really write, but translate, others merely provide versions and most of the time perversions.
Covarrubias, *Tesoro de la lengua castellana o española*, 1611[36]

Out of this relationship between the individual and the State the novel will emerge, as the writer-protagonist of the Picaresque writes a report on his life to an absent authority. The proliferating formulae of notarial rhetoric invaded the writing of history as well, which also reflected the ideology of the State, but through the highflown rhetoric of Renaissance historiography. Law and history are the two predominant modes of discourse in the colonial period. Their truthfulness is guaranteed by the mediating codes of the State, chiefly notarial rhetoric.

The overwhelming presence of the State, a bureaucratized figure of patrimonial authority, or rather, a figural image of authority cast in the rhetoric of the imperial bureaucracy, is at the core of the Picaresque. It would be limiting not to see the development of Latin American narrative against the backdrop of the emerging modern novel in the Picaresque. The two are not only coeval, but are produced within a broader context, or text, of which they are versions and, in some cases, perversions. When seen in the context of the foregoing discussion the Picaresque appears as an allegory of legitimation. The *pícaro* is orphaned or illegitimate. A creature of the city, the center of the new patrimonial bureaucracy, he seeks legitimacy through the codes in which the new authority is hypostatized: the rhetoric of the new State. His conscience is being cleared by this exercise in which he imitates the models furnished by that rhetoric; he belongs, he is like that hypostatized figure. He is made up by its writing.

Compliance with the rhetorical norm on the part of the *pícaro* has a significant counterpart in one of the more remarkable documents of Colonial Spanish America: the infamous *requerimiento*.[37] This text was read to the bewildered natives by a conquering group of Spaniards, informing them that unless they declared themselves to be subjects of the Spanish Crown, they would be attacked, their possessions confiscated and their freedom forfeited. This document was dutifully read before battle, in the presence of a notary who stamped his signature to attest that proper procedure had been followed. Their consciences lightened by the ritual recitation of the *requerimiento*, the conquistadors could then make war on the Indians with as much brutality as they deemed necessary. The performance, like Lazarillo's written confession, is an action that at once shows subservience and grants freedom. Mimicking the rhetorical norm, voicing the text of authority, as it were, frees one, insofar as the action is part of the functionality of the bureaucracy, a functionality that carries its own authority because it, in its turn, stands for the power of the Crown. Reciting the *requerimiento* is an act of imitating the simulacrum of patrimonial authority, of being like the simulacrum of power that rhetoric contrives. In the case of the *pícaro* and many of the chroniclers of America, however, the rhetorical vehicle is not the *requerimiento*, but the *relación* – a report, deposition, or even a confession in the penal sense.

The *relación* pledges to be a textual link with the source of power

through the maze of bureaucratic formulae that supplanted patrimonial authority. A great deal of narrative in colonial Latin
America – Columbus, Pané, Bernal Díaz, Cabeza de Vaca and
countless others – was written in this form. It was a way of ensuring
the enfranchisement of the author and of *lending* credence to his
story. (One might recall here that Sor Juana Inés de la Cruz' famous
Respuesta a Sor Filotea is a plea that is quite similar to these.) The legal
formula, like that of the *requerimiento*, gave formal, bureaucratic
bonding and approval to what the documents contained, as if Don
Quixote could get a notary public to declare officially that the
enchanters exist. The Picaresque, that is to say, the modern novel,
emerges to lay bare the conventionality of this process of legitimation, to uncover its status as an arbitrary imposition from the
outside, rather than inner validation that successfully links the
individual and the story of his life to the State. The *pícaro*-author,
like the *cronista-relator*, struggles within language to show the limits of
the kind of promise such an outside verification entails and to create
a space where the story of the individual can have its own form of
substantiality – the text. This is so because language itself, like the
bureaucracy, is now conceived as a functional system whose
operations override the impact of outside authority. Just as the law
is codified, Nebrija's *Gramática*, and the debates over Erasmianism
in the sixteenth century, are evidence of this conception.[38] The
novel is the process by which language submits to the conventions
of rhetoric at the service of power, in order to show that writing does
not afford the kind of individual self-presence that the bureaucracy
promises, that the letter always remains undelivered like the one in
García Márquez' *El coronel no tiene quien le escriba*. Yet language does
submit to the models of rhetoric, in a mimetic move that appeals to
the freedom from authority afforded by the functionality of rhetoric
and of language itself. Rhetoric is the bureaucratic part of the
patrimonial bureaucratic state, the part that both constrains and
delivers by means of its own rationality, by its own process of
self-verification, a process that is presumably independent of patrimonial authority. Both the novel, and the history of the New World,
merge in their effort to at once legitimate and free the individual.
Pablos, Quevedo's *pícaro* in *El Buscón*, speaks, at the end of the novel
of leaving for America, a voyage Mateo Alemán made and Cervantes wished to make. The New World is an escape because of the very
freedom afforded the new as something not yet codified. The

thematic reflection of this is the topic of utopia that runs through Latin American letters.[39] The novel offers the same kind of liberation by its imitation of the forms through which the state transacts power. This process remains in place in the Latin American narrative until the present, though the kind of mediation varies.

The rhetorical conventions of the *relación*, mimicked by the Picaresque, appear again and again in the extant texts of the colonial period, volumes of which have been published, though it should be obvious that volumes more could be culled from the various existing archives, particularly the one in Seville. Seville, the capital of *picardía*, as well as the gateway to America, is now the site of the largest collection of texts pertaining to the New World, and a veritable textual prison-house.[40] The formula of the *relación* is not only simple but revealing in its own naïveté and seemingly innocuous capacity to contain facts. In 1575 Philip II issued an ordinance concerning the style of these documents. He stated that "el estilo sea breve, claro, substancial y decente, sin generalidades, y usando de las palabras que con más propiedad puedan dar a entender la intención de quien las escribe" ("the style should be brief, clear, informative, and decorous, devoid of generalities, and should use the most appropriate words to express the intention of the person writing").[41] Instructions concerning the style of these letters continued to appear in 1595, 1605, 1634, 1645, and 1748. The prescriptions range from an order to pare down the ritualistic forms of address to the size of the margins and what was to be written in them (sometimes a summary to save the reader time).[42] In the *relación* the author states his name, lineage, place of origin and then goes on to report – for the record, so to speak – what has taken place, be it an expedition, the review of a viceroy's tenure in office, a grievance or a deed leading to a petition. When Lazarillo says that he is writing at the request of Your Worship, he is invoking a formula of legalistic language, the "motivación," or compliance with a request to draw up a document. Compliance with the formulae, the very act of writing according to it, is a way of inscribing oneself in the general functionality of language. The act is crucial in a legal sense; its substance is to imitate, to perform the gesture prescribed (*prescribed*) by the law; to find liberation as well as enfranchisement through the law. "Pues sepa vuestra merced ante todas cosas que a mí llaman Lázaro de Tormes, hijo de Tomé González y de Antona Pérez, naturales de Tejares, aldea de Salamanca"; "Yo, fray Ramón

Pané, pobre ermitaño de la Orden de San Jerónimo, por mandato del ilustre señor Almirante y virrey y gobernador de las Islas y de la Tierra Firme de Indias, escribo lo que he podido aprender y saber de las creencias e idolatrías de los indios, y de cómo veneran a sus dioses." (I leave these quotations in Spanish to preserve the formulaic tone of the naming and the ritualistic cadence.) There is a clear echo of these formulae in the opening sentence of the *Quijote* ("En un lugar de la Mancha, de cuyo nombre no quiero acordarme"), even if the purpose of the *relación* is denied by intentionally omitting the name of the place in La Mancha where the action begins. The first person reporting, even negatively, is performing the act prescribed by the *relación*. The presence of the "I" in the present narrating story, which comes from the *relación*, will give the novel, from the Picaresque on, its autobiographical and self-reflexive cast. Through these humble formulae, the *relación* sought to establish the legitimacy of the author on two counts: genealogical and territorial. Both genealogy and residence are criteria for naturalization in the Spanish Empire, a process that was obviously problematic in the Indies and around which the picaresque novel, of course, revolves, at least until Fielding's *Tom Jones*. Birth and marriage are the acts through which the *pícaro* relates to the law, hence they will be important topics in the novel for centuries to come.[43] Lázaro is not only from Tormes, but of Tormes: Guzmán is both from and of Alfarache. The act of writing seeks self-presence through compliance with the rhetorical mold. It is a legal kind of ontological gesture, and the formulae furnish the symbolic link with family and territory, with lineage and state. Lazarillo, Guzmán, Pablos, and particularly Justina, tear apart these texts because they emphasize the liberating part of the covenant and twirl language in a dizzying demonstration of its radical conventionality. The simulacrum of power replaces power itself in order to void it. Columbus, Cortés, Bernal, and Garcilaso, establish their own precarious and often contested protestations of civil and political being through legal language.[44]

The give and take of legal language issues from its very dialectical and polemical nature. No utterance can occur in legal proceedings without assuming a question or a response, in short, a dialogue of texts. This is no theoretical dialogue, however, but one that is part of legal rhetoric itself; truth, existence in the civil sense, propriety, all emerge from such a confrontation, hence the dialogic nature of the relationship between Lazarillo and Your Lordship, or between Don Quijote and the galley-slaves. Such a dialectical exchange or disposition is also to be found in the different kinds of legal rhetoric through which the story of Latin America was originally told.[45]

Legal language, in the form prescribed by notarial arts, was not the only discourse of the State at the time of the conquest of America. There was a more deliberate way in which the New World was incorporated into the body politic: the language of history, more specifically of Renaissance historiography, at the service of centralized political power.[46] If the key figures of notarial rhetoric were scribes and lawyers, the key figures of historical writing included secretaries as well as appointed and self-appointed court historians. Like notarial rhetoric, historical writing was mediated by very powerful institutions: the Royal Council of the Indies and the *cronista mayor*.[47] By the spring of 1493, Columbus' letter to Luis de Santángel was being translated and disseminated throughout Europe, and by 1500, Peter Martyr d'Anghiera was sending to Italy the first of his *De Orbe Novo decades*, incorporating the New World into history. In seven short years the issue of how to interpret the discovery of the New World, of how to inscribe it into a larger historical pattern, was already being worked out. The question was a matter of great interest to historians, theologians, and philosophers, who would debate it earnestly. But there were also very pragmatic political factors involved in the interpretation of this overwhelming historical event.

The claims of the Portuguese Crown to the newly discovered territories and its active interest in Columbus' exploits was the first such consideration. Later, other powers came to vie with the Spaniards for the newly "discovered" lands. The papal bull of 1493 and the Treaty of Tordesillas gave jurists, philosophers, and theologians their first chance to discuss the problem and to attempt to reach practical solutions. But these arrangements did not quell the desire of powers other than the Spanish for the New World. With the division of Europe as the result of the Reformation, the dispute took on an even more acrimonious tone. In this climate, the writing of history was no innocent activity, and the Spanish State, ever jealous of its hold on its vastly increased territories, was at pains to control it. An overarching ideological construct was erected to justify and ratify Spanish territorial rights.

Another pragmatic consideration that influenced the conception of American history was its bearing on the various legal proceedings involving the conquistadors and the Crown. Marcel Bataillon has shown how official historiographers, from Peter Martyr to Gonzalo Fernández de Oviedo, and Francisco López de Gómara were affected by the disputes between the Kings and Columbus' heirs.[48] Bataillon proves that the omission of Columbus' landings on the Continent – *tierra firme* as opposed to the islands – on the part of court historians obeyed the Crown's desire not to grant control over such a vast territory to the Admiral's family. The bitter disputes concerning the fate of the natives had a similar impact on historiography. It would not be far-fetched to say that Bartolomé de las Casas' voluminous *Historia de las Indias* was written as a legal brief, against the versions offered by Oviedo and others of the treatment given to Indians. The protracted disputes about the New Laws and the encomienda system – which, in some cases, led to sedition – no doubt also affected the writing of history. Legal battles raged at all levels during the conquest of America, determining the way in which the history of this process was written. Garcilaso's *Comentarios reales* are also mediated by such historiographical overdeterminations.

This branch of the State's discourse was not concerned with the tawdry details of everyday life; nor was it usually cast in the formulaic rhetoric of the notarial arts. On the contrary, Renaissance historiography strove for elegance and beauty and couched the ideology of the conquering State in the harmonious prose of humanism and in humanistic conceptions of history. It was only at this level that the most sophisticated justifications for the conquest could be articulated. The most important rhetorical device which structured these histories was of medieval origin: figural interpretation as a way of proving the providential nature of the Spanish enterprise in the New World.[49] There is a homological relationship between the elegance pursued by humanist historians and the organic, systemic organization of the patrimonial bureaucratic state. The former reflects the latter. There is an incompatibility between notarial rhetoric and historiography that takes the form of a legalist dialogue: the historiography of the state is the authority to whom notarial rhetoric addresses itself, the overall archive where information about people and events will be classified and thus submitted to the constraints of power. Knowledge about individual lives and deeds becomes power in the archive or in the text of official historians.

The existence of an official historian in Castile dates back to the reign of John II (1406–54).[50] The first official historians were, significantly enough, notaries who set down the actions of the king, applying the practices of their trade. These notary-historians were usually chosen from among the secretaries of the king, so that in later years the offices of secretary and court historian were usually combined. In the Renaissance, secretaries to princes, kings or otherwise powerful individuals were the keepers of language.[51] They were often great humanists, a practice that continued in Spain in the sixteenth century, as in the case of Francisco López de Gómara, who was not only a remarkable humanist historian but also Hernán Cortés' secretary. In the first half of the sixteenth century, the Spanish Crown attempted to control the flow of information from America by having all documents pass through the Council of the Indies and, of course, by using the Crown's power to license the publication of books, not to mention the watchful eye of the Holy Office of the Inquisition and its vigilant bureaucratic network. It was the Council who determined the legality of documents and issued laws to control what happened in the New World. History was far from exempt from such control.

Peter Martyr, and even Oviedo, wrote like court historians. The latter in particular aspired to be named official historian of the Indies and hence presented a summary of his work in progress to the Emperor in 1526. This *sumario*, which takes its title from legal jargon, is not only a history, but a petition as well. More direct control came to be exercised after the mid-point in the century. Finally, in 1571, Philip II created the position of *cronista mayor* and charged him with writing the official history of the New World. The position existed until the eighteenth century, though often very little was accomplished by those who held it in its latter phases. But what is significant is the way in which the *cronista mayor* was conceived. The document creating the position of *cronista cosmógrapho* (which I am assuming is the same as *mayor*) states that the individual holding the post should be attached to the Council of the Indies, that he should keep the cosmographical charts of the New World, keep strict account of the geographical location of the various parts of the realms, and keep records of eclipses and other natural phenomena, making sure that the time at which they occurred was duly recorded. The 1571 *cédula* goes on to state:

Porque la memoria de los hechos Memorables y señalados que a auido y vviere en las yndias, se conserue, el coronista cosmographo de yndias baya siempre escriuiendo la historia general dellas con la mayor Precision y verdad que ser pueda, de las costumbres, Ritos y antiguedades, hechos y acontecimientos que se entendieren, por las descripciones historias y otras Relaciones y auerigaciones que se enuiaren a nos, en el consejo; la cual historia este en el, sin que de ella se pueda publicar ni dejar leer Mas de aquello, que a los que el consejo pareciere que sea publico.

So that the memory of deeds that are significant and worthy of recollection which have taken place and will take place in the Indies be preserved, the chronicler-cosmographer of the Indies should always be engaged in writing their general history, with as much precision and truthfulness as possible. He should write about the customs, rituals and myths of the people that are known through descriptions, histories and other accounts [*relaciones*] and enquiries sent to us at the Council [of the Indies]. Said history should be in his possession, no publication thereof being made, nor any part be read except what the Council deems should be made public.[52]

The document further stipulates that to facilitate the work of the *cronista cosmógrapho* secretaries and other officials should send him, at the Council, all the documents pertaining to transactions in the Empire and that the historian "guarde y tenga con secreto sin las comunicar ni dejar ver a nadie sino solo a quien por el Consejo se le mandare, y como las fuere acauando, las vaya poniendo en el archiuo del secretario cada Año, antes que se le pague el vltimo tercio del salario que ouiere de auer" ("keep them secret, not communicating them to anyone, nor allowing anyone to see them except as ordered by the Council, and that as he finishes using them, he should deposit them in the Secretary's archive each year, before the last third of his salary is paid to him [the *cronista*]").

The decree of 1571 was followed by a *real cédula* signed by the King the following year, which was sent to the various audiencias, instructing them to make available to the *cronista* all information pertaining to their jurisdiction. The order is remarkably broad and inclusive. I quote from the copy sent to Santa Fe de Bogotá:

Presidente y oidores de nuestra audiencia real, que residen en la ciudad de Santa Fe del nuevo reino de Granada, sabed: que deseando que la memoria de los hechos y cosas acaescidas en esas partes se conserven; y que en nuestro Consejo de las Indias haya la noticia que debe haber de ellas, y de las otras cosas de esas partes que son dignas de saberse; habemos proveido persona, a cuyo cargo sea recopilarles y hacer historia de ellas; por lo cual os encargamos, que con diligencia os hagais luego informar de cualesquiera persona, así legas como religiosas, que en el distrito de esa audiencia hubiere escrito o recopilado, o tuviere en su poder alguna historia, comentarios o relaciones de algunos de los descubrimientos, conquistas, entradas, guerras o facciones de paz o de guerra que en esas provincias o en parte de ellas hubiere habido desde su descubrimiento hasta los tiempos presentes. Y asimismo de la religión, gobierno, ritos y costumbres que los indios han tenido y tienen; y de la descripción de la tierra, naturaleza y calidades de las cosas de ella, haciendo asimismo buscar lo susodicho, o algo de ello en los archivos, oficios y escritorios de los escribanos de gobernación y otras partes a donde pueda estar; y lo que se hallare origi- nalmente si ser pudiere, y si no la copia de ellos, daréis orden como se nos envíe en la primera ocasión de flota o navíos que para estos reinos vengan.

President and judges of our royal court at Santa Fe, in the new Kingdom of Granada, be advised that: wishing to preserve the memory of events occur- ring in this realm, and wishing that our Council of the Indies have the information about them that it should, as well as other things in the realm that it should know, we have provided a person, whose charge it is to gather all this and write a history of them. For this reason we ask you to inform, with all dispatch, all persons, be they secular or religious, who within the jurisdiction of this court has written or compiled a history, or has in his possession a history, commentary or compilation of data about discoveries, conquests, attacks, wars or factional disputes, having occurred in those provinces from the time of its discovery to the present time. We also wish to receive information about the religion, mode of government, rituals and customs that the Indians had and have, also a description of the land, as well as the nature and qualities of the things on it, asking you to search for this too, or whatever there might be about it, in archives, offices and papers of secretaries and anywhere else where such information may be kept. Whatever is found we wish to have in the original, if not a copy, which you should order to have sent to us in the first fleet of ships bound for this kingdom.[53]

Juan López de Velasco (1571–91) and Licentiate Arias de Loyola (1591–96) were the first official historians of the Indies, but it was not until the tenure of Antonio de Herrera y Tordesillas (1596– 1625) that an individual took to heart the task of compiling a general history of the Indies worthy of the orders issued by the Crown. His compendious *Historia general de los hechos de los castellanos en las islas i tierra firme del mar Océano*, published in Madrid from 1601 to 1615 is as monumental a task of re-writing as has perhaps ever been accom- plished. Herrera, who was a contemporary of Mateo Alemán,

Miguel de Cervantes, and Garcilaso, lists at the beginning of his work his historical sources: these include all of the great histories of the New World published or unpublished (including the Inca's). Composed in an impeccable style, his *Historia general* is a wide-ranging apology for the conquest of America and the glory of the Spanish (particularly Castilian) State.[54]

Herrera y Tordesillas' official history did not go unchallenged, which proves the dialectical nature of the relationship between historiography and notarial rhetoric. In 1600, Francisco Arias Dávila y Bobadilla, a personage with the quaint title of Count of Puñonrostro (Fist-on-Face), took Herrera y Tordesillas to court for what he was about to publish about his grandfather Pedrarias Dávila, the ferocious conqueror of Darien. Although Herrera tried to appease Arias by making slight changes in his manuscript, the litigious count continued to sue until 1610, when a court finally decreed that Tordesillas was not obliged to change anything unless he was confronted with more reliable testimony than he had.[55] Given that the actions in question had taken place nearly a century before, the only way to challenge the historian was by producing notarial documents of the period that would question the veracity of his writing. The decision in favor of the court historian is ample proof of where power lay in the confrontation between the documents in the archive and the overarching history that was charged with giving them a certain organization and meaning. It is well worth keeping this in mind when considering Garcilaso's *Historia general del Perú*.

"Language is the handmaiden of Empire," said Nebrija in the dedication of his *Gramática* to the Catholic Kings in 1492.[56] Writing was a fundamental feature of the Spanish Empire, not only for the reasons given, but also because Spain's was the first large state to be created after the printing press was perfected.[57] The Spaniards taught the Indians how to read and write with the purpose of integrating them more effectively into their polity. Never was an empire more permeated by the letter. In the sixteenth century there was already a university in Hispaniola (The University of St. Thomas Aquinas) and the College of Santa Cruz de Tlatelolco was founded in Mexico City in 1536 with the express purpose of teaching bright natives Latin and rhetoric. In 1512, the Franciscans had printed in Seville 2,000 ABC primers to teach the Indians how to read, and the bishop of Mexico, Juan de Zumárraga, acquired

12,000 copies in 1523 in Alcalá de Henares.[58] The Spanish Empire was ruled by the law, and the law could only be learned, disseminated and obeyed by people who knew how to read and write. Writing, as we have seen, was a form of legitimation and liberation. Garcilaso wrote, and wrote well, because he was encouraged to do so by the socio-political context in which he grew up.

But how, specifically, did Garcilaso learn to write? There are poignant pages in the *Comentarios* in which the Inca reminisces about how a priest took him and the other mestizos under his wing to teach them Latin, rhetoric and history. Garcilaso remained in touch with his classmates throughout his life, and some of them sent him information for his book from Peru. His experience with them was obviously an important and memorable part of his childhood. There are also moving scenes in which Garcilaso portrays himself as his father's scribe or secretary, when the latter was corregidor and chief justice of Cuzco. In book 8, chapter 6 of the *Historia general del Peru*, after relating an incident involving an exchange of letters between Sebastián Garcilaso de la Vega and Viceroy Hurtado de Mendoza, the Inca writes: "Yo tuve ambas las cartas en mis manos, que entonces yo servía a mi padre de escribiente en todas las cartas que escribía a diversas partes de aquel imperio; y así respondió a estas dos por mi letras" ("I had both letters in my hands, for I then served my father as secretary for all the correspondence he had with various parts of the Empire, and I wrote the replies to these letters in my own hand").[59] The Inca must have already been a good writer when his father employed him as a scribe, and as a scribe Garcilaso must have mastered the legal or notarial rhetoric of the time. This was to be an experience as crucial as learning to write. In carrying out his duties as a scribe, the young mestizo had ample evidence of the power of writing in the Empire. Taking dictation from his father, the Inca learned, at the very foot of authority, the link between writing and legitimation, as he drew up briefs, wills, petitions, and other documents. Writing hypostatized the voice that rang so near him, carefully modulating the tropes and the formulae of the state. Writing would become the Inca's obsession.[60] This practice was to have a telling effect on the *Comentarios reales*. The scene of the mestizo taking dictation from his father can be seen as an emblem of Latin American writing in colonial times.

This notarial rhetoric, which may appear to us today as the least interesting kind of writing, was an important area of Renaissance humanistic activity, and in the history of its development many issues relevant to students of literature come up: not only matters of style but of point of view, the intended reader, rules for glossing a text, and so forth. The law (*legislar*, from "to read") is above all a system of reading and writing, a prescribed way of interpreting. The great humanists who rekindled classical rhetoric were the same ones who codified legal or notarial rhetoric.[61] In fact, rhetoric was rediscovered in Bologna by these very humanists, who were charged with creating a discourse capable of acting as a system of exchange for the bankers and merchants of the Italian cities. It was, above all, Rolandino Passagieri who, in his *Summa* and *Aurora*, fixed the rules and gave the models that, from the thirteenth century on, would be used in the rest of Europe and in Latin America, in some cases until the eighteenth century. He is the forefather of the *letrados* who came to the New World. Notarial rhetoric became an important branch of rhetoric in Spain during the reign of the Catholic Kings due to the fundamental changes in the legal system mentioned before and as a reflection of the great impulse given to learning by Cardinal Jiménez de Cisneros. *Artis notariae*, or manuals for the notary, appeared in the Peninsula, and the Italian models themselves were imported. These arts of the notary contained rules for writing. In some cases they were mere formulae, in many others they were very much like the manuals of style still used today to teach effective writing. Sentence construction, the use of tropes, and instructions for the redaction of the various parts of the documents are given, along with specific models to copy and forms for inserting in the appropriate places the contingent details of a given case. A student is taught how to write a letter asking his parents for money. A letter teaches a wayward woman how to ask her husband to take her back. If one were to make up a list of these *exempla*, it would be easy to come up with a project for a kind of *Decameron*. Indeed, I suspect that this kind of manual may be the model used by Rodríguez Freyle in planning *El Carnero*, which contains precisely such an array of cases. Notarial rhetoric furnished a method for incorporating into writing the events of everyday life; in fact, those that escaped the law: adultery, illegitimacy, delinquency in general; all the individual cases that deviated from Natural Law. In this, notarial rhetoric plays a more decisive role in the development of realistic prose than the *sermo humilis* to which Auerbach refers.[62] Notarial rhetoric is connected to society's codes much more directly and significantly. It is a mode of representing that which escapes, and by doing so brings it back into line. It is the fine mesh that traps everything into writing, from domestic quarrels to the discovery of the Pacific. The *pícaro* writes to exculpate himself; the very act of writing is a way of coming clean, of using formulae through which his actions are harnessed by society's rules of representation. Of course, submitting to such formulae was also a way of liberating oneself from the authority that purported to control writing from without by mimicking the simulacrum that took its place.

The *letrados* were the keepers of writing in the colonial period, not only in their official capacity as rhetoricians and scribes, but also as men of letters – lettered men, men of the letter, who lived by and of the letter. The tradition of the lawyer-writer, so prevalent to this day in Latin America, began with these humble officials of the State bureaucracy. Don Nicolás de Irolo Calar, author of the first Latin American treatise of notarial art, the *Política de escrituras* (Mexico, 1605), was also a poet. He summarized his doctrine, which he backs up with numerous examples to be used according to the individual cases, as follows:

La cual [brevedad], de más de lo dicho, es motivo, incita y anima a aprender lo que se pretende saber: supuesto lo cual y que de ir las escrituras con no más de lo que han menester son mejor y más bien entendidas, y que por poner lo que no es de importancia arguye ignorancia, y que iría muy fuera de camino el que viendo dos caminos para ir a una parte, dejase el más corto y más llano, y finalmente el mejor, y quisiese ir por el otro, debe el que quisiera acertar no poner más de aquello que sea necesario a la escritura, dando de mano a prolijidades y vejeces que todavía usan algunos, como si no tuviéramos hoy mejor lenguaje, más elegante y más pulido. Usese en cada tiempo lo que corre, y adviértase que cada día se ponen las cosas en mayor policía y primor, y también en que por lo dicho no se quiere decir que se ponga sólo lo esencial y sustancial en las escrituras, que esto sería llevar mucha sequedad y mostrarse por ellas ser poco práctico el escribano, que adornadas han de ir y parecerá bien que vayan con algunas razones que hagan buena consonancia. Y porque no puedan tener ningún defecto, y en efecto tengan toda perfección, se llevará, cuando se fueren ordenando, cuidado con tres cosas. La primera y principal que vayan con las fuerzas que requieren. La otra, con claridad. Y la otra, que cada cosa se ponga y asiente en su lugar, y todo de manera que lo uno llame a lo otro.[63]

[Brevity] is, in addition to what has already been said, an incitement and encouragement to learn that which one aspires to know. And besides documents are easier to understand if they contain only the necessary information. To do otherwise would be as clear a proof of one's ignorance as if, on being shown two ways to reach a certain place, one rejected the best route, the most direct one over flat ground, in favor of the other more difficult route. The key to success is to include in the document only what is essential, leaving out the long-winded phrases and old-fashioned flourishes that some still use, as if we did not have access to a better, more polished and elegant language. Always use the most up-to-date language and notice the greater care and order with which documents are more and more being written. Do not, however, take this to mean that one should include only the bare minimum in documents. This would make them very dry and make all too evident the inexperience of the scribe. Documents need some adornment and a good impression will be made if they contain sentences in keeping with the subject-matter ... and in effect, reach the highest degree of perfection. Documents should be written according to three rules. First and foremost they should have the necessary proofs. Secondly, they should be clear. Thirdly, everything should be written down and recorded in its proper place, and the whole be organized in such a way that each part relates to all the others.

Irolo's concern with beauty, as well as with notarial thoroughness, is evidence of the *letrados'* literary bent, and of the role they played in the production of the language of the narrative of Latin America in the colonial period. Irolo was not exceptional in his poetic inclinations. Silvestre de Balboa y Troya de Quesada, author of the epic poem *Espejo de paciencia* (Puerto Príncipe, Cuba, 1608), was an *escribano*. The list of modern Latin American authors who studied law or actually became lawyers would be a very long and illustrious one, including José Martí, Carlos Fuentes, and Gabriel García Márquez, to name but three.

The preceding could be summarized as follows. The novel, as well as much of the history of the New World, was told within the rhetorical constraints imposed by the new, centralized state of Spain. It was through the rhetoric of the notarial arts, and not as a result of a literary tradition, that the authors of *La Celestina* and the picaresque novels were able to incorporate the details of everyday life into their fictions. These fictions involved the life of the disenfranchised of society, who sought legitimation through the very act of writing. Thematically this was expressed in *La Celestina* and the Picaresque by the orphanage or illegitimacy of the protagonist, in the chronicles by the real issue of enfranchisement in the new society (the *encomienda*, the state bureaucracy). The novel and the history of the New World – as well as later narratives concerned with the uniqueness of Latin America – are like letters written to a central authority, because legal rhetoric always implies a textual exchange or dialogue, a petition or appeal or an answer to some sort of accusation. Like the pillory, which served to let the individual expiate his deviance in a public display of shame, writing, coming clean, is an act through which pardon, reunification with the body politic is pursued. This dialogue or exchange inherent in legal rhetoric is present within the text of the novel or chronicle in various ways. In the chronicle, the *relación*, or written report, is to be subsumed within the larger rhetoric of Renaissance historiography, which is the global text that will then incorporate its trivial details into an overall, harmonious formulation wherein power is contained. In the Picaresque the dialogue is implicit in the exculpation and in the protestations of innocence. It is also present in the act of conversion, which presumably leads the *pícaro* to write because he has converted to the good life. This conversion is present in the chronicle, as well as in the novel, in the very act of compliance with the rhetorical norm, which is a form of mimicking authority, of assuming its form thereby freeing itself from the outside source of power that determines it. The dialogic exchange is also evident in the fact that a *relación* could also be a reading of the record to summarize or refute the allegations and the evidence; the *relación* can be a commentary, and there were *relatores* in charge of summarizing the lengthy proceedings. In any *relación* the *pícaro*-chronicler is not only recounting his life but revising the version of it previously given to the authorities. Lázaro answers "Your Worship" to correct versions of his activities reported to that personage. Garcilaso (and Bernal, of course) writes his *Comentarios* as a *relación* in this respect. Ultimately, what the mimicking of legal rhetoric accomplishes is the legitimation of the voice which narrates the story. How else could the likes of Lazarillo, Garcilaso or Bernal presume to write about themselves? In that legitimation of the voice in the present lies the creation of the novelistic voice, capable of recording events that have not been consecrated by literary or rhetorical tradition.

Garcilaso wrote well because his good rhetoric was a simulacrum of the order of the Empire, an order that is itself a simulacrum of the authority invested in the figure of the King. Garcilaso was his father's scribe in two senses: he wrote on his behalf and in his stead, that father being the hypostasis of power that rhetoric itself and the figure of the King represented. Just as he assumed his father's name to write, Gómez de Figueroa becoming Garcilaso de la Vega, el Inca, his writing replaced the father. The better the Inca wrote, the closer he came to gaining the ever-elusive legitimacy that writing, as a mediation between the source of power and the individual, promised. The *Comentarios reales de los Incas* is an allegory of legitimation parallel to the one contained in the Picaresque, only that here the allegory extended to include the whole New World as well as the mestizo.

4

Since Your Worship writes me to relate these matters very fully, I have thought it best to start not in the middle but at the beginning. In this way Your Worship and others may receive a complete account of my life.

La vida de Lázarillo de Tormes, 1554[64]

Most readers of Garcilaso's *Comentarios reales de los Incas* would be hard put to identify Garcilaso's book with notarial rhetoric or with the Picaresque, but this is because only the first part of the work is commonly read. That is the part dealing with Garcilaso's Incaic background; it is a history of pre-Hispanic Peru, particularly the succession of the Inca monarchs until the arrival of the Spaniards, and a thorough account of Inca culture, specifically their religious beliefs. Post-romantic ideology, most notably *indigenismo*, has made this part much more attractive than the second one, which is concerned with the conquest of Peru and the civil wars that followed it. Yet this second part is essential to the book's plan, perhaps the very spark that inspired the Inca to write. What makes the Inca's story so Latin American is not the narrative of his non-European origin, but the need to include it as part of the scheme of his legitimation. In a sense, one could say that the first part fits within the design of the second and is dependent on it, rather than the other way around. The *Historia general del Perú* is mostly concerned with the heroic yet sordid affairs of the Spaniards, in their savage struggle for the spoils of conquest. It is the paternal side of the book, as it were, where the issue of the patrimonial bureaucracy and its authority over writing are most clearly at stake.[65] It is also the most autobiographical part of the *Comentarios*, for it is concerned with Garcilaso's own times, not with that of his forebears. Published posthumously, the book was conceived as a second part of the

Comentarios reales, and Garcilaso had named it as such, but the publishers, for reasons that are not entirely clear, changed the title.[66]

Garcilaso begins this second part with a detailed account of how the precious metals extracted from the mines in Potosí and other regions of Peru brought great wealth to Spain and Europe in general. He aims to prove the value of what the first conquistadors, among them his father, accomplished: "ganaron un imperio tan grande y tan rico que ha enriquecido a todo el mundo" ("they won a great and wealthy empire that has enriched the whole world").[67] With an eye for economic detail worthy of a modern historian, Garcilaso compares the price he paid for a pair of shoes upon his arrival in Spain to what the same pair would cost at the time he is writing. Hunger for wealth and power moves men in the *Historia general del Perú*, and Garcilaso relishes examples of the resulting corruption, violence, and chicanery. He recounts the civil wars from the privileged and legally valid perspective of an eyewitness; an eyewitness, moreover, who at the time of the action saw events as a child (like Lázaro's feigned perspective), and thus with a fresh, not to say astonished vision of things. The story is an appeal for legitimacy not only in the political world of the times, but also within the text itself, as Garcilaso's protestations about the validity of his point of view reveal. Here Garcilaso's training as a scribe no doubt served him well, for the presence of notarial rhetoric is especially prominent. But there is an even more compelling and concrete reason to view the entire book as in many ways determined by the *artis notariae*.

Sebastián Garcilaso de la Vega, Garcilaso's father, belonged to one of the most distinguished families in Spain.[68] The Inca could count among his paternal ancestors a very illustrious line of personages of rank, some of them the best poets of the language, from Jorge Manrique to his namesake Garcilaso de la Vega, the great lyricist. But Sebastián was a *segundón*, that is to say, not a first-born male, who had gone to the New World in search of fortune, as was frequently the case. While his actions in the conquest and civil wars bore eloquent testimony to his zeal and desire to live up to very high social ambitions, Garcilaso's father had faltered once. In the midst of the Battle of Huarina, Sebastián apparently offered his steed Salinillas to the dismounted Gonzalo Pizarro, the leader of the seditious group (he was at the time a prisoner of

Pizarro's, but trusted to roam about freely on his honor, an ambiguous position at best in a very muddled political situation). This act of either gallantry or of political prudence would cost Sebastián and Gómez de Figueroa, the future Inca, dearly. Owing to the thoroughness of the bureaucratic system and the increasing importance of writing and archival practices, this stain – if, indeed, there was one – remained indelibly stamped upon Sebastián's record, hampering his son's efforts at court to make good his demands as a direct descendant of a conquistador. Historians, whose record was a relevant part of legal proceedings, also recounted the incriminating scene at Huarina. Garcilaso struggled against the version in the legal record and in the historians' writings through appeals against the former and through corrections of the latter in his own history. The *Comentarios reales* are woven around that scene of the horseless traitor being offered a mount by Garcilaso's father. In this sense, the book is actually a *relación*, a letter of appeal to the Council of the Indies to have Sebastián's name cleared and Garcilaso's petitions granted. It also resembles a *relación* in the sense that it is a summary of the record, a culling of the written evidence and a commentary on it. Prior to writing the book Garcilaso had appeared in person before the Council of the Indies to argue his case. After quick deliberations, the decision went against the Inca. It was never reversed despite his untiring efforts, which followed the line, though on a smaller scale, of the great legal proceedings involving Columbus, Cortés, Cabeza de Vaca, and the Pizarros. The story of Garcilaso's fruitless appeals to the Council, along with his version of the story, appears in the second part of the *Comentarios reales*.

Agustín de Zárate, whose work Garcilaso often glosses, comments at the start of his *Historia del descubrimiento y conquista del Perú* (1555) that he was unable to write the book while in the New World for fear that Francisco de Carvajal, one of Gonzalo Pizarro's minions, would slay him.[69] Writing the history of Peru in the sixteenth century was a dangerous political act. The history of Peru involved heroic deeds on a huge scale, given the nature and extension of the terrain and the civilizations that the Spaniards conquered, but mostly it involved the wars that erupted among the Spaniards themselves which taxed to the limit the system of government and law sketched before.

The civil wars of Peru were a result of the struggle between the central government in Spain and the conquistadors in the New

World. In brief, in 1542 the Crown passed the New Laws limiting the *encomienda* system which allotted land and Indians to worthy conquistadors. The untiring efforts of Bartolomé de las Casas and others on behalf of the Indians had a good deal to do with the issuance of these laws. But they were also the result of political and economic calculations on the part of the Crown. With the aid of the *encomienda* system, the early conquistadors had become a *de facto*, if not a *de jure*, landed aristocracy with a ready supply of serfs (the Indians). Not only had they become dangerously powerful and hence capable of secession (as happened more than once), but they also hoarded land and Indians in a way that made it difficult to reward new waves of conquistadors who would be willing to extend the territories and wealth of the Crown. The New Laws came as a shattering blow to the first conquistadors because they limited the number of "lives" for which an *encomienda* lasted, as well as the ways in which it could be inherited.[70] While in Mexico a revolt was averted, in Peru one broke out. The revolts continued throughout Garcilaso's childhood and early life until he left for Spain in 1560.

Let us review more closely what was at stake and how Garcilaso stood on the political issues being fought over. The main one was the New Laws limiting the *encomienda* system. The limits were as follows: *encomiendas* would henceforth not be hereditary; officials of the government could not have *encomiendas* and had to turn theirs over at once; and, finally, anyone implicated in the revolts of Peru, on whichever side, would have to relinquish his *encomienda* and henceforth be unable to have one. Sebastián, and by implication Garcilaso, was affected by all three provisions. Blasco Núñez Vela was sent by the Crown to enforce the laws, but was opposed by Gonzalo Pizarro, who defeated him. Núñez Vela was killed in battle. Licentiate la Gasca took his place and did battle with Pizarro, but was soundly defeated at the battle of Huarina. The fact that the Crown's forces were routed at Huarina surely explains the obstinacy with which the authorities remembered Sebastián's generosity toward the rebel leader.

The *letrados*, who replaced the conquistadors, came to enforce the laws. They had the backing of the Crown and of the disenfranchised soldiers who expected rewards for every deed performed in favor of the King. But the civil wars continued, many disenchanted soldiers joined the ranks of the rebels because they felt that they had not been properly rewarded for their loyalty to the Crown. Loyalty and legality were difficult to establish, since all sides often claimed both. As in the peninsula, the popular classes sided with the Crown against the aristocracy. Eventually, with the abrogation of many of the laws, peace was established, but the legal status of the estate of many a conquistador remained a tangled affair, complicated by questions concerning their marriages to women from Spain.[71]

Garcilaso made his claim before the Council of the Indies as the son of a first conquistador, a nobleman, and of an Indian woman of noble rank – the aristocracy of the Incas having been recognized in certain cases.[72] But Sebastián's lapse at Huarina and his complicated marital situation made things difficult for the Inca. Garcilaso's father married Doña Luisa Martel de los Ríos, a Spanish lady, and married off Chimpu Ocllo, Garcilaso's mother, to Juan del Pedroche, a Spaniard of lesser rank. The Inca's illegitimacy and the lack of legal foundation for his appeals were unequivocal, yet his book, and his adoption of the name Garcilaso de la Vega, is a homage to his father, in whose defense he wrote, and whose identity he seemed to want to assume. Varner writes:

But Gómez' eventual decision to adopt the name Garcilaso de la Vega was inspired by an intense devotion to his father and was made in a passion of defense and pride. Under the name which Lope García Castro [a member of the Council of the Indies who suspected the loyalty of Sebastián] had sullied, he would attempt to forge a new route to fame and fortune, and he would wear it proudly when he renewed his pretensions at Madrid. Be that as it may, from this time forward Gómez referred always to himself as Garcilaso de la Vega, though when clarification demanded it he frequently added "who was known in the Indies as Gómez de Figueroa." And then as the years passed and he began to awaken to the former glories and the current miseries of his mother's people, the mestizo, again in a passion which mingled both pride and defense, embellished his adopted name with "el Indio" or "el Inca."[73]

Francisco de Carvajal, Gonzalo Pizarro's ruthless field marshal, liked to refer to those who changed allegiance during the civil wars as *tejedores*, weavers, because they went back and forth. The weave of Garcilaso's *Comentarios* is so complex because his father was a weaver of sorts, and Garcilaso's own position was not simple either. Garcilaso's claim involved the ownership of Indians as well as that of land. To adopt his father's identity, he had to be the lord of his mother's people. Garcilaso also would have had to abandon his role as scribe, as *letrado*, assigned him by Sebastián. Given the politics of the time, Sebastián had to be opposed to the *letrados* (when answering other accusations regarding his performance as corregidor of Cuzco, Sebastián once protested emphatically that he was not a *letrado*). Which was Garcilaso to represent, the voice of the master or the letter of the scribe?

The *relación*'s narrative situation (answer or appeal to higher authority) is evident in the entire *Comentarios reales*, once one takes into consideration the legal struggle in which the Inca was engaged when he thought of writing the book. The *Comentarios* were conceived as part of the record in a legal petition that required the Inca to give proof of his worthiness. Such worthiness could only be proven by furnishing evidence of the noble lineage of his father and mother and of the former's service to the Crown in the New World. The first part of the *Comentarios* is written with the purpose of showing the nobility of the Incas, that is to say, of establishing the noble lineage of the maternal side of Garcilaso's family. On this side his claim is based on the fact that the Incas were lords of Peru because of their heroic and civilizing activities against the barbarism of previous Indian cultures. In the last chapter of the *Historia* Garcilaso makes explicit his purpose in writing both parts:

Habiendo dado principio e esta nuestra historia con el principio y origen de los Incas, reyes que fueron del Perú, y habiendo dado larga noticia de sus conquistas y generosidades, de sus vidas y gobierno en paz y en guerra y de la idolatría que en su gentilidad tuvieron, como largamente con el favor divino lo hicimos en la primera parte de estos *comentarios*, con que se cumplió la obligación que a la patria y a los parientes maternos se les debía. Y en esta segunda, como se ha visto, se ha hecho larga *relación* [my emphasis] de las hazañas y valentías que los bravos y valerosos españoles hicieron en ganar aquel riquísimo imperio, con que asimismo he cumplido (aunque no por entero) con la obligación paterna que a mi padre y a sus ilustres y generosos compañeros debo ... (IV, pp. 173–4)

Having begun this history with the commencement and origin of the Inca kings in Peru, and having noticed at length their conquests and generous deeds, their lives, their government in peace and war, and the idolatrous religion they had in heathen times – all of which were performed at length in the first part of these *Commentaries*, with divine aid – we fulfilled the obligation we felt toward our mother country and our maternal stock. In the Second Part, as we have seen, a long account was given of the deeds and heroic actions that the brave and valiant Spaniards performed in conquering that wealthy empire, wherein we have fulfilled, even though not completely, our paternal obligations, which we owe to our father and his illustrious and generous companions.[74]

The Incas were "kings in Peru" and carried out "conquest and generous deeds," making that part of the world fit for the advent of Christianity. The *primera parte* is a lengthy plea attempting to establish the splendor of Inca (not Indian) culture, based on oral and written testimony, leading up to the "treachery" of Atahualpa, who usurps the rightful claims of Garcilaso's maternal relatives. Atahualpa's culpability is a cornerstone in the rhetorical structure of the *Comentarios*. With it the Inca justifies the Spanish invasion and exonerates his maternal relatives from having surrendered too easily to the conquering Europeans. In any case, the *primera parte* is part of the whole appeal, but it involves only one aspect of it; proving that the Incas were noble by lineage and deed, and that they were civilized people worthy of retaining their privileges in the new society. In a sense, Garcilaso is complying with the 1571 *cédula* by writing about "the customs, rituals and myths of the people," but he is also pleading for their recognition. Garcilaso is arguing in favor of a caste – the Incas – not of a race. The *segunda parte*, in contrast, is a complex, multilevel plea to exculpate Garcilaso's father and the Spaniards as a whole, to make good the Inca's pretensions in Spanish society. In this sense, the first part fits within the design of the second; it is a necessary first step in the process of exculpation and restitution through writing. Like Lázaro, Garcilaso wants to tell the entire story, which involves the lives of both of his parents. As he says in the last book of the *Historia*, his claim is "acerca de los servicios de mi padre y la restitución patrimonial de mi madre" ("with reference to my father's service and the restoration of my mother's inheritance").

The legal efficacy of the first part of the *Comentarios* in one instance gratified Garcilaso greatly, and revealed better than anything else, the nature of his historiographic enterprise. He writes the following in the penultimate chapter of the *Historia*

El gobernador Martín García de Loyola dejó una hija habida en su mujer la infanta, hija del príncipe don Diego Sairi Tupac. La cual hija trajeron a España y la casaron con un caballero muy principal llamado don Juan Enríquez de Borja. La católica majestad demás del repartimiento de indios que la infanta heredó de su padre le ha hecho merced (según me lo han escrito de la corte) de título de marquesa de Oropesa, que es un pueblo que el visorrey don Francisco de Toledo fundó en el Perú, y le llamó Oropesa porque quedase memoria en aquella tierra de la casa y estado de sus padres y abuelos. Sin esta merced y título me dicen que entre los ilustrísimos señores presidentes del concejo de Castilla y de Indias y el confesor de su

majestad y otros dos oidores del mismo concejo de Indias se trata y
consulta de hacerle grandes mercedes en gratificación de los muchos y
señalados servicios que su padre el gobernador hizo a Su Majestad y en
restitución de su herencia patrimonial. A lo cual me dicen que no sirven
poco nuestros *Comentarios* de la primera parte por la *relación* [my emphasis]
sucesiva que ha dado de aquellos Incas. Con esta nueva me doy por
gratificado y remunerado del trabajo y solicitud de haberlos escrito sin
esperanza, como en otras partes lo hemos dicho de galardón alguno.

Governor Martín García Loyola left a daughter by his wife, the princess,
the daughter of Prince Don Diego Sairi Túpac. This daughter was brought
to Spain and married to an eminent gentleman called Don Juan Enrique de
Borja. His Catholic Majesty, as I hear in letters from the capital, has
conferred on her, in addition to the allocation of Indians which the princess
inherited from her father, the title of marquesa de Oropesa, a town founded
in Peru by Viceroy Don Francisco de Toledo and called Oropesa to
commemorate in Peru the house and estate of his parents and ancestors. In
addition to this grant and title, I am told that the illustrious presidents of
the Royal Council of Castile and of the Indies, His Majesty's confessor, and
two other judges of the Council of the Indies, are considering the question
of bestowing other great favors on her in recognition of the many notable
services her father the governor rendered His Majesty, and in restitution of
her patrimonial inheritance. I am informed that the First Part of our
Commentaries has been of no little assistance in this, by reason of this account
there given of the Inca kings. This news gratifies and rewards me for the
labor and care I have taken in the writing of the work, which I undertook,
as I have said elsewhere, without any hope of reward.[75]

The parallels between the princess and Garcilaso are striking. Like
her, he is of noble lineage on both sides, and like her, his father (in
his view) performed valuable services to the Crown. It follows that if
his account of Incan grandeur is admitted as evidence in her case, it
should also be in his, and his specific mention of the officials at both
the councils who favored her is clearly a reference to his own failure
before them. In Garcilaso's mind, the princess's claims are no more
valid than his. But the point is that the first part of the *Comentarios*,
the one most commonly thought of as merely a memoir or a vague
plea in favor of the recognition of Inca culture, is no less a part of
Garcilaso's *relación* to the authorities.

The restitution of Chimpu Ocllo's patrimony in the general sense,
not merely as inheritance, was a vast historiographic and legal task,
for it involved a revision of the record that cast the development of
Andean history as a teleology leading up to Inca civilization. It

necessitated a thorough philological and historical commentary on Spanish histories, as well as a translation of oral records and personal recollection into the language of Renaissance historiography. A succession of monarchs worthy of Rome demanded a history told in the high style, and Garcilaso endeavored to do so whenever possible.[76] But the restitution of Sebastián Garcilaso de la Vega, for reasons that have been described, was an even more complex problem, because it involved the very conception of the whole work and Garcilaso's relation to authority; that is to say, of writing within the patrimonial bureaucracy of the Empire, the question of representation and self-representation. The central issues at the core of the narrative of Latin America and the origins of the novel are contained in that relationship.

Varner has told in great detail and with no small measure of eloquence of Garcilaso's efforts before the Council of the Indies, so I need not go over the details here. Suffice it to say that, in Spain, Garcilaso led a relatively modest life. He was partially dependent on the generosity of his paternal relatives, a situation that no doubt irked him given his pretensions concerning the lineage of both of his parents. In a society as stratified as Spain's was then, and as concerned with purity of blood, Garcilaso's anxieties had a real basis. Without his lineage Garcilaso was a mere *letrado*; with it he was a man of substance. The *Historia general del Perú*, the debt that Garcilaso pays his father and his companions, is also an investment he makes to acquire such substance. In contrast to the first part of the *Comentarios*, the *Historia* deals with what could roughly be called the present, although Garcilaso is writing about events that took place fifty years before he commits them to paper.[77] In this history of the present – of events that have *vigencia*, currency, even in legal terms – the discursive elements typical of the *relación* are more evident. Garcilaso is narrating here the fine mesh of contemporary history, sometimes from day to day and from hour to hour, events that he himself witnessed. He emphasizes throughout the book that he saw the events he narrates with his own eyes and uses legal terminology (*testigo de vista*) to validate his position as witness. Legalisms abound in the *Historia*, and the very nature of the text is that of a *relación*, both as an account of his and his father's life and deeds and as a culling and summary of the documentary evidence of the case.

The *Historia General del Perú* is an oblique biography of Sebastián

Garcilaso de la Vega and an even more indirect autobiography of Garcilaso de la Vega, el Inca, the narrator. The book is a *relación* in the guise of an *historia*; the history of the conquest of Peru is the framing narrative, but the focus of the overall, broad picture is blurred, while the marginal figure of Sebastián, in a corner, appears in sharp relief, but if observed closely, one can also see the contour of Garcilaso's own profile. The history begins with the legal establishment of a corporation by the triumvirate that will undertake the conquest of Peru, as if to set down the legal foundations of the enterprise, and winds up with the trial and execution of the last Inca claimant to the Crown, Tupac Amaru. The story, then, ranges from the first legal acts leading to the conquest of Peru to the final subordination of the kingdom to the Spanish Crown, sealed at the pillory. Garcilaso objects to the harsh treatment of the last Inca and invests his story with a tragic tone.[78] As a *mestizo* with royal Inca blood, he does not wish to see the claims of his maternal forebears threatened. The history also encompasses the life of Sebastián, who dies shortly before the execution of Tupac Amaru. History and biography run parallel courses and blend with one another; in a sense, the history of Peru is the life of Sebastián, replaced in the writing by his pleading son, his scribe.

Sebastián's biography begins with his arrival in Peru with the Pizarros and continues until his death. It contains a detailed and touching account of his expedition to conquer Buenaventura, a tale of survival in the jungle that anticipates some of the pages in modern Latin American novels such as *La vorágine* and *Los pasos perdidos*. This account is of paramount importance because it establishes Sebastián as one of the original conquistadors, therefore entitled to their privileges and exemptions. Most important, it establishes that he obtained new territories for the Crown, hence he is due land and Indians. The story of Sebastián's life continues with his participation in the quarrels among the conquistadors and later the civil wars that raged after the arrival of viceroy Blasco Núñez Vela. Garcilaso's father is mentioned hundreds of times in the *Historia*, a rare privilege for one whose highest rank in the government was corregidor of Cuzco for a few years and who was a mere captain in the army.[79] His son is careful to mention Sebastián among those on the side of the Crown, and he is at pains to show him in a good light at every turn. Garcilaso is, of course, careful to review the record of what happened at the Battle of Huarina, collating the various published versions and questioning their validity. He winds up this oblique biography with a panegyric of Sebastián, allegedly written as a funeral oration by a ecclesiastic who begged the Inca not to reveal his name. The oration takes ten pages of two columns in the Biblioteca de Autores Españoles edition, and it is yet another biography of Sebastián, in the elegiac mode. The oration appears in the middle of the last (eighth) book of the *Historia*. Whether or not Garcilaso himself wrote it is difficult to say and perhaps of little importance. What matters is that he chose to include it. It is a summary of the details of Sebastián's life scattered in the text, one of the devices used to finish the *Historia*.

Except for this oration, Garcilaso's biography of his father is not told in the pure Renaissance style of, for example, López de Gómara's portrait of Cortés, but there are traces of it in the *Historia*. There is, in fact, throughout this second part an effort to write the history of Peru in the style of the great Renaissance historians, like Guicciardini.[80] This is evident particularly in the descriptions of battles, in the account of political maneuvering, and in the eloquence of some of the speeches recreated by the Inca. The providentialist unfolding typical of Spanish Habsburg historiography is also much in evidence, and the meshing of Sebastián's life with the political history of Peru, which obeys a Renaissance conception of man as hero and protagonist of history. This is also true of the descriptions of the original conquistadors, who appear as heroes in search of fame and power, as veritable princes in the Machiavellian sense, even if they really turned out to be so mostly in the pejorative meaning of the term. This is the way in which Garcilaso's book complies with the higher forms of the State's discourse, the way in which his text appears to reflect the harmony of political and social power that the State wishes to convey in the representations of its machinery at work. It is the all-encompassing, capacious Archive to which all the well-written *relaciones* are sent, with the voice of "Your Worship" modulating the totalizing discourse of the State. This side is paternal in the sense of being a simulacrum of the father through the eloquence of the authoritative State.

But this is not the only form of compliance with the discourse of the State. There is a second, conflicting model that dismantles the other and predominates in the Inca's discourse: the notarial rhetoric of the appeal, of the *relación*. The history of the civil wars is fraught with legalisms both in the telling and in the story itself. Garcilaso wants to date, name, place, validate and corroborate. He offers his own eyewitness account as well as those of others, such as Gonzalo Silvestre, an old conquistador he meets in Spain who gave Garcilaso much information for his *Florida*.[81] He is sedulous in following the formulae of notarial rhetoric to establish the veracity of his text. He often recounts individual cases, which turn out to be like short stories, describing the lives of the protagonists, large and small, of the conflict.[82] This part reads like a picaresque novel, not only because it is full of characters and incidents that appear to have come out of the *Guzmán de Alfarache*, but because the style itself, with its emphasis on the concrete, the quotidian, the base, is very much like that of Mateo Alemán and other novelists, and also because the narrative perspective is that of a child.

It is as a witness that Garcilaso inserts himself in the narrative and tells his autobiography. We see him listening to stories from his classmates about what happened in this or that event or taking position at his father's house in order to be able to observe festivities or other events taking place in the plaza in front. We also see him taking refuge in the house with his mother as his father's enemies lob cannonballs at it. It is as a witness that he can refute what historians have said or add what they, for whatever reasons, have left out. Garcilaso wants to correct the record, giving a truer *relación*. Consequently, he is careful to cite those whose names do not figure in a battle or conspiracy, and to tell the true story of what happened at such and such an event. Legal language avails him of that possibility.

Needless to say, some of these events are exceedingly dramatic, as when a dinner is interrupted by a bevy of conquistadors who come to murder the king's envoy, and Garcilaso and Sebastián escape over the roofs of neighboring houses. Or when Garcilaso relates as a witness what happened at the execution of Almagro, or one of the Pizarros, and how he and his childhood friends played with a rotting part of Francisco de Carvajal's dismembered corpse. Details, from the color of the putrid flesh of the cadaver, to the qualities of a given horse, are offered. The *Historia*, then, is filled with the documentary need to name, place, and date. The Archive absorbs the wayward, the trivial, and the marginal and turns them into knowledge and power.

Garcilaso is scrupulous about mentioning everyone present at every event. He is also careful to place and date each event with reference to details of his own life that sustain the truthfulness of the account. He is, naturally, diligent in consulting written sources, from the published histories to letters from his friends back in Peru. In all this it is evident that he wishes to set the record straight, that his text aspires to get at a truth that is not only the historian's elegant verisimilitude but the judge's executive kind of verification and action. Writing is a legal act.

The most carefully planned aspect of this notarial style are the lists of conquistadors present at actions that favored the Crown, where Sebastián's name never fails to appear. Careful planning is also evident in passages where Garcilaso feels that the historians have unfairly left out the names of conquistadors, or where some of their deeds have not been sufficiently recorded. But this concern emerges most clearly in the reading of the written sources. One cannot take lightly the title Garcilaso gave his most sustained narrative enterprise: *Comentarios*. As a genre, the commentary spanned both the humanistic and the notarial sides of the work. Commentaries were often written to explicate a classical text or even a fairly contemporary one like the commentary on the poetry of Garcilaso's namesake that Fernando de Herrera published. There is an inherent humility in the genre that fits in with the narrative situation of the *relación*. The commentary is an answer to an authoritative text: a fragment that depends for its form on that of the mastertext. A commentary is a parasitic text and Garcilaso in part develops a parasitic relationship with the texts of his predecessors. But a commentary is also a legal text, the sort of text composed by a *relator* who, culling from the available record, submits a summary of a case to test its validity.[83] And that is very much the mode of the entire *Comentarios reales*.

Garcilaso is pleading before the Archive, before knowledge classified and stored by the State, which has determined that his father is guilty. To establish his case Garcilaso has to review the record and interpret it. He has to create his own archive, which will compete with the one the Council of the Indies has at its disposal. He reads the Spanish historians, particularly Francisco López de Gómara, Agustín de Zárate and Diego Fernández de Palencia, to sift from them the most truthful version of events. The *Historia*, in particular, is a tissue of quotations from these authors. A large percentage of the body of Garcilaso's text has been literally copied – *a la letra*, as he says so many times – from the historian's books. The

Comentarios, particularly the *Historia*, is like a large quilt, made up of patches of other works. It is a dialogue of texts, within the larger dialogue of the text with the authority of the Archive.

5

> In the beginning I was the notary,
> dust covered and in no hurry,
> inventor of the inventory.
>   Nicolás Guillén[84]

Nowhere is this process more clearly displayed than in the description of the Battle of Huarina and the entire chapter Garcilaso devotes to reviewing the versions given by the historians about his father's actions. The scene, in which the mestizo pleads his case in person, and Lope García de Castro thunders accusations about his father at him, dramatizes the whole structure of the book.

Garcilaso first gives his own version of Huarina, based on what he heard from combatants on both sides and on what Gonzalo Silvestre, who fought on the side of the Crown, told him. He is extremely careful to establish the validity of his point of view by giving minute details, even the color of some of the horses, and by citing testimony from both sides. What is at issue, of course, is whether his father did indeed give Gonzalo Pizarro his horse, because that leader's own horse had been killed or maimed in the battle, and whether in so doing, Sebastián saved the rebel from death, defeat, or both. Garcilaso's account is based on what Gonzalo Silvestre told him, and Silvestre was precisely the one who wounded Pizarro's horse while trying to capture him. No witness could conceivably offer a more reliable testimony. According to what Garcilaso says Silvestre told him, the wound to Pizarro's horse was very slight and could not have incapacitated the animal. But the incident is further clouded by the fact that Pizarro's horse died shortly after the battle, and Gonzalo kept Salinillas for quite a long time. Garcilaso, who fancied himself as an expert on horses, goes on to explain that Gonzalo's horse died far from the battlefield, not from a wound, but from having been allowed to drink too much water. He further shows that by the time his father allowed Pizarro to use Salinillas, the battle was over, hence his action could have had no bearing on the outcome.

These laborious justifications appear in what is also a very minute description of the battle, showing how Pizarro emerged victorious because of Carvajal's superior ability as a field marshal. Garcilaso is anxious to prove that Carvajal was a great soldier and Pizarro a worthy leader whose claims were not entirely without merit, in part to dispel the accounts given by other historians. It is to these accounts that the whole description of the battle is aimed, for reasons that Garcilaso makes quite explicit. The Inca vows that the historians meant no evil to his father, that they wrote according to the testimony given them, but argues that the testimony was false. He remembers his classmates telling him about his father's apparent misdeed at Huarina, and also that his father had a notary public draw up a document dispelling the rumor, signed by over twenty combatants on the Crown's side. Garcilaso goes on to tell the story of his dramatic appearance before the Council of the Indies, a story that is the origin of the *Comentarios reales* and that is an enactment of the *Picaresque–relación* narrative situation:

De manera que no sin causa escribieron los historiadores lo que dicen, y yo escribo lo que fué, no por abonar a mi padre, ni por esperar mercedes, ni con pretensión de pedirlas, sino por decir verdad de lo que pasó, porque de este delito que aplican a Garcilaso, mi señor, yo tengo la penitencia sin haber tenido la culpa: porque pidiendo yo mercedes a Su Majestad por los servicios de mi padre y por la restitución patrimonial de mi madre, que por haber muerto en breve tiempo la segunda vida de mi padre quedamos los demás hermanos desamparados y viéndose en el consejo real de las Indias las probanzas que de lo uno y de lo otro presenté, hallándose convencidos aquellos señores con mis probanzas, el licenciado Lope García de Castro, que después fue por presidente al Perú, estando en su tribunal, me dijo: "¿Qué merced queréis que os haga Su Majestad, habiendo hecho vuestro padre con Gonzalo Pizarro lo que hizo en la batalla de Huarina y dándole aquella tan gran vitoria?" Y aunque yo repliqué que había sido testimonio falso que le habían levantado, me dijo: "Tiénenlo escrito los historiadores ¿y quereislo negar?" Con esto me despidieron de aquellas pretensiones y cerraron las puertas a otras que después acá pudiera haber tenido . . .

The historians therefore did not write as they did without cause; and I write what passed, not to justify my father, or in the hope of reward or with any idea of claiming one, but merely to tell the truth about what happened. For this crime has been imputed to my lord Garcilaso, and I have done the penance for it without any guilt or blame. I asked His Majesty to reward my father's services and restore my mother's property – for as my father's other widow died soon after him, we brothers and sisters were all impoverished. But when the Royal Council of the Indies studied the evidence I presented about all this, and they were convinced of the solidity of my case, a member of the court, Licenciate Lope García de Castro, who was after president of Peru, said to me: "What reward do you expect His Majesty to grant you when your father did as he did at the battle of Huarina and gave Gonzalo Pizarro that great victory?" And although I replied that this was false witness that had been brought against me, he said: "The historians have written it: are you going to deny it?" With this they dismissed my claims and closed the door against others I might have made since . . .[85]

The historians in question are the same three that Garcilaso has been glossing and correcting throughout his text: Agustín de Zárate, Francisco López de Gómara, and Diego Fernández, el Palentino. Gómara, whom Garcilaso calls on occasion "that Imperial Chaplain," was not only the historian of the conquest of Mexico, but one of the greatest humanists of sixteenth-century Spain, totally devoted to the policies of Philip II, to whom he dedicated his compendious and elegant *Historia general de las Indias* (Antwerp, 1553).[86] His tone is triumphant verging on the propagandistic. Agustín de Zárate, author of an *Historia del descubrimiento y conquista de la provincia del Perú y de las guerras y cosas señaladas en ella* (Antwerp, 1555), was a royal accountant, sent to the New World with Blasco Núñez Vela.[87] He was rewarded for his good services there by being put in charge of the royal treasury in Flanders, where he published his book, also dedicated to the Emperor. Garcilaso tends to favor his testimony because Zárate was present at many of the events he describes, though he also corrects him when necessary. Diego Fernández, a resident of Palencia, hence el Palentino, was a shadowy figure, obviously a notary or scribe turned historian. His *Historia del Perú*, published in 1569, shows signs of his having had access to private documents, which may mean that he was a secretary.[88] The book is also dedicated to Philip II. Although Garcilaso quotes other histories, these three books are the ones he obviously has at hand as he writes, for they are quoted extensively in the *Historia*. These are the historians to whom Licentiate García de Castro confidently alluded in his encounter with the mestizo in the chambers of the Council of the Indies. They constitute the most resilient vault of the Archive.

   The voice of the witness rings feebly against Lope García de Castro's blast, which probably echoed in the chambers of the council. Like Garcilaso's commentary, woven around the text of the archival historians, the voice is in a parasitic relationship to the unwavering core of the story. Garcilaso pits the details of his knowledge against the overarching, absorbing truth of the Archive, the account of Gonzalo Silvestre against the harmonious prose of López de Gómara. It is at this point that Garcilaso offers a direct statement about the importance of his own life that echoes the one in *Lazarillo*'s prologue: "Perdónenseme estas impertinencias, que las he dicho por queja y agravio que mi mala fortuna en este particular me ha hecho y quien ha escrito vidas de tantos, no es mucho que diga algo de la suya" ("I hope I may be pardoned for this tiresome outburst, which I have included in dudgeon against my ill fortune in this matter: one who has written the lives of so many others can hardly be criticized for saying something of his own").[89] The *particularidades* that Garcilaso always gives and insists upon are the wayward details, the criminal, as it were, which can only be trapped by a particularized *relación*. His book is ultimately both a *relación* and a history, better yet, the dialectical interplay between the two. Writing, by appearing in the guise of the State's rhetoric, acquires an illusory freedom by compliance, a mimetic process that will determine from now on the form of the novel and the narrative of Latin America.

A late historian of the discovery and conquest of America, Juan Rodríguez Freyle, a bureaucrat at Santa Fe de Bogotá, wrote a book well into the seventeenth century, that lays bare the structure of Garcilaso's and its relation to the origins of the novel. The book is commonly known as *El Carnero* and was published in 1636. The fact that Garcilaso wrote at the end of the sixteenth and beginning of the seventeenth century makes his work contemporary to the picaresque novels which pick up the legacy of *Lazarillo de Tormes* (1554) and, in a deliberate and reflexive way, create the picaresque genre. I refer especially to *Guzmán de Alfarache* (1599) by Mateo Alemán, but also to Francisco de Quevedo's *El buscón*, written earlier but not published until 1626, and Francisco López de Ubeda's *La pícara Justina* (1605), already mentioned. The work of the Inca, as I have observed, shares fundamental features with the Picaresque, but it cannot be a reaction to it since it is a parallel phenomenon. This is not the case with Rodríguez Freyle, whose book takes into account not only the principal aspects of the picaresque tradition, but also the most important chronicles of the discovery and conquest of the Indies. The work of Rodríguez Freyle is a crepuscular, disbelieving and irreverent synthesis of Latin

American history, one that tilts more decisively in the direction of the novel than Garcilaso's text. Rodríguez Freyle's critical perspective is what allows for the kind of reading proposed here. He is the theoretician of the Archive.

The settings, events and characters of *El Carnero* are the same as those of the Picaresque, but the work offers itself as, or pretends to be, a history of the Viceroyalty of New Granada, together with a series of more or less impudent stories, none of which is narrated in the first person like the stories of Lázaro, Guzmán, Pablos, Justina and the others. Because several of the stories contained in the book are so anthological, no critic has stopped to ask what *El Carnero* is as a whole. As with the *Comentarios reales*, however, the issue of what the book is or pretends to be is a crucial one that can only be answered in the context of my discussion of notarial rhetoric and renaissance historiography.

Rodríguez Freyle dramatizes, in the global construction of his work, the quarrel among the various rhetorical forms from which the Picaresque emerges as a result of the socio-political evolution of the Spanish Empire. The principal contestants in that quarrel are history, as conceived by the humanists who construct the overarching ideological legitimation of the State, and the bureaucratic rhetoric also created by the Empire, through which the individual communicated to acquire his or her own legitimacy. The disposition of the battle is already evident in the title of the book, which reads in its entirety: *El Carnero. Conquista y descubrimiento del Nuevo Reino de Granada de las Indias Occidentales del Mar Océano y fundación de la ciudad de Santa Fe de Bogotá primera de este reino donde se fundó la real audiencia y cancillería, siendo la cabeza se hizo Arzobispado. Cuéntase en ella su descubrimiento, algunas guerras civiles que había entre sus naturales, sus costumbres, gentes, y de qué procedió este nombre tan celebrado de El Dorado. Los generales, capitanes y soldados que vinieron a su conquista, con todos los presidentes, oidores y visitadores que han sido de la Real Audiencia. Los Arzobispos, prebendados y dignidades que han sido de esta santa iglesia catedral, desde el año de 1539 que se fundó, hasta 1636, que esto se escribe; con algunos casos sucedidos en este Reino, que van en la historia para ejemplo, y no para imitarlos por el daño de la conciencia.*[90] Intrigued, and for good reason, by the brief title by which the work came to be known (whose meaning I will examine), few readers have stopped to note the irony of the complete title, especially seen in relation to the contents of the book, and without skipping over its outrageous length. The work which the title names is the opposite of what the latter proclaims. The "casos sucedidos en este Reino," which the title mentions at the end as a mere addition, are the predominant element, while the history proper is only a pretext for framing the stories. This pretext is of great significance, but the inversion must be underlined: instead of the stories being an aggregate of or complement to the history, the history itself has become a rhetorical addition. Like the major histories of the New World *El Carnero* begins at the beginning, from discovery and conquest to the Foundation of the City, but this whole cycle is given as a brief, introductory summary. Years of bloody battles, heroic deeds and the founding of cities occupy a few chapters, while the adventures and misadventures of don Juan-like husbands and not too virtuous married women are historicized with a wealth of details. The *casos* practically take up the whole book. It is evident that *El Carnero*, seen in its totality, is a corrosive critique of the chronicles of the discovery and conquest of Latin America, beginning with the title itself, which reminds one of Herrera y Tordesillas' *Historia general de los castellanos en las islas y tierra firme.*

The model parodied in *El Carnero* is the ideal of Spanish historiography in the sixteenth century and beyond, analyzed above, which combines rules of stylistic decorum with an overall providentialist plan of medieval origin. Opposing that model was notarial rhetoric, which, as we also saw, is the more humble means of expression through which the common people carried out their transactions with the State. In *El Carnero*, as in the *Comentarios*, there is a confrontation between the vast program of Habsburg historiography, whose principal exponent was probably López de Gómara, and the narration of an individual life. The former implied a lineal and harmonious evolution of history reflected in the elegant and coherent organization of the text, while the latter, in contrast, narrates an individual existence, trapped in the trifling network of daily life cast in a text whose model and sources are not literary but bureaucratic. The historiography of the Indies searches for general laws of historical evolution and attempts to codify them in an organic text. The *casos* that Rodríguez Freyle relates are concerned with the law in a most concrete and social sense. From the perspective of López de Gómara, the historiography of the Indies is related to poetics, to the chivalric romances, to the most elevated models of Renaissance prose; from the perspective of the *casos*, it is related to the Picaresque which sought its form not in literature but in legal formulae such as the *relación*. In *El Carnero* history, presumably the essence of the book, becomes a pretext, whereas the stories, the gossip, which could have been a mere rhetorical ornament or *exempla*, became central and more substantial. This bold inversion on the part of Rodríguez Freyle is mainly a critical move: like the *pícaro*'s *relación*, his entire book is a contrived act of mimicking, a liberation through feigned compliance.

Susan Herman's brilliant discovery of the meaning of the short title *El Carnero* clarifies the significance of Rodríguez Freyle's critique. Herman has succeeded in establishing that "carnero" refers neither to the leather in which the book was bound, nor to that which adorns the foreheads of several husbands in the story; rather it is derived from *carnarium* and alludes by analogy to the place where discarded papers were thrown.[91] "Carnero" meant the wastepaper basket at the Santa Fe de Bogotá *audiencia*, the bin where the textual remnants of a variety of legal cases were discarded. The Picaresque, whose world of "casos" (like Lazarillo's) Rodríguez Freyle evokes by means of this founding metaphor, is also the product of those textual byproducts of the penal bureaucracy. The wastepaper basket of the Santa Fe court is a mock Archive, a textual storehouse which contains, in pell-mell fashion, the lives and deeds of *pícaros* and individuals like Garcilaso who lived almost virtually on the margins of the law. The wastepaper basket of the court at Bogotá is not Don Quijote's library; what matters in the new literature inaugurated by the Picaresque and colonial Latin American narrative is precisely that it pretends not to be literature.

The cases that make up the major portion of *El Carnero* are about illicit sexual activities; that is to say, in the context of the functions performed by the lawyers who drew up the documents that wound up in the trash bin of the *audiencia*, about marriage and the transgressions committed against the institution. The classical and medieval literary tradition behind this theme is well-known, and it would be foolish not to recognize its importance in *El Carnero*. In many ways Rodríguez Freyle's book is a sort of colonial *Decameron*. But the combination of transgressions against the institution of marriage and its legalistic background is more properly part of the picaresque tradition as I have been analyzing it here, which is already part of the Renaissance. The all-important issue of legitimacy, which is also at the core of Garcilaso's literary enterprise is at stake in the prurient elements of *El Carnero*. There is a connection between the illegal and indiscriminate sexual activity *El Carnero* portrays and the proliferation of writing as law. It is by revealing the connection that Rodríguez Freyle provides the most significant insight into the origins of the novel.

Harry Sieber and Javier Herrero have demonstrated convincingly how sexuality permeates *Lazarillo* at all levels, and in a study of two of Cervantes' exemplary novels I have shown to what extent matrimonial vicissitudes play an important role in the founding fable of the Picaresque.[92] Lázaro, Guzmán, Pablos, Berganza, Cipión and other *pícaros* are either offspring or parents of dubious conjugal fidelity. Lázaro and Pablos end up marrying or living with women whose sexual activities are anything but legal. There is no contract that legitimizes the *pícaro*'s relationship with society or the state, except the *relación*, the report or letter that he himself writes. Both the *pícaro*'s marriage as well as the document he writes about his life are proof that writing, in its proliferation, reflects the disorder of the world, not its submission to the law. This is the same conclusion at which the reader has to arrive in Garcilaso's review of the record concerning the Battle of Huarina – the text of the Archive contains power but not truth, it punishes but does not exculpate. The document written by the *pícaro*-novelist unveils this. The *pícaro*'s text is ambiguous, proliferating, polysemic, while taking the form of a legal document that is expected to guarantee its fidelity to the facts, and beyond that, the cohesiveness of the State, which authorizes and backs up truth and its circulation. Just like the laws making up the *derecho indiano*, marriage in the Picaresque and *El Carnero* "se acata pero no se cumple," its authority is recognized, but not obeyed except in its external form. This is the most subversive aspect of the Picaresque and the *Comentarios reales* that *El Carnero* brings out, one that points at the process whereby the texts that most forcefully attempt to rule society and reflect its values are shown to labor in the opposite direction; it is the process through which the discourse of the novel is created. *El Carnero* performs this critical function in relation to the language of the law much in the same way as the *Comentarios reales* performs it in relation to the language of history. The emerging novel is the meeting place of both critiques.

El Carnero also exposes another fundamental feature of the novel, which persists until today and that is the starting point of this study;

that it is not derived mainly from a literary tradition, but from other manifestations of language closer to the functioning of the modern state. The novel imitates not reality but the conventions of those other manifestations of language, using them as founding fables to show that in their origin and functioning they are similar to literature.

3

A lost world re-discovered: Sarmiento's *Facundo* and E. da Cunha's *Os Sertões*

An English traveler at the beginning of the nineteenth century, referring to the journey by canoe and mule that could last as long as fifty days, had written: "This is one of the most miserable and uncomfortable pilgrimages that a human being can make." This had no longer been true during the first eighty years of steam navigation, and then it became true again forever when the alligators ate the last butterfly and the maternal manatees were gone, the parrots, the monkeys, the villages were gone: everything was gone. Gabriel García Márquez, *El amor en los tiempos del cólera*[1]

The opening sentence of Esteban Echeverría's "El matadero" is ambiguous, but at the same time clearly programmatic: "A pesar de que la mía es historia, no la empezaré por el arca de Noé y la genealogía de sus ascendientes como acostumbraban a hacerlo los antiguos historiadores españoles de América que deben ser nuestros prototipos" ("Although the following narrative is historical, I shall not begin it with Noah's ark and the genealogy of his forbears as was wont once to be done by the ancient Spanish historians of America who should be our model(s)").[2] This is quite a portentous beginning for a mere novella, but Echeverría's is a very ambitious text. The Argentine writer wanted to depict in his story the ruthless repression to which opponents of Rosas' dictatorship were being subjected. The explicit scenes of mayhem are presented in the clinical tone of a scientific observer describing natural phenomena. In the story, a young man who is very clearly a projection of the author is assaulted by the rabble who work or just assemble at the Buenos Aires slaughterhouse. These thugs represent the barbaric supporters of dictator Juan Manuel Rosas, who ruled Argentina from 1829 to 1852. The young man is slain as if he were just another animal. "El matadero" is a political allegory, but also much more. Echeverría's statement about history is important for two reasons. First, it acknowledges a desire for continuity of purpose in Latin American history. The historians to whom Echeverría refers are obviously the chroniclers of the discovery and conquest of America. Like them, he wishes to place the New World within a large historical outline, hence his allusion to the Bible. Writing the narrative of Latin America involves writing about the beginning of history. But, at the same time that Echeverría invokes the chroniclers as his models, he signals a break with them. This break is evidence of the emergence of a new masterstory in the narrative of Latin America. The story will not depend on a providentialist design reaching back to biblical events for coherence and meaning, like the Spanish chronicles did, yet it will have a beginning just as powerful as theirs in determining the unfolding of Latin American history. Echeverría's history will be of the present. After the sentence just quoted, Echeverría writes: "Tengo muchas razones para no seguir ese ejemplo [that of the chronicler's], las que callo por no ser difuso. Diré solamente que los sucesos de mi narración pasaban por los años de Cristo de 183 ..." (pp. 12–13) ("Numerous reasons I might adduce for not following their example, but I shall pass them over in order to avoid prolixity, stating merely that the events here narrated occurred in the 1830's of our Christian era" [p. 210]). In the vast expanse of time encompassed by the Christian era, within which the chroniclers assembled their capacious historical machines, Echeverría's own time in the present is privileged as the start. That present is distinctive and historical because Latin American nature endows it with the power to break with the past and create a new and distinct sequence. The break is represented by violence in "El matadero," the violence whose victim is the educated young observer, who could not remain detached enough from the phenomena that he watched. The violent present is its own antecedent, its own start. Echeverría's novella marks the beginning of a new Latin American masterstory, mediated by the most authoritative discourse produced in the West since the eighteenth century: modern science. "El matadero" may very well contain all of the most important elements in that masterstory.

It is not by chance that Echeverría should be the writer to signal in such a clear fashion a break with the previous masterstory, which was based on the relationship between writing and the voluminous legal production of the Spanish Empire. The decadence of the Spanish Empire since before the eighteenth century is a fact that need not be belabored here. What is important, however, is that powers such as England, who were taking a forward leap to modernity through the industrial revolution came increasingly into contact with territories in the Spanish Empire. Spain, which had obviously lagged behind in the development of science and technology, was either being replaced by independent republics, or its control was so weak in the territories it did hold that communication with other European powers via contraband was extensive.[3] Illegal commerce with England and France was a fact of life in Spanish colonies from the beginning of Spanish rule, but as the Spanish Empire lost its grip, smuggling increased or was replaced by outright takeovers, as in the case of the English occupation of Havana in 1762 and that of Buenos Aires in 1806. Contacts such as these with Spanish territories were often decisive in changing colonial societies, propelling them sometimes ahead of Spain into the new mercantilist world created by the Industrial Revolution.[4] In a sense, whether the territory in question was independent of Spain or not, it was often entangled in a web of commercial and cultural relations with other European powers that turned it into a neo-colony of such growing empires. In Spain itself, after the accession to power of the Bourbon dynasty, and particularly during the reign of Charles III, a sizeable elite, sometimes with the support of the Crown, tapped into the sources of the Enlightenment, and attempted to bring about radical reforms. The gyrations of Spanish law became ever more abstract, increasingly less concerned with the reality of the new societies, except where it constrained the native, creole oligarchy, which was European and U.S. oriented. Hence a new kind of hegemonic discourse emerged. Perhaps the last important work to emerge from the law–narrative relationship was Alonso Carrió de la Vandera's *El Lazarillo de ciegos caminantes* (1773), which turns out to be about the circulation of documents in Spanish America, and where the complex games of authorship lead to the inescapable conclusion that the book is its own picaresque protagonist, as Karen Stolley has brilliantly shown.[5]

Given the kind of relationship the former Spanish dominions established with the new powers, one in which furnishing raw materials was the most important role, it is not surprising that nature should be the focus of such discourse, though this is not the only motive. And given the advancement of Argentina with respect to the rest of Latin America as well as its apparently boundless natural resources, it should come as no surprise that Argentine writers should be the focus of attention, though similar examples abound in the rest of Latin America. This new masterstory does not derive its cogency from a direct observation and imitation of Latin American nature, but from the mediation of works by numerous scientific travelers who should rightly be considered the second discoverers of the New World. If the first discoverers and settlers appropriated Latin America by means of legal discourse, these new conquistadors did so with the aid of scientific discourse, which allowed them to name again (as if for the first time) the flora and fauna of the New World. This discourse had its own rhetoric, which differs considerably from what we identify as scientific today. These travelers wrote accounts in the form of diaries and travelogues that did not fall entirely outside literature. There was, in fact, a promiscuous complicity between literature and scientific reportage that made it relatively easy for Latin American writers to assimilate these narratives. The new Latin American narrative absorbs this second voyage, this pilgrimage in search of Latin American historical uniqueness through the textual mediation of European science.

But the law does not disappear altogether from these narratives. Echeverría's scene of frenzied lawlessness also reveals the transformation of legal discourse in this second masterstory, and how it continues to appear as an important vestige until the present. I refer to the law in the literal sense as legal codes, not to the more abstract sense in which I use it in this book as the hegemonic discourse that mediates the narrative; the law which, under different guises, serves as the model the narrative follows. The law as penal code appears again through individuals who are outside of it, who have committed an infraction that isolates them from the norm, like the thugs in Echeverría's story. Whereas in the colonial period lawlessness centered on questions of legitimacy – bastardy, adultery, secession – now violence is the issue, a violence that excludes yet does not threaten legitimacy. Being outside the law in the sixteenth century meant one did not exist in a civil sense. In the nineteenth century and after, lawlessness does not exclude; the criminal Other is an Other Within, created by the split of Latin American society into urban and rural worlds as a result of modernity. That Other is within a law that includes the observer, an observer who, in the case of the narrative, both fears and desires to be like him. This inclusiveness does not mean, of course, that the Other Within will be given a place in Latin America's stratified society, but rather that he represents a nature which, newly interpreted by science, beckons as an all-inclusive law that will explain the otherness of the New World as a whole. From now on the Latin American narrative will deal obsessively with that Other Within who may be the source of all; that is, the violent origin of the difference that makes Latin America, distinct, and consequently original. This problematic will remain as a strong vestige not only in obvious texts such as Horacio Quiroga's stories, but also in more recent ones like Cortázar's "Axoltl." Facundo Quiroga, Antonio Conselheiro, Doña Bárbara, Demetrio Macías, become the central characters of their respective books because they are lawless and violent in some way. Their grandeur is a measure of their otherness, of their straying from the norm; in their cases, literally from the law. The Latin American self both fears and desires that Other Within, because of his lawlessness, and travels to meet him. But the only way to apprehend him is through the mediation of a hegemonic discourse, which is now that of modern science, as disseminated by the naturalists who turned the New World into their living laboratory.

As with legal discourse, the new is a dialectical process of imitation and distortion, a process that becomes itself the subtext or true masterstory. No book exemplifies this operation more dramatically and no book leaves a deeper imprint on Latin American narrative, than Sarmiento's *Facundo* (1845), a near contemporary of "El matadero," perhaps even its full-blown version.

2

Facundo is a book that is impossible to pigeonhole; it is a sociological study of Argentine culture, a political pamphlet against the dictatorship of Juan Manuel Rosas, a philological investigation of the origins of Argentine literature, a biography of the provincial *caudillo* Facundo Quiroga, Sarmiento's autobiography, a nostalgic evocation of the homeland by a political exile, a novel based on the figure of Quiroga; to me it is like our *Phenomenology of the Spirit.* Whatever one makes of the book, *Facundo* is one of those classics whose influence is pervasive and enduring and which is claimed by several disciplines at once. The fact that Sarmiento rose to become president of Argentina and put into practice policies that had such a tremendous impact on the course of his country's history adds to the canonical status of his book. The most recent evidence of *Facundo*'s lasting relevance are the debates around the figure of Caliban as symbol of Latin American culture, a polemic whose origin is found in Sarmiento.[6] Another, perhaps more durable resurgence is the proliferation of dictator-novels in Latin America, all of which have their common source in *Facundo*.[7] Carpentier's *El recurso del método* (1974) pays the most explicit homage to the Argentine, not only in such thinly veiled allusions as giving the name of Nueva Córdova to the provincial town in which part of the action takes place. Carpentier's novel is a critical reflection of the mimetic process between European and Latin American texts that *Facundo* sets in motion. That process is one of the reasons for its continued presence in the Latin American literary imagination. It is, therefore, not by accident that *Facundo* centers on the issue of authority and power.

Facundo o civilización y barbarie en las pampas argentinas was written while Sarmiento was in political exile in Chile, fleeing from the dictatorship of Rosas. As with many classics, much to the frustration of positivistic critics, the text evolved through various editions, so that it is really impossible to say which is the definitive version of *Facundo*. When it first appeared in 1845 in Santiago de Chile, the book was called *Civilización y barbarie. Vida de Juan Facundo Quiroga y aspecto físico, costumbres y hábitos de la República Argentina*. The second edition dropped the pair *civilización y barbarie*, a formula that would spawn a progeny of commentators and become a topic of Latin American literature and thought. The book is now simply called *Vida de Facundo Quiroga y aspecto físico, costumbres y hábitos de la República Argentina, seguida de apuntes biográficos sobre el general Fray Félix Aldao* (1851). There are several other editions in Spanish, including one printed in New York in 1868 and one in Paris in 1874. Whatever the changes, the core of Sarmiento's book continued to be the life of Facundo Quiroga, a *caudillo*, or strong man, from the Argentine pampas, whom Sarmiento wishes to study in order to better understand Rosas and the genesis and exercise of political power in his country. By studying Facundo Quiroga, Sarmiento hopes to isolate an early stage in the development of dictatorship, its seed, as it were. Although he was Sarmiento's contemporary, Facundo Quiroga's violent present harks back to the origin – a present origin. The study of Facundo Quiroga leads Sarmiento to his description of the pampas and the society of gauchos from which the *caudillo* emerged (though, strictly speaking, Facundo was from Llanos de la Rioja). Power and authority are somehow lodged in the seminal figure of Facundo Quiroga, a barbaric product of the land who, Sarmiento knows, is at the contradictory core of Argentinian, and by extension, Latin American culture (what Hegel, when he spoke of Napoleon, called a world-historical individual).[8] Yet he, Sarmiento himself, is also a part of that culture; the part that will be, he hopes, its civilized future. It is with fascination and repulsion that Sarmiento approaches Facundo Quiroga, like someone delving into the darker recesses of his or her own subconscious. The grandeur of the book is predicated on this antithetical origin, a cauldron of warring contraries in which author and protagonist embrace like Dioscuric twins, joined and separated by their correlative differences.

Facundo Quiroga was not, of course, the only *caudillo*, nor was he necessarily the most ferocious. He was one of many who emerged after Independence, and who vied with each other in a struggle for life that certainly appeared to be based on the survival of the fittest. (Their wars reappear in those of Colonel Aureliano Buendía in *Cien años de soledad*.) By 1819 the *caudillos* with their gaucho bands were the lords of much of the countryside: Estanislao López was master of Santa Fe, Francisco Ramírez controlled Entre Ríos, Aráoz ruled Tucumán. Quiroga was the strongman of Rioja, where he had been born to a family that prospered, but he had wandered off to war, winding up in a Chilean cell, where he is reported to have killed the Spaniard who helped him escape. Though notorious, Facundo Quiroga was not necessarily unique. It was the group of outlaws, of *caudillos*, not Facundo Quiroga himself, who eventually gave one of them, Rosas, power. (*Stricto sensu* Rosas' title continued to be Governor of the province of Buenos Aires, though the other Governors delegated to him the power to represent them abroad.) But when he was ambushed and killed at Barranca Yaco, reportedly on direct orders from Rosas, his life acquired a neatness that elevated him from mere type to legend.[9] To understand him Sarmiento needs the aid of science.

Sarmiento's relationship to Facundo Quiroga is homologous to the one his book establishes with the discourse of scientific travelers and thinkers whose names he mentions and whose texts he quotes or uses as epigraphs throughout. The role of this web of texts – some placed in liminal positions, others quoted in the body of the work – is to lend authority to Sarmiento's discourse, to serve as a model, and to give Sarmiento legitimacy as author. For Facundo Quiroga to be intelligible (that is, to be legible), he has to conform to the scientific categories and rhetoric of modern science; yet, to be compelling and worthy of attention he has to fall out of them. To be readable to Europeans or to those steeped in European culture, Sarmiento has to write a book that conforms to their discourse; yet, to be himself and hence interesting to them, he has to be different and original. As established by the relationship between the discourse of the law and narrative in colonial times, the mimetic act will serve as a form of liberation, both because of the formal compliance implicit in the very act of representation, and because of the self-annulment that takes place in that process of compliance, in the absorption and denial of the authoritarian relationship established. The dimensions and reach of this subtext increase from Sarmiento to Euclides da Cunha. But let me first turn to the mediation or model.

3

To be able or not to perceive the distinctive hues of that which is creole [i.e. Latin American] may be insignificant, but the fact is that of all the foreign travelers (not excluding, by the way, the Spaniards), no one perceives them better than the English: Miller, Robertson, Burton, Cunningham, Graham, Hudson.   J. L. Borges[10]

Travel literature has been a mainstay of writing about the New World and, in fact, many, if not all, of the *relaciones* mentioned in the previous chapter were *récits de voyage*, beginning with Columbus' *Diario*. The discovery and conquest of America gave rise to a great deal of travel literature, much of it concerned, even if at times incidentally, with scientific reportage. The *cronista cosmógrafo*, as seen before, was expected to tally as much information as possible about natural phenomena, such as volcanic eruptions and storms. Travel literature, as Percy G. Adams has shown in his compendious book, has been an important part of European letters since Herodotus, and has evolved according to changing historical conditions without ever becoming a genre, or even being confined to prose. Adams has also shown how travel literature may have influenced the emergence of the modern novel, mostly though parody.[11] The fact that parodies of travel books as influential as *Gulliver's Travels* and *Candide* appeared already in the eighteenth century (with the latter including a journey to South America) is evidence of the influence of travel literature in the period that I am concerned with, and of its being one of the forms the novel assumes. The travel literature relevant to my purposes here, however, is specifically related to the rise of modern science. Hence, while the history furnished by Adams, which only reaches to the end of the eighteenth century, is relevant as background, scientific travel to Latin America in the modern era has characteristics of its own, determined by the new conception of nature formulated by modern science.

The importance of the copious travel literature produced by the numerous scientific travelers who criss-crossed Latin America in the eighteenth and nineteenth centuries has not been totally overlooked, though as a body of writing it has yet to be systematically studied. To date Edward J. Goodman's is the best general introduction to the subject.[12] In Latin America, the only important work on the travelers was done by Carlos J. Cordero, whose *Los relatos de los viajeros extranjeros posteriores a la Revolución de Mayo como fuentes de historia argentina* is much more than the title announces.[13] The relevance of travel literature to Latin American literary history has all but been ignored. The overall import of travel literature in the general context of Latin American culture was established in 1944 by Mariano Picón Salas, who wrote, with his customary perspicuity:

The growing interest of European countries, notably England and France, in assuring the freedom of the seas for their own international trade, together with the spirit of research in natural history characteristic of the age, made the eighteenth century a period of scientific expeditions [...] Commercial and political advantage was thus identified with scientific curiosity. Some of these eighteenth-century travelers, Louis de Bougainville for instance, cleverly combined a scrutiny of nature with adventure and brought back information of interest to both their monarchs and their academies of science. With specimens from so many distant places, botanical gardens, mineralogical collections, and museums of "curiosities" were established in European capitals from Madrid to Saint Petersburg.[14]

The combination of economic interest, scientific inquisitiveness, and desire for adventure characterized the travels of European scientists for nearly two centuries. Picón Salas lays out most of the major characteristics of European scientific travel literature in the modern era. Modern imperial powers, through institutions charged with acquiring and organizing knowledge (scientific institutes, *jardins des plantes*, museums of natural history, *Tiergarten*), commission individuals possessing the scientific competence to travel to their colonies or potential colonies to gather information.[15] Once there, these often colorful individuals engage in a variety of adventures in the pursuit of knowledge and profit. The result is thousands of books describing, analyzing, and classifying the flora, fauna, landscape, social organization, ethnic composition, fossil formations, atmosphere, in short, everything that could be known by nineteenth-century science. The equation between power and knowledge, between collection and possession could not be clearer, particularly when one takes into account that many of the travelers, as in the case of Captain Francis Bond Head, were representatives of corporations involved in some sort of economic exploitation, such as mining. In many other instances the exploration and research carried out by the travelers had a direct or indirect military application, and in fact, travelers like Captain Richard Burton were military men. The various attempts that the British Empire made to occupy territories vacated by the Spanish are less mediated manifestations of this relationship between knowledge and power, as were those by the United States when it emerged on the world scene as an economic and military power in its own right (there were quite a few travelers from the United States).[16] This means, paradoxically (given that they were often active agents in fierce economic exploitation), that these scientific travelers were more often than not agents of progress, and that their efforts had in some instances a revolutionary impact on Latin American societies. The case of Alexander von Humboldt is, of course, the most notorious in this regard.

Backed as they were by the might of their empires and armed with the systemic cogency of European science, these travelers and their writings became the purveyors of a discourse about Latin American reality that rang true and was enormously influential. Their entire discursive activity, from traveling itself to taxonomical practices, embodied truth and exuded authority through its own performance. The influence of this travel literature was immense, not only on political developments within the very reality they described, but on the conception of that reality that individuals within it had of it and of themselves. A crucial component in that Creole mind was the scientific knowledge of Latin American nature, which was in many cases made available or possible by scientific travelers. Strong evidence of the enduring influence of scientific travel books in Latin America since the beginning of the nineteenth century can be found in a journal such as *El Plantel*, published in Cuba by Domingo del

Monte and the group of Romantic writers who first conceived the notion that there could be a Cuban literature. In addition to poetry, essays and history, the journal contained long pieces by the Cuban naturalist Felipe Poey, accompanied by drawings of animals and plants much like those found in the travel books.[17]

The obsolete legal discourse of Spanish colonization was replaced by scientific discourse as the authoritative language of knowledge, self-knowledge, and legitimation. This scientific discourse became the object of imitation by Latin American narratives, both fictional and non-fictional. Conventional literary history, which focuses on works that fall within the sphere of influence of European literature such as Jorge Isaacs' *María* (1867) and José Mármol's *Amalia* (1851, 1855), hardly take into account the powerful influence of scientific travel books on those very novels and on Latin American narrative of the nineteenth century in general. The mediation of the travel books is present as much in Sarmiento's *Facundo* and Lucio V. Mansilla's *Una escursión a los Indios Ranqueles* (Argentina, 1877) as in Cirilo Villaverde's description of sugarmill life in *Cecilia Valdés* (Cuba, 1880) and, as will be seen in greater detail, Euclides da Cunha's *Os Sertões* (Brazil, 1902).[18] It is the hegemonic model in Latin American narrative until the 1920s and appears as a strong vestige in archival fictions from *Los pasos perdidos* to *Cien años de soledad* and *Yo el Supremo*.

Although one would look in vain for traces of it in manuals of literature and specialized journals, the sheer volume of books about Latin America by European and U.S. scientists is staggering. As indicated in the first chapter, thousands of these books are listed in the recent bibliography published by Thomas L. Welch and Myriam Figueras, *Travel Accounts and Descriptions of Latin America and the Caribbean 1800–1900: A Selected Bibliography* (1982), and I am sure that many more could be added if the temporal span were broadened backwards and forwards. I am also certain that research in the publications of the various learned institutions of France, Germany, Belgium, England, and the United States would reveal many more names and texts that were not published separately as books. This proliferation is comparable only to that of legal documents during the first 200 years of Spanish domination, or until the famous *Recopilación* of 1681.

The travel books play a similar role in relation to the narrative, though the differences are also quite significant. To begin with, these scientific texts obeyed no anonymous rhetorical rules, nor were they penned by notaries. The scientific travelogues had authors with resounding names, like Charles-Marie de la Condamine, Louis de Bougainville, Alexander von Humboldt, Charles Darwin, Peter Wilhelm Lund, Captain Francis Bond Head, Robert and Moritz Richard Schomburgk, Captain Richard Burton. Not all the books were written by scientists in the strict sense, or even in the more inclusive sense prevalent in the nineteenth century. As S. Samuel Trifilo says with reference to English travelers in Argentina: "The accounts were written by a wide cross-section of British society – soldiers, merchants, naturalists, diplomats, businessmen, engineers, miners, missionaries, adventurers, tourists, and many others."[19] Again, as opposed to the humble formulae of the Spanish bureaucracy or even the sophisticated histories written by humanists, the scientific travelogues are literary by almost any standard.

These scientists were as much imbued with literature as the poets of the era were fascinated and influenced by science (Goethe, for instance). Besides, the travelogues not only gave an account of the objects found but also of the process by which they were found, that is, the story of the traveler's life as he journeyed in search of the secrets of nature, which of course also turns out to be a voyage of self-discovery. These travelers were powerful writers, and the stories they told are fraught with dangerous and droll adventures. Their passion for nature, as intense as that of the poets, produced compelling examples of the romantic sublime.[20] This is true not only in the masterworks, like Von Humboldt's *Voyage aux régions équinocciales du Nouveau Continent*, but also of the minor ones, like *Reisen in Britisch-Guiana in den Jahren 1840–1844*, by his disciple Moritz Richard Schomburgk. In addition, some of the travelers were themselves artists or carried artists in their retinue for the purpose of drawing or painting the landscape or the specimens under scrutiny – in some cases because they could not be preserved, in others so that the reader could "see" them in their natural habitat. The practice appears to have its remote antecedent in the so-called Drake Manuscript of the sixteenth century, which contains a remarkable array of drawings in color.[21] As a result, the books these travelers produced were remarkably valuable objects, containing beautiful illustrations of the flora, the fauna, geological formations, human types, and occasionally the party of scientific adventurers.

The prevalence of journeys of this type during the nineteenth century was such that they became a topic in Western popular fiction up to our times, when, almost as a subgenre, travel adventures have invaded the cinema and television. In the nineteenth century the most notable examples are, of course, the novels of Jules Verne and, closer to our time, Sir Arthur Conan Doyle's *The Lost World* (1912), which some have mentioned as a possible source of Carpentier's *Los pasos perdidos*. Professor Challenger's journey in search of living specimens from the prehistoric era takes him to a plateau, deep in the South American jungle, where plant and animal life have been kept outside of the evolutionary process.[22] The scientific result of the expedition consists not only of the account we read, but also of some pictures of the prehistoric monsters, needed to convince the general public as well as the properly skeptical scientific societies. The scientific traveler's human and technical probe into the uncharted regions of the colonial world was literary not only in his own perception of nature, but increasingly as a literary topic as well.

If one were to single out the most important element in the scientific travelogues and the one that had the most powerful influence on narrative, their own and others modeled after it, it would have to be time, or more precisely history, and even more specifically natural history.[23] Latin American nature had been a source of wonder to Europeans since the discovery, and the Spanish chronicles are filled with quaint descriptions of natural objects, beings and phenomena that were strange, or out of the ordinary to the author, and for which there was no word.[24] The stranglehold of Neo-Scholastic philosophy was too tight to allow the Spanish to conceive of Latin American nature as a system obeying a different history, to think actually that Latin American nature could in fact be Other. A great deal of intellectual energy was spent on forcing divergent natural phenomena into Aristotelian categories, as in the case of Father José de Acosta's monumental *Historia natural y moral de las Indias* (1590). It was like fitting a square peg into a round hole, and the results were not surprisingly monstrous, as parts from various classifications were invoked to account for animals that seemed to have been put together with pieces from different puzzles. An animal was not the result of a unique history, but a collage of parts drawn from other creatures, out of whose unchanging shape a wing, a leg or a claw had been borrowed. Much of the charm and power of baroque Latin American literature is based on the tropological contortions required to describe the New World as a set of reshuffled bits from the Old. The European travelers brought an idea of history that would allow Latin American nature to provide the basis for an autonomous and distinct Latin American being; this, along with the truth-bearing power of their discourse, is their lure to the Latin American imagination. On the political side, the result was independence from Spain. On the narrative side it provided a new masterstory, the one Sarmiento attempted to write.

The elements of that masterstory are determined as much by science as by the voyage. The voyage of scientific or quasi-scientific travelers was part of the romantic *Bildungsreise*. Traveling is the emblem of time, both personal and historical. Not only is natural history a kind of clockwork ticking away the complicated periodicity of evolution, but the observing self of the traveler is also swept along in the swirl of time. This double movement of subject and object creates an asymptote whose expression is the romantic topic of longing for a lost unity of self and cosmos, an organicity that would include the observing self. In Europe the poets always traveled south, preferably to Italy, like Goethe, Byron, or Musset, to regions where nature, together with the ruins of a splendid pagan past, could kindle or rekindle inspiration, and actually transform the self. As Goethe writes in his *Italian Journey*: "Above all, there is nothing that can compare to the new life that a reflective individual experiences when he observes a new country. Though I am still always myself, I believe I have been changed to the very marrow of my bones."[25] That symbolic South is analogous to the world of nature found elsewhere in Africa or Latin America in that it is outside the modern world that the poet flees; a modern world whose most bewildering and perverse feature is that it determines that flight from itself and absorbs it. Within that "visionary South," as Wallace Stevens would call it many years later, poets traveled to the provinces, as in the case of the Spaniard Mariano José de Larra, Echeverría himself, or Villaverde in his *Excursión a Vuelta Abajo*.[26] Extremely revealing figures in this respect are those of Latin Americans, or descendants of Latin Americans, who return to their countries of origin and write travel books in languages other than Spanish. One is Ramón Páez, a son of Venezuelan *caudillo* José Antonio Páez, who was educated in England and wrote *Wild Scenes in South America or Life in the Llanos of Venezuela* (New York, 1862), after an 1847 journey, a book that would influence Venezuela's most important fiction, *Doña Bárbara*. Another is María de las Mercedes Santa Cruz y Montalvo, Countess of Merlín, a Cuban aristocrat married to a French general in Madrid during Bonaparte's occupation, who wrote *La Havane* in 1844.[27] For these travelers, the predicament of scientific travel becomes literal – they wind up being both subject and object of their gaze, and the language they use detaches them artificially from who and what they are in the same way that scientific discourse presumably establishes a distance between naturalists and the world they study. The narrator of *Los pasos perdidos* is their anguished descendant.

Traveling was an ordeal, a detachment from the world known to the traveler in search of knowledge of nature and of himself. The ideal was, of course, a self-discovery in which nature and the self would be one, in which the luxurious and even somber beauty of the natural world would be in harmony with the soul in search of its secrets. Thomas Belt intones, in his remarkable *The Naturalist in Nicaragua*: "Alone on the summit of a high peak, with surging green billows of foliage all around, dim misty mountains in the distance, and above the blue heavens, checkered with fleecy clouds, that have traveled hundreds of miles from the north-east, thoughts arise that can be only felt in their full intensity amid solitude and nature's grandest phases. Then man's intellect strives to grapple with the great mysteries of his existence, and like a fluttering bird that beats itself against the bars of its cage, falls back baffled and bruised."[28] The rhetoric of scientific travel narrative is permeated by the figure of this narrator-hero who undergoes trials for the sake of knowledge. These trials were not trivial, given the primitive means of transportation available, the weight, volume, and fragility of the cumbersome scientific instruments, the epidemics to which the traveler was exposed and to which his body was far from immune, and the difficulties in communicating with the "natives" of the various regions visited. Many European scientists succumbed to diseases; others lost their reason. Belt, for instance, died in Denver, Colorado, at age forty-five, of a "mountain fever," while Joseph Juissieu, a botanist who accompanied La Condamine, lost his mind when, according to Goodman, "the collection of plants he had so laboriously gathered with the greatest of effort was lost through carelessness."[29] To these difficulties one might add those involved in securing specimens of plants, rocks, or animals, preserving them through taxidermy or some other method if necessary, and sending them back to the metropolis for analysis, classification, and eventual display. Von Humboldt's many trunks filled with desiccated specimens made long and circuitous voyages of their own. Some still have not arrived at their destination.

The most arduous trial, however, was for the traveler to retain his sense of self at the same time as he searched for knowledge, and not any kind of knowledge, but one with cosmic implications, for it involved the origins of time and the innermost secrets of a natural world to which he too belonged. Specialization had not yet dulled the sensibility of scientists, and their awareness of the literary dimensions of their enterprise made them receptive to their personal involvement in the reality they observed. Hence, it was not easy to be detached from the reality described and at the same time not distort it, and it was difficult to write with detachment in the midst of a world that threatened to unveil secrets that could conceivably jolt the traveler out of his identity. This was so, particularly in the case of travelers like Francis Bond Head, whose exploits as a horseman made him akin to the gauchos, in such a way that one feels that he was becoming one with them. But, to write for a European public, scientific or otherwise, the traveler had to remain European, had to persevere in his identity in spite of the lures of the wild. His discourse demanded it. The rhetorical strategy that kept this distance was the constant expression of wonder, of surprise, achieved through repeated comparisons between the European and the colonial world. But distance was created mostly by the practice of classification and taxonomy (for which Linnaeus had provided a whole new language). The other world, or the world of the Other, is classifiable, apt to become the object of a taxonomy. The soul, the spirit of the traveler, interposes the grid of classification between his desire to fuse with the object of his study and that object itself. In these books, Latin America becomes a museum of living natural history, a zoological and botanical garden in which, in contiguous enclosures, animals or plants live separated sometimes by centuries of evolutionary history.

In some of the voyages this perseverance in European identity is manifested in a spectacular fashion, as when the Schomburgk brothers, who are traveling under British auspices, fire salvos in the midst of the jungle to celebrate the Queen's birthday. Their expedition into Guiana and Venezuela is like a capsule of European time within the vast time-machine of nature. In popular fiction this element of the voyage is expressed in the elaborate preparations that the travelers make to carry with them a European environment. In Jules Verne's *La Jangada*, a novel about the Amazon, for instance, the huge raft built by French travelers becomes a Noah's ark for European life, an island of civilization floating downriver through the deepest jungle. European paraphernalia insulates the traveler from the reality outside, but as in Verne's contrived vehicles, ornate windows are built to observe and classify flora, fauna, and human samples. "Civilized" impedimenta are both a form of isolation and a point of view; both instruments and means of travel are representations of method, emblems of the travelers' discourse. Hence Captain Nemo's observatory-like window in the Nautilus, which allows him to view rare fish and plants in the depths of the ocean.

The image of Captain Nemo peering into the depths at unusual specimens allows us to posit the characteristics of travel narrative derived from science, the previous ones having been derived from the very activity of travel itself. The notion of depth expresses the conception of reality as natural history; an unfolding, or, of course, an evolution in time, which accounts for differences in flora and fauna because evolution took diverse paths in different regions. Time, in other words, is not the same in every place. A given evolutionary path leads to a different set of species. Travelers journeying through the colonial world searched for those differences in the hope of finding a master combination, the key to history, or the beginning or beginnings of it all. But Nemo is also looking at animals that belong to a prehistory, animals that were somehow left out of the evolutionary process and either became extinct or very rare. In the nineteenth century Latin America became the field of study of a significant group of paleontologists who hoped to find the secrets of evolution in prehistoric animals preserved by a quirk or accident of history. This is what Professor Challenger – the protagonist of Sir Arthur Conan Doyle's *The Lost World* – searches for on that fictional plateau in the South American jungle, a plateau which, given its elevation, due to a violent upsurge of the earth, isolated its flora and fauna from the rest of the jungle, creating some sort of natural genetic laboratory. (The model for Conan Doyle here is obviously the Galapagos Islands and the role they played in Darwin's observations and theories.) This "splendid isolation," as George Gaylord Simpson described it in one of his fascinating books on the subject, preserved the origins in the present.[30] Scientific travelers in Latin America looked not only for current specimens of flora and fauna, but for specimens that represented a backward leap into the origins of evolution. Hence, to travel to Latin America meant to find history in the evolution of plants and animals, and to find the beginning of history preserved – a contemporary, living origin. It is the present depicted in Echeverría's "El matadero" as the violent time of the narrative.

4

Nos instruments de physique et d'astronomie excitaient à leur tour la curiosité des habitants.

A. von Humboldt, Cumaná, 16–18 November 1799[31]

Sarmiento's fascination with the work of European travelers is well-known. He quotes them often, and even states: "A la América del Sud en general, y a la Argentina sobre todo, ha hecho falta un Tocqueville, que, premunido del conocimiento de las teorías sociales, como el viajero científico de barómetros, octantes y brújulas, viniera a penetrar en el interior de nuestra vida política, como en un campo vastísimo y aún no explorado ni descrito por la ciencia, y revelase a la Europa, a la Francia ..." (p. 10) ("South America in general, and Argentina in particular, has needed a de Tocqueville who, armed with the knowledge of social theory, like the scientific traveler with his barometers, octants and compasses, would come and penetrate into the depths of our political life, as if it were a vast territory still unexplored by science, and reveal it to Europe, to France ...")[32] (These instruments that Sarmiento longs for and that travelers lugged through Latin America will appear in *Cien años de soledad* as part of Melquíades' equipment.) Sarmiento's fascination with the methods and practices of modern science was undeniable and unabashedly expressed in other writings. What is revealing here, however, is that he equates social and natural science. He believes that the instruments of both are alike. Hence this is not an empty pronouncement on the part of Sarmiento. Given the significance of the instruments as a representation of method, Sarmiento's pronouncement is like a methodological profession of faith and an identification of the model of his discourse (in a sense the instruments play a role analogous to that of the notarial arts in the colonial period). De Tocqueville's gaze upon North American social life is the optical perspective – the instrument mediated or enabling point of view – that Sarmiento wishes to attain to look at South America. He is himself the de Tocqueville that he claims "South America" needs. De Tocqueville, however, is a mere emblem of the scientific travel book that determines *Facundo* as a text. How do the characteristics of scientific travel narrative sketched above appear in Sarmiento's book?

Sarmiento's journey away from Argentina may have had a political motive, but it is also analogous to the ordeal of separation discussed in reference to the travel books. It is the trial that leads to writing. In fact, the very act of leaving Argentina, which appears in a kind of prologue or epigraph (not included in the English translation), is directly linked to writing. Sarmiento scribbles a political harangue, in the form of a French quotation:

A fines del año 1840 salía yo de mi patria, desterrado por lástima, estropeado, lleno de cardenales, puntazos y golpes recibidos el día anterior en una de esas bacanales sangrientas de soldadesca y mazorqueros. Al pasar por los baños de Zonda, bajo las armas de la patria que en días alegres había pintado en una sala escribí con carbón estas palabras: ON NE TUE PAS LES IDEES.
El gobierno, a quien se comunicó el hecho mandó una comisión encargada de descifrar el jeroglífico, que se decía contener desahogos innobles, insultos y amenazas. Oída la traducción: "¡Y bien! – dijeron – ¿qué significa esto?" Significa simplemente que venía a Chile, donde la libertad brillaba aún, y que me proponía hacer proyectar los rayos de las luces de su prensa hasta el otro lado de los Andes. Los que conocen mi conducta en Chile, saben si he cumplido aquella protesta. (no page)

Toward the end of the year 1840 I was leaving my homeland, exiled by pity, beaten up, full of welts and cuts inflicted upon me the previous day by the blows of the soldiery and government thugs. On passing the Zonda Baths I wrote the following words in charcoal beneath the national coat of arms, which in happier times I myself had painted on the wall of one of the rooms:
ON NE TUE PAS LES IDEES.
Informed of the deed, the Government sent a committee charged with interpreting the hieroglyphic, which was reputed to contain vile impudences, insults and threats. Upon hearing the translation they said: "So what? What does this mean?" It simply means that I was on my way to Chile, where freedom still shines, and that I intended to project the rays of Chile's bright press upon the other side of the Andes. Those who are familiar with my activities in Chile can say whether I have been true to my intention. (my own translation)

It is revealing how much Sarmiento here resembles the hero of Echeverría's "El matadero," and how much his leaving is the result of an act of violence. Leaving and writing are violent acts inscribed in this liminal text, not quite yet in the book, but projecting upon it the reason for beginning it. Leaving and writing are linked in *Facundo* as they are in the travel books. They represent an ordeal, a separation. Sarmiento will discover his own self and delve into Argentine culture by moving away and seeing it from afar. He has been routed away from it, as if he were the issue of a violent and bloody rebirth. Of course, he is at once moving from his own culture and to it as object of study, as opposed to the travelers who move from their culture to an alien one which they will study. This difference is crucial because it denotes one of the productive contradictions in *Facundo*: The terrain actually to be traveled is not that of Argentina but that of the texts by the European travelers. It is a known fact that Sarmiento's acquaintance with the pampa came mostly through books, particularly the one by Sir Francis Bond Head, *Rough Notes Taken During Some Rapid Journeys Across the Pampas and Among the Andes*, a work he quotes in French.[33] The self-discovery in *Facundo* is thoroughly mediated by texts, just as the texts of the travelers are mediated by scientific discourse. This double mediation is Sarmiento's version of the perseverance in a European self, the equivalent of the scientist's European impedimenta. Only here the manifestation of that perseverance is textual and corresponds to the intertextual web of quotations, epigraphs, and allusions in the book. Legitimation, self-recognition, power, authority are all invested in the chameleon-like ability of Sarmiento's text to blend in, not with the land, but with the European texts about the land. Discourse and its object are one, because the object is always already discourse.

The literary character of that mediation is also revealed in a curious feature of Sarmiento's discourse: He often compares gaucho life to various oriental societies as they are described by European orientalists.[34] If the gaucho is the origin of Argentine culture, the deep stratum of the Argentine self, that origin is the solidly literary figure of a gaucho dressed in the garb of a bedouin as described by French, German and British travelers. At times the gaucho is compared to unabashedly literary texts by the likes of Victor Hugo. The congruence of European science is to the discourse of the scientists what this textual prisonhouse is to Sarmiento's: the grid that presumably keeps him from becoming one with his object of study, which, paradoxically, becomes his object of study because he too is a product of that construct. The origin, the self, and the history of the self, are literary figures, fictions of the European literary imagination as much as products of scientific inquiry.

There is a sense in which Sarmiento's mixing of European texts from scientific and literary origins unveils the profound complicity between those forms of discourse, disavowing the possible objectivity and scientific truth-bearing quality of the scientists' books. Surely the scientists project onto their object of study a vision as charged with values and desires as that of literature itself. The European gaze is one, whether it be scientific or artistic; its object is an Other created out of its longing for an origin and organicity, an Other that it depicts, classifies and describes as it creates a discourse of power predicated on the adequation of scientific discourse and an object that it has molded for itself. It is in this circularity that science and modern literature reflect each other, as Sarmiento's use of both kinds of texts reveals because of his ambiguous position as both subject and object. It is by revealing this circularity that *Facundo* breaks free of the mimetic bond out of which it was created as a text.

There are other characteristics drawn from scientific travel books in *Facundo* beyond this double mediation, most notably Sarmiento's classificatory practices, particularly of the gaucho. Among the most memorable pages in *Facundo* (the ones that most of us remember from elementary and high school) are those devoted to the description of the various kinds of gauchos: the minstrel, the pathfinder, the track-finder, the outlaw. Each of these types is described minutely, from his attire to his daily routines. The gaucho is to Sarmiento like a species of vegetable or animal life whose various families he finds, describes, and classifies for the European observer. The same taxonomical compulsion is carried over to larger blocks of Argentine life, as when the various kinds of cities are analyzed and contrasted, for instance, Córdoba vs. Buenos Aires.

What is remarkably modern about this classification is that it holds simultaneously multiple layers of time, that it reflects depth in the sense discussed before. Buenos Aires and Córdoba occupy the same time in the present, but belong to two different eras separated perhaps by centuries. The pampa may be the remote origin of all and if so, is contemporaneous with later manifestations of Argentine culture that it has determined. Facundo Quiroga is an earlier stage of Juan Manuel Rosas, though they are contemporaries (they were both born in 1793, but the *caudillo* was cut down in 1835, while the dictator lived a long life in exile until 1877):

Desenvolviéndose los acontecimientos, veremos las montoneras provinciales con sus caudillos a la cabeza; en Facundo Quiroga últimamente, triunfante en todas partes la campaña sobre las ciudades y dominadas éstas en su espíritu, gobierno y civilización, formarse al fin el gobierno central, unitario, despótico del estanciero don Juan Manuel Rosas, que clava en la culta Buenos Aires el cuchillo del gaucho y destruye la obra de los siglos, la civilización, las leyes y la libertad.   (pp. 54–5)

As events succeed each other, we shall see the provincial montoneras headed by their chiefs; the final triumph, in Facundo Quiroga, of the country over the cities throughout the land; and by their subjugation in spirit, government, and civilization, the final formation of the central consolidated despotic government of the landowner, Don Juan Manuel Rosas, who applied the knife of the gaucho to the culture of Buenos Ayres, and destroyed the work of centuries – of civilization, law and liberty.

(p. 55)

Another significant feature of the book's temporality is the way in which the origin is conceptualized. Although Sarmiento often alludes to the Spanish and even Indian history of Argentina, the origin is the pampa, which appears as an absolute beginning, prior to history, represented by the topic of nomadic, shepherd societies, an origin shared with other cultures, such as the Oriental ones. In Argentina, however, that origin is present at the same time as the history that has followed it. *Facundo*, like the books by the travelers, purports to display the dynamics of history in a spatio-temporal display, a kind of arrested-animation exhibition, highlighting the various shapes that the accidents of evolution have created in the specific region described. The book is like a gallery of types and epochs, held in synchrony by the machinery of scientific discourse.

Perhaps the best way to visualize this kind of representation is through a painting. In 1859, the U.S. artist Frederick Church unveiled his enormous canvas "Heart of the Andes," based on two expeditions to South America, but mostly inspired by Alexander von Humboldt's writings. Church followed von Humboldt's perception that, in the Andes, "at a single glance, the eye surveys majestic palms, humid forests [...] then above these forms of tropical vegetation appear oaks and sweetbriar, and above this the barren snow-capped peaks." A disciple of the renowned artist

Thomas Cole, Church was a member of what is known as the Hudson River School of painting, which delighted in portraying the beauty of the North American landscape. In "Heart of the Andes," however, he attempted to give an all-encompassing view of nature's history in the manner of von Humboldt's ambitious *Cosmos: A Sketch of a Physical Description of the Universe*.[35]

Sarmiento, of course, is not missing from that picture. Like the travelers, his life is part of the narrative, as we saw in the quotation from the book's prologue or epigraph. Sarmiento weaves himself in and out of the picture as observer, classifier and commentator, as much as author of the account. His authority is bolstered not only by the extensive quotations from scientific and literary texts, but by the sense of his having been there, of his having a special knowledge garnered through the ordeal of travel and observation. He often refers to his life in Chile, where, as a foreigner, he is naturally the object of attention. The sense of being out of his home country, often expressed by the travelers, appears in these vignettes in which Sarmiento recounts how Chileans dealt with him, and what is of interest to them about him because he is different and foreign.

These laborious preparations – a propadeutic – lead Sarmiento to his specimen: Facundo Quiroga, whose life is set in the center of the book like an odd insect trapped in a glass paperweight. The story of Facundo Quiroga's life obeys no conventional rhetorical rules for writing a biography. Life, biography, has the emphasis here on the *bio* – life is biological. Life is a concept much in vogue in nineteenth-century science, and the debate between organicists and mechanicists is well-known. It is a concept that left a deep imprint on European thought and literature, culminating perhaps in Nietzsche or in Unamuno, and the Hispanic versions of *Lebensphilosophie* called *vitalismo*. Sarmiento accounts for Facundo Quiroga's character and fate in scientific terms. The *caudillo* is motivated by an excess of life, a thrust that leads him inevitably and tragically to Barranca Yaco, where he knows he will be slain. Facundo Quiroga's surfeit of life is visible in the shape of his head, in his stoutness, and in his fiery eyes. These are biological accidents that determine his fate, that make his life conform even more to a tragic pattern. Just as Facundo Quiroga's originality is the result of accidents, so is the whole of gaucho culture, a serendipitous accumulation of random events. The *pulpería*, the social nucleus of gaucho life, develops from the chance meetings of gauchos:

Salen, pues, los varones sin saber fijamente a dónde. Una vuelta a los ganados, una visita a una cría o a la querencia de un caballo predilecto, invierte una pequeña parte del día; el resto lo absorbe una reunión en una venta o pulpería. Allí concurren cierto número de parroquianos de los alrededores; allí se dan y adquieren las noticias sobre los animales extraviados; trázanse en el suelo las marcas del ganado; sábese dónde caza el tigre, dónde se le han visto rastros al león; allí, en fin, está el cantor, allí se fraterniza por el circular de la copa y las prodigalidades de los que poseen ... y en esta asamblea sin objeto público, sin interés social, empiezan a echarse los rudimentos de las reputaciones que más tarde, y andando los años, van a aparecer en la escena política.   (pp. 50–1)

The men then set forth without exactly knowing where they are going. A turn around the herds, a visit to a breeding-pen or to the haunt of a favorite horse, takes up a small part of the day; the rest is consumed in a rendezvous at a tavern or grocery store [pulpería]. There assemble inhabitants of the neighboring parishes; there are given and received bits of information about animals that have gone astray; the traces of the cattle are described upon the ground; intelligence of the hunting-ground of the tiger or of the place where the tiger's tracks have been seen, is communicated. There, in short, is the Minstrel; there the men fraternize while the glass goes around at the expense of those who have the means as well as the disposition to pay for it ... yet in this assembly, without public aim, without social interest, are first formed the elements of those characters which are to appear later on the political stage.   (pp. 48–9)

Even the gaucho's poetry is due to accidents of the terrain, irregularities like those of his body: "Existe, pues, un fondo de poesía que nace de los accidentes naturales del país y de las costumbres excepcionales que engendra" (p. 36) ("The country consequently derives a fund of poetry from its natural circumstances [accidents] and the special customs resulting [being engendered] from them" [p. 27]).

The notion of accident is decisive because it determines Facundo Quiroga's freedom, his flight from the norm, his originality. When he defeats regular armies he does so because he is free to use non-conventional tactics that befuddle his enemies. An accident is inaugural by definition: it is an event independent of the past which becomes a unique form of present violently broken off from history, a new form of temporality, like the series of tumultuous acts narrated in Echeverría's story. An accident is a beginning like those that paleontologists hope to find in caves and digs; Facundo Quiroga's penchant for brutality is an expression of his freedom. As an origin in the present, he validates Rosas' inclination to violence, and Sarmiento's own escape from the model furnished by the scientific travelers.

When Sarmiento finally arrives at the beginning of his *life* of Facundo Quiroga, we read:

Media entre las ciudades de San Luis y San Juan un dilatado desierto que, por su falta completa de agua, recibe el nombre de *travesía*. El aspecto de aquellas soledades es, por lo general, triste y desamparado, y el viajero que viene de oriente no pasa la última *represa* o aljibe de campo sin proveer sus *chifles* de suficiente cantidad de agua. En esta travesía tuvo lugar una vez la extraña escena que sigue. Las cuchilladas, tan frecuentes entre nuestros gauchos, habían forzado a uno de ellos a abandonar precipitadamente la ciudad de San Luis, y ganar la *travesía* a pie, con la montura al hombro, a fin de escapar a las persecuciones de la justicia. Debían alcanzarlo dos compañeros tan luego como pudieran robar caballos para los tres.

No eran por entonces sólo el hambre o la sed los peligros que le aguardaban en el desierto aquel, que un tigre *cebado* andaba hacía un año siguiendo los rastros de los viajeros, y pasaban ya de ocho los que habían sido víctimas de su predilección por la carne humana. Suele ocurrir a veces en aquellos países en que la fiera y el hombre se disputan el dominio de la naturaleza, que éste cae bajo la garra sangrienta de aquélla; entonces el tigre empieza a gustar de preferencia su carne, y se le llama *cebado* cuando se ha dado a este género de caza; la caza de hombres. El juez de la campaña inmediata al teatro de sus devastaciones convoca a los varones hábiles para la correría, y bajo su autoridad y dirección se hace la persecución del tigre *cebado*, que rara vez escapa a la sentencia que lo pone fuera de la ley.

Cuando nuestro prófugo había caminado cosa de seis leguas, creyó oír bramar el tigre a lo lejos y sus fibras se estremecieron. Es el bramido del tigre un gruñido como el del cerdo, pero agrio, prolongado, estridente, y que, sin que haya motivo de temor, causa un sacudimiento involuntario de los nervios, como si la carne se agitara ella sola al anuncio de la muerte.

Algunos minutos después el bramido se oyó más distinto y más cercano; el tigre venía ya sobre el rastro, y sólo a una larga distancia se divisaba un pequeño algarrobo. Era preciso apretar el paso, correr, en fin, porque los bramidos se sucedían con más frecuencia, y el último era más distinto, más vibrante que el que le precedía.

Al fin, arrojando la montura a un lado del camino dirigióse el gaucho al árbol que había divisado, y no obstante la debilidad de su tronco, felizmente bastante elevado, pudo trepar a su copa y mantenerse en una continua oscilación, medio oculto entre el ramaje. De allí pudo observar la escena que tenía lugar en el camino: el tigre marchaba a paso precipitado, oliendo el suelo y bramando con más frecuencia a medida que sentía la proximidad de su presa. Pasa adelante del punto en que ésta se había separado del camino y pierde el rastro; el tigre se enfurece, remolinea, hasta que divisa la montura, que desgarra de un manotón, esparciendo en el aire sus prendas. Más irritado aún con este chasco, vuelve a buscar el rastro, encuentra al fin la dirección en que va, y, levantando la vista, divisa a su presa haciendo con el peso balancearse el algarrobillo, cual la frágil caña cuando las aves se posan en sus puntas.

Desde entonces ya no bramó el tigre; acercábase a saltos, y en un abrir y cerrar de ojos sus enormes manos estaban apoyándose a dos varas del suelo sobre el delgado tronco, al que comunicaban un temblor convulsivo que iba a obrar sobre los nervios del mal seguro gaucho. Intentó la fiera dar un salto impotente; dio vuelta en torno al árbol midiendo su altura con ojos enrojecidos por la sed de sangre, y al fin, bramando de cólera se acostó en el suelo, batiendo sin cesar la cola, los ojos fijos en su presa, la boca entreabierta y reseca. Esta escena horrible duraba ya dos horas mortales; la postura violenta del gaucho y la fascinación aterrante que ejercía sobre él la mirada sanguinaria, inmóvil, del tigre, del que por una fuerza invencible de atracción no podía apartar los ojos, habían empezado a debilitar sus fuerzas, y ya veía próximo el momento en que su cuerpo extenuado iba a caer en su ancha boca, cuando el rumor lejano de galope de caballos le dio esperanza de salvación.

En efecto, sus amigos habían visto el rastro del tigre y corrían sin esperanza de salvarlo. El desparramo de la montura les reveló el lugar de la escena; y volar a él, desenrollar sus lazos, echarlos sobre el tigre, *empacado* y ciego de furor, fue la obra de un segundo. La fiera, estirada a dos lazos, no pudo escapar a las puñaladas rápidas con que en venganza de su prolongada agonía le traspasó el que iba a ser su víctima. "Entonces supe qué era tener miedo", decía el general don Juan Facundo Quiroga, contando a un grupo de oficiales este suceso.

También a él le llamaron *Tigre de los Llanos*, y no le sentaba mal esta denominación, a fe.   (pp. 71–3; emphasis in the original)

Between the cities of San Luis and San Juan, lies an extensive desert, called the Travesía, a word which signifies *want of water* [on the contrary, it means a watercrossing]. The aspect of that waste is mostly gloomy and unpromising, and the traveler coming from the east does not fail to provide his *chifles* [canteens] with a sufficient quantity of water at the last cistern which he passes as he approaches it. This Travesía once witnessed the following strange scene. The consequences of some of the encounters with knives so common among our gauchos had driven one of them in haste from the city of San Luis and forced him to escape to the Travesía on foot, and with his riding gear on his shoulder, in order to avoid the pursuit of the law. Two comrades were to join him as soon as they could steal horses for all three.

Hunger and thirst were not the only dangers which at that time awaited him in the desert; a tiger that had already tasted human flesh had been following the track of those who crossed it for a year, and more than eight persons had already been the victims of this preference. In these regions, where man must contend with this animal for dominion over nature, the former sometimes falls a victim, upon which the tiger begins to acquire a preference for the taste of human flesh, and when it has once devoted itself to this novel form of chase, the pursuit of mankind, it gets the name of *man-eater*. The provincial justice nearest the scene of his depredations calls out the huntsmen of his district, who join, under his authority and guidance, in the pursuit of the beast, which seldom escapes the consequences of its outlawry.

When our fugitive had proceeded some six leagues, he thought he heard the distant roar of the animal, and a shudder ran through him. The roar of the tiger resembles the screech of the hog, but is prolonged, sharp, and piercing, and even when there is no occasion for fear, causes an involuntary tremor of the nerves as if the flesh shuddered consciously at the menace of death.

The roaring was heard clearer and nearer. The tiger was already upon the trail of the man, who saw no refuge but a small carob-tree at a great distance. He had to quicken his pace, and finally to run, for the roars behind him began to follow each other more rapidly, and each was clearer and more ringing than the last.

At length, flinging his riding gear to one side of the path, the gaucho turned to the tree which he had noticed, and in spite of the weakness of its trunk, happily quite a tall one, he succeeded in clambering to its top, and keeping himself half concealed among its boughs which oscillated violently. Thence he could see the swift approach of the tiger, sniffing the soil and roaring more frequently in proportion to its increasing perception of the nearness of its prey. Passing beyond the spot where our traveler had left the path, it lost the track, and becoming enraged, rapidly circled about until it discovered the riding gear, which it dashed to fragments by a single blow. Still more furious from this failure, it resumed its search for the trail, and at last found out the direction in which it led. It soon discerned its prey, under whose weight the slight tree was swaying like a reed upon the summit of which a bird has alighted.

The tiger now sprang forward, and in the twinkling of an eye, its monstrous fore-paws were resting on the slender trunk two yards from the ground, and were imparting to the tree a convulsive trembling calculated to act upon the nerves of the gaucho, whose position was far from secure. The beast exerted its strength in an ineffectual leap; it circled around the tree, measuring the elevation with eyes reddened by the thirst for blood, and at length, roaring with rage, it crouched down, beating the ground frantically with its tail, its eyes fixed on its prey, its parched mouth half open. This horrible scene had lasted for nearly two mortal hours; the gaucho's constrained attitude, and the fearful fascination exercised over him by the fixed and bloodthirsty stare of the tiger, which irresistibly attracted and retained his own glances, had begun to diminish his strength, and he already perceived that the moment was at hand when his exhausted body would fall into the capacious mouth of his pursuer. But at this moment the distant sound of the feet of horses on a rapid gallop gave him hope of rescue.

His friends had indeed seen the tiger's foot-prints, and were hastening on, though without hope of saving him. The scattered fragments of the saddle directed them to the scene of action, and it was the work of a moment for them to reach it, to uncoil their lassoes, and to fling them over the tiger, now blinded with rage. The beast, drawn in opposite directions by the two lassoes, could not evade the swift stabs by which its destined victim took his revenge for his prolonged torments. "On that occasion I knew what it was to be afraid," was the expression of Don Juan Facundo Quiroga, as he related this incident to a group of officers.

He too was called "the tiger of the Llanos," a title which did not ill befit him ...   (pp. 73–6)

Sarmiento has encrypted in this story, on the threshold of Facundo Quiroga's life, the central tropological mechanisms of his book. The story can be read as an allegory not only of the *caudillo*'s life, but more interestingly of the life of *Facundo* the book; of its existence in relation to Sarmiento and the books by the scientific travelers. This quasi-liminal text, on the verge of the full story, is a version of that masterstory of the narrative of Latin America whose kernel is Echeverría's "El matadero": both center on violence and sacrifice. Here, however, the internal dialectics from which the story issues are more forcefully present.

It is a curious fact that the first sentence of the life of Facundo Quiroga already contains a trope that announces the mastertropes of the story, as if beginnings always had to contain in embryonic form middles and ends. The desert between San Luis and San Juan is called a *travesía* because of its absolute lack of water; yet one normally calls a *travesía* the crossing of a body of water. Hence the name means, in this specific context, the opposite of what it ordinarily does; it is a kind of natural catachresis, as if language communicated in a mysterious, non-rational way, by doing violence to conventional relationships between signifier and signified. To understand language we have to be able to master a code that is not the universal one, which we presume to be based on a layered memory of human exchange. The desert is called a water-crossing because of its absolute lack of water, therefore we must be ready to read the opposite of what words appear to mean. We know from Amado Alonso and others, of course, that a term like *travesía* entered Argentine Spanish as far back as 1575 like many other words borrowed from the language of seafaring that the colonists brought with them after the inevitable crossing of the ocean, a linguistic phenomenon common to the Spanish of the Americas.[36] Be that as it may, the inversion remains, whether it is a historical retention or a renewed misnomer.

The watery metaphor is continued when we are told that travelers must store up water before embarking on a journey through the desert at the last *represa*, that is to say, the last dam or lock. Now, *represa* is given here as synonymous to *aljibe*, a well or cistern, which does contain water, but it seems that it gets its name because it marks the boundary of the desert, not because it provides water. The metaphoric body of water to be crossed is fenced in by dams where the traveler must load up on that which is missing from the area thus contained. If we remember that the vast wastes of the pampa are often compared to the sea in *Facundo*, we can understand better that, within the tropological system of the text, which seems to be made up of a series of inversions, the earth can be water. What all these inversions have been preparing the reader for is the unusual, the out-of-the-ordinary, the "strange scene" about to be narrated, one in which man is the object of the chase, not the other way around. Strangeness, uniqueness, pervades the story of Facundo Quiroga, the singular specimen, the mutant that is going to explain a distinct Latin American strain.

The singularity of the gaucho, his existence outside the norm, is expressed by the fact that he is often an outlaw. This gaucho in particular flees the city because he has stabbed a man to death in one of the frequent outbursts of violence against fellow men and animals that punctuate the life of a gaucho. The gaucho's violent nature makes him both a man of nature and a man outside the law. Like the catachresis that describes his habitat, the gaucho lives in a world of transgressions, of rupture, of breaks. This condition is further emphasized in this particular case by the gaucho having to travel on foot. The horse was the gaucho's way of life, practically from birth. The "strange story" is not only about an individual who functions outside the law, but one who is, at this specific moment, outside his own law, where he can be prey to an accident like the one that in fact befalls him. The story is about an instance, original and unique, hence capable of engendering an individual as exceptional as Facundo Quiroga.

The tiger enters the "strange scene" also under the banner of a misnomer. We are dealing here not with a tiger, of course, but with a species of jaguar, "tiger" being one of the approximations used by Europeans to name American natural phenomena that did not quite conform to their categories. Be that as it may, like the gaucho, the tiger is running away from the law because he kills men. This is no ordinary tiger. He belongs to a special kind that is partial to human flesh. Once he has tasted a human, the tiger acquires a predilection for humans, a predilection that is based on a very intimate, secret, and forbidden knowledge. To be *cebado* means to be "primed," to have a foreknowledge that incites desire; to have or have already had a morsel of what one desires, a teasing, partial sampling. This knowledge and desire for more of the same – a same that is already part of one, being inside, consumed – is the aesthetic counterpart of the scientific curiosity of the travelers; the literary aspect that Sarmiento unveils through the pell-mell mixing of textual tidbits from science and literature. The tiger's ability to capture humans, his technique in following a scent, his hermeneutic power to interpret the signs of human presence, are predicated on this foreknowledge. Like the textual doubling in the mediation of discourses, knowledge is predicated on foreknowledge, on capturing an object that discourse has itself molded. There is, precisely, a sense in which this knowledge exceeds the norm, goes beyond mere need for food. To be *cebado* means not only to be primed, but to be fat, to be satiated. One can *cebar* an animal, fatten him for the kill and the table. Hence the taste for human flesh on the part of the tiger is a forbidden knowledge in that it is like a vice, a desire that exceeds need. There is in the beautiful descriptions of the animal, particularly of his violent acts and perseverance in his pursuit of his prey to the point of giving his life in the effort, a reflection of this doubly vicious character, at once meanness, and addiction to pleasure. To be *cebado* is to have a penchant for extravagance, for luxury, to be driven by an excess of life, like Facundo Quiroga. This foreknowledge acquired through the taste of flesh is in consonance with the communication established between the tiger and the gaucho, which is not merely a digestive one.

The gaucho learns of the tiger's presence through the roar of the animal, in reaction to which "sus fibras se estremecieron," meaning, of course, his muscle fibers, his flesh. Taste is not the only sense through which the flesh of the gaucho and the tiger communicate. It is explained in the next line that the roar of the tiger is like the grunt of a pig, but shrill and long. Even when there is no reason for fear (*motivo* here has to be translated thus), it causes one's nervous system to shudder involuntarily, as if the flesh itself became agitated "al solo anuncio de la muerte" ("by the mere announcement or threat of death"). The tiger's roar establishes a communication with the gaucho's flesh that bypasses language. Later on, the same kind of understanding is established when the tiger communicates a tremor to the tree that acts directly upon the nerves of the gaucho. As opposed to the vagaries of communication through language and its tropological relays, delays, and detours, the language the tiger speaks to the gaucho communicates directly, producing in him a contradictory feeling of fascination and mortal fear. Tiger and gaucho understand each other subliminally, that which is being communicated being itself sublime: terror and desire. This identification and communication between tiger and gaucho by means of a sublime language says much about the masterstory embedded in Sarmiento's book.

The language of the pampa, as shown, breaks with the received language of social communication; words often mean, irrationally, against history, the opposite of what they normally signify. That language is like the one the tiger and the gaucho speak. Meaning is not conveyed by the established code but by a given feeling, a feeling that stands at the threshold of the need to trope, at the very origin of language. The pampa is not merely a plain – a blank page – but a silence whose vastness provokes, like the sea, a feeling of the infinite that incites both fear and longing. The "strange story" narrates an accident; an accident cannot have an antecedent, otherwise it would not be one. Since it does not have anything prior that explains it, the accident has to be narrated in a catachretic language, whose odd signs are like the unique specimens involved. The fact that Facundo Quiroga acquires his *nom de guerre* from this scene is a clear indication of how naming proceeds in this language. The gaucho steals from the animal his already mistaken name. By killing the tiger, the gaucho names himself. Naming is a violent activity, a break with the norm, with the law. This would be of no particular interest if the story were narrated with detachment by the voice Sarmiento uses for classification, the rhetoric of the travelers that allows him to hold up as distinct, strange and uncivilized that which he is describing. But this is not the case.

Until Facundo Quiroga breaks in to explain that it was then that he learned about fear, the reader does not know that it was *the caudillo himself who was telling the story*. Sarmiento has almost imperceptibly surrendered the narrative voice to the protagonist himself. This prosopopeia creates an identification between Facundo Quiroga and Sarmiento that is parallel to the one just established between the tiger and the gaucho. The gaucho cannot evade the bloodthirsty stare of the tiger, which both attracts him and threatens him, drawing him toward the animal's enormous mouth. A mouth with a voice, but with no articulate language, a language that is also spoken through the eyes, as if being deflected, monstrously, through another organ. A language of gazes, of looks, that returns the inquisitive stare of the gaucho, that classificatory, affixing glance of man. The gaucho cannot speak out of fear. The mouth of the tiger has stolen his voice, like Facundo Quiroga stole Sarmiento's. Is Sarmiento the detached, civilized observer, or is he, like the gaucho up in the tree, vibrating with the sublime language of fear? Or, again, like the tiger, drawn in opposite directions by the two lassoes, pulled by fear and desire toward certain annihilation? If one takes into account that time and again Sarmiento insists that Rosas commands through fear, then the chain of identifications becomes even more interesting: the tiger is like Facundo Quiroga, who is like Juan Manuel Rosas, who is like Domingo Faustino Sarmiento. The language of the text is not that of the scientific travelogue but the accidental language of literature, a subliminal language whose system is that of breaking the system, and whose aim is to be unique, like the gaucho and the tiger, to partake of their violent beauty.

Sarmiento, or better, Sarmiento's discourse is like the tiger's, made up of misnomers, of violence represented as catachreses, motivated by a desire for the object that turns him into the object, as Facundo Quiroga's and the tiger's voice blend one with the other. Sarmiento's discourse is *cebado*, primed, satiated, yet desirous for more, and reveals at the same time this quality to be the fundamental one in the scientific traveler's discourse. It is the artistic, the aesthetic excess in those books, which Sarmiento feeds on to create an outlaw discourse, beyond the taxonomies of science. For, to capture that unique, monstrous prey, that mutant that marks the foundation of Latin American narrative discourse, his own discourse has to be unique and monstrous, the product of a different time. It is for this reason, and for no other, that *Facundo* is a founding text in Latin American narrative; it contains in a dramatic fashion the second masterstory, one that will prevail until the *novela de la tierra*, and remain a strong vestige until the present.

But there is more, of course, for in killing the tiger the gaucho is killing himself, or at least prefiguring his own death in Barranca Yaco. Facundo Quiroga's life is the stuff of tragedy. His excess of life, like a tragic hubris, leads him to the grandeur of his power as well as to his death, about which he is warned on several occasions. He cannot escape his fate because, in order to be free, his life has to be determined by accidents that release him from the norm. Fear, the language he knows, can make his flesh shudder in anticipation of death, but fear cannot tell him what to do to avoid death; if anything, fear leads him to death. Sarmiento, the omniscient narrator in the book, is caught in the same trap. Given his identification with Facundo Quiroga and Rosas, their demise is his own demise. He too is blind to his own fate, which is to be like them. In literary history Sarmiento lives because of Facundo Quiroga. What Sarmiento has found in his voyage of discovery and self-discovery is a present origin, one that speaks through him, hollowing out the voice of his scientific language. His authority will not be attained by it, but by the tragic sacrifice of his protagonist, which he re-enacts in the text. This tragic fusion is a reflection of the linear time introduced by the evolution of nature, which brings everything to an end, inexorably, so that it will be reborn in a different guise. Fusion with the object of analysis is the escape from the hegemonic discourse, the subplot of this second masterstory, a flight into the abyss of time. Escape from mediation is figured in nineteenth-century narrative by this joining with the object of observation, which is a fusion with mutability. This vertiginous sense of time will remain in Latin American fiction in the endings of novels like Carpentier's *El reino de este mundo* and García Márquez' *Cien años de soledad*, narratives in which the action is brought to a close by a violent wind that blows everything away. That wind first swept across the pampas in Sarmiento's *Facundo*.

4

... because races condemned to one hundred years of solitude did not have
a second chance on earth.   Gabriel García Márquez[37]

In a prefatory note to the first edition of *Os Sertões* (Rio de Janeiro,
1902), Euclides da Cunha writes that he is moved to publish the
book, even with considerable delay after the events that it recounts,

porque a sua instabilidade de complexos de fatores múltiplos e diver-
samente combinados, aliada às vicissitudes históricas e deplorável situação
mental em que jazem [subraças sertanejas do Brasil], as tornam talvez
efêmeras, destinadas a próximo desparecimento ante as exigências cres-
centes da civilização e a concorrência material intensiva das correntes
migratórias que começam a invadir profundamente a nossa terra.

the instability of the multiple factors and diverse combinations that go to
make up this ethnic complex [the "subraces" in the backlands of Brazil],
together with the vicissitudes of history and the lamentable lack of mental
enlightenment which prevails among them, is likely to render these races
short-lived, destined soon to disappear before the growing exigencies of
civilization and the intensive material competition offered by the stream of
immigrants that is already beginning to invade our land.[38]

This urgent conception of the fleeting nature of time and the
mutability of the real world, as shown by the swift evolution and
disappearance of entire human groups, is at the very core of
Euclides' compelling masterpiece.[39] *Os Sertões* is a book that owes
much to *Facundo*, but it is much greater, and provides a grandiose
synthesis of Latin American narrative in the nineteenth century,
whose impact can still be felt in novels like Severo Sarduy's *Colibrí*
(1983).[40]

As was the case with Sarmiento, the gap between the author's
intention in writing the book and the final product is quite wide; it is
a chasm into which Euclides' "scientific racism" sinks, and his
pessimism acquires a tragic hue that exceeds the scope of the prosaic
positivistic doctrine that guided him. Euclides' efforts to preserve for
future historians a sketch of the history of Canudos and its protagonists develop into an in-depth study of Brazilian history and identity,
an analysis whose very grandeur is a consequence of its failure. In
spite of Machado de Assis' distinction as a novelist, it is Euclides'
hybrid book – half reportage, half scientific analysis and all literature – that has had the widest circulation and impact in the rest of

Latin America, as Mario Vargas Llosa's recent rewriting of *Os Sertões* in *La guerra del fin del mundo* has confirmed once again.[41]

Like *Facundo*, *Os Sertões* centers on an extraordinary figure who embodies the backward forces of the hinterlands, engaged in mortal combat with "civilization," represented by the cities on the seashore. In *Os Sertões* the eccentric figure is not a strongman like Facundo Quiroga, but Antonio Conselheiro, the leader of a grassroots religious movement that mobilized the dirt-poor people of the remote flatlands of the northeast – the *sertão* – in the last decade of the nineteenth century. These *sertanejos*, many of them criminals (*cangaceiros*), fugitives and convicts, become a significant force, and make themselves strong in a makeshift citadel, Canudos. The events that make up the story of *Os Sertões* are of stark and redundant simplicity. The recently installed (1889) Republic considers the religious movement a threat to its political stability and sends a military expedition to suppress it. But, to the embarrassment of the government, the army is soundly routed by the rebels. Three military expeditions of increasing might fail to take Canudos, until a fourth one manages to reduce it to the ground – literally, for the army uses dynamite to smash every building, in what we would call today a scorched-earth campaign. But Canudos never surrenders and the paroxysmal violence lasts until the very end, with an appalling death toll on both sides.

The story is worth retelling to chart its crescendo, as well as to note its repetitive nature. What begins as a minor conflict in a remote hinterland escalates into a confrontation of national and even international proportions, whose most significant character is that it continually thwarts prediction and defies conceptualization. Cause and effect seem to have an incremental rather than a sequential relationship. This unpredictability foils the politicians and the military in their interpretation of events. They are the first "readers" of Canudos who fail in their interpretive effort and suffer the consequences. The Republic is ridiculed and the government is destabilized. Politicians in the capital claim the rebels are supplied by foreign powers interested in reinstating the monarchy, while the *sertanejos* believe that the Republic is inspired by the Devil himself. These colossal misreadings define what takes on the aura of a confrontation between eras and civilizations, not between opposing factions within a single country. The repeated failure of the military expeditions acquire in Euclides' Miltonian style a nightmarish quality. The Republic's errors are re-enacted by *Os Sertões*, a rare coincidence that gives the book its poignancy and pathos.

Os Sertões is a blow-up of *Facundo*, but as with most enlargements, it is not simply a bigger copy but also a distortion. There is a monstrous progression from Sarmiento to Euclides da Cunha. The scientific instruments that Sarmiento wished to turn upon Latin America have metamorphosed in Euclides into the machines of war made possible by modern science, and which are turned upon the backlands of Brazil in order to possess it in the most tangible and forcible way. There is a rigorous correlation between instruments of war and methods of scientific inquiry, between the planning of military campaigns, and Euclides' own deployment of his scientific discourse. The violence that marked the passage of time in *Facundo* has become a generalized and convulsive state of war in *Os Sertões*, a constant escalation without a discernible rate that winds up in an orgy of bloodshed and indiscriminate destruction that blurs the difference between soldiers and *sertanejos*. It is a violence without measure and without end, for Canudos never surrenders. The synchrony between nature and culture that made Facundo Quiroga a freak embodying the latter, becomes in Euclides a vast cosmic coalescence of deviant forces that ranges from geological upheavals to the shape of Conselheiro's head. Time is abnormal growth; violence a general deviance from, sometimes literally a rupture with, the norm, the law. Nature, in *Os Sertões*, expresses a tragedy of cosmic proportions, one that the text itself can embody because of its own hubris and anagnorisis, because of its own inherent aberrancy.[42]

If it is true that Euclides was not as prominent a figure as Sarmiento, he was, on the other hand, more systematically imbued with the spirit and methods of nineteenth-century science. A military engineer by training and profession and later an engineer in civilian life as well as a scientific traveler (to Peru) in his own right, Euclides voices throughout *Os Sertões*, to the very last line, a faith in science that is manifest in his ceaseless allusions to major and minor figures of the various disciplines, ranging from geologists to psychopathologists, and including some of the many naturalists who traveled through and described Brazil.[43] In a way Euclides reflects Brazil's commitment to science in the nineteenth century, which for various reasons outstripped that of the rest of Latin America. One was that for most of the nineteenth century, under the monarchy,

Brazil retained more ties with Europe than the nations whose independence had led immediately to the formation of republics. Another was the discovery of precious metals in the interior of Brazil, which led to much scientific travel connected with mining. Be that as it may, from early on Brazil established institutions for the promotion of scientific research and exploration such as the Imperial Museum, founded in 1818, and the Sociedade Velosiana de Ciências Naturais, which was created in 1850. As far as scientific exploration is concerned, Nancy Stepan writes the following in her authoritative *Beginnings of Brazilian Science*, from which I have obtained the information offered above:

The tradition of scientific exploration of South America established by Humboldt gained momentum in Brazil with the opening of Brazil to European trade after 1808. Many expeditions were sponsored, some privately and others by foreign governments. The travels of the French naturalist Auguste de Saint-Hilaire in 1816 were followed by those of Alcide d'Orbigny, who was sent by the Muséum d'Histoire Naturelle de Paris, and by those of the German Prince Maximilian of Wied-Neuwied, who was accompanied by the botanist Friedrich Sellow. With the marriage of the Archduchess Leopoldina, daughter of the Austrian Emperor, to the Brazilian Prince Regent, Dom Pedro, a number of scientists came to Brazil with her court to examine Brazilian vegetation and animals. Most famous were two Bavarians, Karl Friedrich Philipp von Martius and Johann Baptist Von Spix, whose massive, many volumed *Flora brasiliensis* (the first volume of which was published in 1829) eventually took sixty-six years to complete, and remained the standard textbook on Brazilian botany until well into the twentieth century. In the steps of the French and Germans came the Russian-sponsored expedition of Baron Georg Heinrich von Langsdorff, a German diplomat in the service of the Tsar, who collected a herbarium of 60,000 specimens for St. Petersburg. The English were well represented with the visits to Brazil of Charles Darwin, Henry Bates, Alfred Russell Wallace, and the botanist Richard Spruce. American [i.e. U.S.] science began its own tradition of scientific exploration in Brazil when the Thayer expedition, led by the distinguished Swiss-born zoologist Louis Agassiz, came to Brazil in the winter of 1865–1866 to explore the Amazon. This stage of exploration led to the amassing of a large amount of important scientific data.[44]

In more ways than one Euclides is heir to the tradition of Brazilian science sketched by Stepan, and more specifically to the engineering school at the Military Academy that had been founded in 1810.[45] The school was to "prepare them [the cadets] for the surveying and exploration of what was virtually unknown land" and "represented a deliberate effort by the Prince Regent to alter the traditionally literary mentality of the country" (p. 25). In *Os Sertões*, Euclides made a heroic attempt to stave off the literary by sedulously heeding the voice of the land surveyor in him, and by remembering the scientific authorities that he had learned to trust.

Euclides casts a fine net of scientific studies over the *sertão* to capture the essence of the events at Canudos, an exceptional historical upheaval that has to be brought to order through the discourse of knowledge and power. His original reports on Canudos, which he wrote as war correspondent to *O Estado de São Paulo*, were intended for an urban public that shared his confidence in science and the military.[46] Euclides' trust in science is as manifest as the Republic's in the efficacy of conventional warfare to overrun the rebels. A detailed inventory of Euclides' references to scientific authorities would no doubt reveal the depth and breadth of his readings.[47] Particularly in the first section of *Os Sertões* the number of references is considerable, and they include the names of Alcide d'Orbigny, Karl Friedrich Philipp von Martius, and others mentioned by Stepan. But he also appeals to geologists, paleontologists, botanists, pathologists. A list of names mentioned in the first two chapters reads as follows (in order of appearance): Rocha Pita, Buckle, Eschwege, Lund, Liais, Huxley, Fred Hartt, Gerber, Martius, F. Mornay, Wollaston, Herschel, Barón de Capanema, Tyndall, Saint-Hilaire, Humboldt, Andrés Reboucas, Beaurepaire Rohan, J. Yofily, Morton, Meyer, Trajano de Moura, Broca, Bates, Draenert, Aires de Casal, Varnhagen, Taunay, Orville Derby, Foville, Gumplowicz, Maudsley, Vauban ... On occasion Euclides assumes the perspective of a scientific traveler as he describes the landscape: "E o observador que seguindo este itinerário deixa as paragens em que se revezam, em contraste belíssimo, a amplitude dos gerais e o fastígio das montanhas, ao atingir aquele ponto estaca surpreendido ..." (p. 96) ("The observer who has followed such an itinerary, leaving behind him a region where the broad sweep of the Campos forms a most beautiful contrast with the mountain summits, upon reaching this point stops short in surprise" [p. 8]). Sometimes Euclides even encourages the reader to travel with him, as if reading *Os Sertões* were like a geographical exploration: "E a paragem formosíssima dos *campos gerais*, expandida em chapadões ondulantes – grandes tablados onde campeia a sociedade dos vaqueiros ... Atravessemo-la" (p. 95) ("This is the exceedingly beautiful region of the Campos Gerais, an expanse of undulating hills – an enormous stage where the rude company of vaqueiros, or cowboys, holds forth. Let us cross this stage" [p. 7]). At other times, he evokes a traveler as he "passes" by a given landscape: "Vai-se de boa sombra com um naturalista algo romântico imaginando-se que por ali turbilhonaram, largo tempo, na idade terciária, as vagas e as correntes" (p. 103) ("It is one that well accords with the fancies of a somewhat romantic naturalist who imagined that here, a long time ago, in the Tertiary period, the waves and swirling currents of the ocean were to be found" [p. 15]).

Although Euclides' first versions of the events were the reports that he wrote as a correspondent for O Estado de São Paulo, Os Sertões is not structured by the author's actual journeys as a war correspondent, or even by a chronological unfolding of the events – even though, when they are recounted, the events do appear sequentially, and the travel books leave an imprint of a different kind. Like Sarmiento and the scientific books they both used as models, Euclides structures his book following an approach to the subject from large to small, from the general to the particular. Consequently he first describes the "Land" (A terra), the "Man" (O homem), and then moves on to relate the "Struggle" (A luta), and each of the expeditions (Putnam's division of the book in his translation does not reflect this structure faithfully). Leopoldo Bernucci writes, perceptively, that this division obeys Euclides' deterministic vision, that it is informed by causal succession.[48] Like Sarmiento, Euclides focuses on Conselheiro as the central specimen of his herbarium, detailing as much as possible his biography and subjecting him to the scientific theories about human character typical of nineteenth-century science, which were founded predominantly on physiology. Character, determined by race and other often "abnormal" physical forces, is destiny. Like Facundo Quiroga, Conselheiro is a kind of monster, a mutant, an accident. His elusiveness, as the object of observation and military pursuit by the Republic, owes much to this freedom from chartable antecedents.

Scientific travel does leave an imprint on the structure of the book, but on a metaphorical level. If there is an analogue to the deployment of the material it is the military campaigns, which also begin by "taking" the territory, and wind up by capturing the citadel and finally the leader, albeit only his body. The voyage was implicit in the military operations, which could be seen as a grotesque but not totally inaccurate figure for a scientific probe, as performed by European travelers to the colonial world. Thirst for knowledge and power conspire in these operations to bring the wayward into line, dead or alive, to subject him to the predictable periodicity of nature, as represented by nineteenth-century science, or to declare him an aberration inhabiting an origin in existence before the beginning of order, and which may explain the order. The mutant must be pinned like a rare bug in a display case, as much a spectacle as a specimen. But like the military campaigns conducted by the Republic, Euclides' plan is often frustrated by the vagaries of chance and the ever-present menace of the mutable. The gigantic and burdensome Krupp guns, mired in mud and unable to destroy a city too flimsy to offer resistance to cannonballs, is the most dramatic representation of the failure of the "instruments" of science to reduce the Other to discourse. The guns have been hauled there as an extension of knowledge, like the very mind of the naturalist, like the textual web with which Euclides wishes to cover the events.[49]

Though not determining the structure of *Os Sertões*, Euclides' journeys and his presence at some of the events do evoke an additional element of scientific travel. He occasionally writes, as we saw, as if he were traveling along with the reader over the terrain. More often than not, however, the echo of the naturalists' travelogues is heard in Euclides' own surprise and marvel at the beauty or grotesqueness of the scene he is describing. Euclides is an alien presence who attempts to reduce the odd to the familiar, and breaks in with astonishment and wonder when he cannot find the means to do so. The scientific traveler interposed the grid of classification between his evolving self and the reality he described, as a way of defending himself from the possibility of collapsing into that other-reality, of becoming one with it. Euclides, like Sarmiento and the travelers, often appeals to classification, though more systematically than the Argentine. But he also appeals to the rhetoric of amazement, to the language of the sublime, to account for the presence of his fragile and transfiguring self before a reality that is bewildering as well as compelling. Euclides' evolving conscience, his heightened awareness of failure, is also an important representation of the unfolding of time – his version of his own interiority as it grinds on, asynchronous both with nature and his own intentions.

The representation of time and change is much more impressive in *Os Sertões* than in *Facundo* because of the repetition and the asynchrony between the time of the city and that of the hinterland, between the grid of science and the lay of the land. A persistent source of irony in Euclides' book is the constant exhibition of this disparity. Until the very end, the Republic miscalculates how much time it will take to overpower Canudos. The forecasts are always wide of the mark. A campaign expected to take but a few days intensifies into a war that lasts many months. It is, in fact, a war without end, for the citadel never surrenders, and even when the soldiers are busy ensuring that not a stone is left standing, resistance reappears. The time of Canudos expands into infinity, marked by the asynchrony of convulsive violence.

Time appears unique in the *sertão* because it is construed as being the time of the origin. Like *Facundo*, Euclides' book purports to be a probe into the origin, an origin that is found in the Other, that Other Within who is a purveyor of violence. Like Facundo Quiroga, Antonio Conselheiro is a unique specimen, living in a unique time and in a unique place. But Conselheiro is a specimen that speaks, one, in fact, whose chief feature is his ability to mesmerize the multitudes with his rhetoric. His oratory is designed to frighten and to persuade:

Era assombroso, afirmam testemunhas existentes. Uma orátoria bárbara e arrepiadora, feita de excertos truncados das *Horas Marianas*, desconexa, abstrusa, agravada, às vezes, pela ousadia extrema das citações latinas; transcorrendo em frases sacudidas; misto inextricável e confuso de conselhos dogmáticos, preceitos vulgares de moral cristã e profecias esdrúxulas ... Era truanesco e era pavoroso. Imagine-se um bufão arrebatado numa visão do Apocalipse ...   (p. 221)

Those persons still living who heard him preach tell us that his sermons were barbarous and terrifying, calculated to send chills down the spines of his listeners. They were made up of mutilated excerpts from the *Hours of Mary*; they were disconnected, abstruse; and at times, to make matters worse, he daringly had resort to Latin quotations. Couched in broken phrases, they were a hopelessly confused mixture of dogmatic counsels, the vulgar precepts of Christian morality and weird prophecies. It was a clownish performance, but dreadful. One has but to imagine a buffoon maddened with a vision of the Apocalypse.   (p. 133)

In spite of Euclides' repugnance, the characterization of Conselheiro's rhetoric could not be more apt and forceful. Conselheiro's singularity is verbal expression, like the uniqueness of Euclides' own text, which is as much a pell-mell collection of disparate fragments as the Counselor's sermons. Uniqueness, then, is expressed in *Os Sertões*, through a language that, ultimately, must partake of the singularity of nature's flawed products, of the tragic grandeur of her mutants, as was the case with Facundo Quiroga and the tiger in Sarmiento. As with *Facundo*, but on a much larger scale, the uniqueness of *Os Sertões* is that it posits and enacts a transcendental language that is like nature's own, a language like the one in which the gaucho and the tiger communicate. It is a language capable not so much of capturing the Other as of allowing the Other to capture the Self. It is a language of inversion in which the beautiful and the frightful mingle. It is a language that can translate the gazes, the muscular vibrations and the piercing roars of the beast. Consequently, Conselheiro's speech is termed *pavoroso*, capable of instilling terror.

It is a language whose transcendence lies in its ability to absorb error.

Os Sertões recounts an escalation of errors that lead to a paroxysmal synthesis of truth and aberrancy. While the Republic increases the volume and might of its expeditions, what eventually brings it victory – or the semblance of victory – is that its soldiers become *jagunços*,[50] or discover that they had been *jagunços* all along. In other words, Canudos absorbs the Republic, which can only defeat it by becoming like it. There are many instances in the concluding chapters of the book in which this identification is clear. It is Euclides' greatest insight, powerfully dramatized in the scenes of frenzied mayhem during the last moments of the campaign, in which he asserts that he is describing actions that cannot be covered by history, that antecede human history:

Realizava-se um recuo prodigioso no tempo; um resvalar estonteador por alguns séculos abaixo. Descidas as vertentes, em que se entalava aquela furna enorme, podia representar-se lá dentro, obscuramente, um drama sanguinolento da Idade das cavernas. O cénario era sugestivo. Os atores, de um e de outro lado, negros, caboclos, brancos e amarelos, traziam, intacta, nas faces, a caracterização indelével e multiforme das racas – e só podiam unificar-se sobre a base comum dos instintos inferiores e maus. A animalidade primitiva, lentamente expungida pela civilização, ressurgiu, inteiriça.   (p. 538)

An astounding miracle was accomplished, and time was turned backward for a number of centuries. As one came down the slopes and caught sight of the enormous bandits' den that was huddled there, he well might have imagined that some obscure and bloody drama of the Stone Age was here taking place. The setting was sufficiently suggestive. The actors, on one side and the other, Negroes, caboclos, white and yellow skinned, bore on their countenances the indelible imprint of many races – races which could be united only upon the common plane of their lower and evil instincts. A primitive animality, slowly expunged by civilization, was here being resurrected intact. (p. 444)

That cauldron of primitive perversity incorporates both soldiers and fanatics; it is the ultimate truth. Nature's capacity for mutation can recover the wayward and the weird, if there is a special space for its teratology. The *sertão* is the blank page, without brilliance ("esta página sem brilhos," p. 538), in which all mutations are possible, even rivers that appear to flow from the sea (p. 155). This is the reason why nature "expresses" itself in *Os Sertões* through a rhetoric and a poetics. This "translation" (a very common term in the book) of nature's mutability into rhetorical figures and poetic categories (there have already been *profecias esdrúxulas*) is Euclides' attempt to have his discourse overcome its contradictions, that which ulti-mately turns the limp language of classification into the enervated speech of literature, the way by which discourse escapes the hegemony of the model discourse by joining its elusive object. In *Os Sertões* mutants are tropes. Let us look at this a little more closely.

In *Os Sertões* nature is a menagerie of tropes, mutants of rhetoric that reflect the mutants in the hinterlands. It is difficult to forget the monstrous tree that grows underground, to survive the droughts:

Vêem-se, numerosos, aglomerados em *caapões* ou salpintando, isolados, as macegas, arbúsculos de pouco mais de um metro de alto, de largas folhas espessas e luzidias, exuberando floração ridente em meio da desolação geral. São os cajueiros anões, os típicos *anacardium humile* das chapadas áridas, os *cajuís* dos indígenas. Estes vegetais estranhos, quando ablaque-ados em roda, mostram raízes que se entranham a surpreendente pro-fundura. Não há desenraizá-los. O eixo descendente aumenta-lhes maior à medida que se escava. Por fim se nota que ele vai repartindo-se em divisões dicotômicas. Progride pela terra dentro até a um caule único e vigoroso, embaixo.

Não são raízes, são galhos. E os pequeninos arbúsculos, esparsos, ou repontando em tufos, abrangendo às vezes largas áreas, uma árvore única e enorme, inteiramente soterrada. Espancado pelas canículas, fustigado dos sóis, roído dos exuros, torturado pelos ventos, o vegetal parece derrear-se aos embates desses elementos antagônicos e abroquelar-se daquele modo, invisível no solo sobre que alevanta apenas os mais altos renovos da fronde majestosa. (p. 120)

Grouped in clusters or standing about isolated here and there are to be seen numerous weedy shrubs of little more than a yard in height, with thick and lustrous leaves, an exuberant and pleasing flora in the midst of the general desolation. They are dwarf cashew-nut trees, the typical *Anacadia humilis* of the arid plains, the *cajuys* of the natives. These strange trees have roots which, when laid bare, are found to go down to a surprising depth. There is no uprooting them. The descending axis increases in size the further they are scraped, until one perceives it parting in dichotomous divisions which continue underground to meet in a single vigorous stalk down below.

These are not roots; they are bows. And these tiny shrubs, scattered about or growing in clumps, covering at times large areas, are in reality one enormous tree that is wholly underground. Lashed by the dog-day heat, fustigated by the sun, gnawed by torrential rains, tortured by the winds, these trees would appear to have been knocked out completely in the struggle with the antagonic elements and so have gone underground in this manner, have made themselves invisible with only the tallest shoots of their majestic foliage showing aboveground. (pp. 31–2)

Through adaptation, these trees survive the struggle for existence. The process involves a radical transformation, an inversion of how a tree is made. This inversion allows the tree to turn adverse conditions to advantage. The tree absorbs the error of nature – the lack of water – and turns it into its strength by deforming itself. It is this tumultuous power of transfiguration that astonishes and frightens the traveler – causes him "pasmo" (p. 125) ("astonishment" [p. 36]) – as Conselheiro's oratory does to his listeners. Consequently rhetorical terms are used to describe the convolutions of nature, and the word "expressive" appears regularly to designate a peculiar twist of the land, or an arresting weather phenomenon. Erosion, for instance, leaves "expressive" furrows upon the mountains: "Os sulcos de erosão que as retalham são cortes geológicos expressivos" (p. 94) ("The erosion furrows that cut them offer significant geological cross-sections" [p. 6]).[51] At other times, a peculiar manifestation of nature is depicted in terms drawn from poetics, for instance, a worm that is eating away the body of a dead soldier is termed: "o mais vulgar dos trágicos analistas da matéria" (p. 112) ("most vulgar of the tragic solvents of nature" [p. 24]). Conselheiro, because of his apocalyptic millenarianism, appeared "no epílogo da Terra" (p. 222) ("at the time of earth's epilogue" [p. 135]). "Tragedies" and "parodies" abound in Euclides' characterization of the *sertão* and the actors of the events at Canudos. Conselheiro possesses, in the imagination of the people, "um traço vigoroso de originalidade trágica" (p. 219) ("a tragic power...and a high degree of originality" [p. 131]). The *jagunços* often seem to be parodying the military strategies of their adversaries: "No dia 15, como se ideassem atrevida paródia à recente vinda do comboio..." (p. 441) ("On July 15, as if they had been staging a bold parody of the latter event..." [p. 351]). There is no question that this natural tropology is to be reflected in the text. Euclides writes: "Se nos embaraçássemos nas imaginosas linhas dessa espécie de topografia psíquica, de que tanto se tem abusado, talvez não os compreendêssemos melhor. Sejamos simples copistas" (p. 178) ("Were we to encumber ourselves with the imaginary outlines of this species of psychic topography, which has been so much abused, we should not thereby make ourselves any more clearly understood; we should be a mere copyist" [p. 89]).

As in *Facundo*, all of the abnormalities, all the transfigurations, occur within an anomalous time and space, which is described in two crucial instances, appropriately, as a "hiatus." The first instance is at the beginning, when Euclides is reporting on the uniqueness of the land:

Abordando-o, compreende-se que até hoje escasseiem sobre tão grande trato de territorio, que quase abarcaria a Holanda (9°11′ – 10°20′ de lat. e 4°-3°, de long. O.R.J.), notícias exatas ou pormenorizadas. As nossas melhores cartas enfeixando informes escassos, lá têm un claro expressivo, un hiato, *Terra ignota*, em que se aventura o rabisco de um rio problemático ou idealização de uma corda de serras.   (p. 96)

As one approaches it, one begins to understand why it is that, until now, the data or exact details concerning this vast tract of territory, which is almost equal to the land of Holland in extent (9°11′ – 10°20′ of latitude and 4°-3° of longitude), have been so very long scarce. Our best maps, conveying but scant information, show here an expressive blank, a hiatus, labeled *Terra ignota*, a mere scrawl indicating a problematic river or an idealized mountain range.   (p. 9)

The second instance appears as the concluding massacre is being portrayed: "Canudos tinha muito apropriadamente, em roda, una cercadura de montanhas. Era un parêntese; era um hiato; era um vácuo. Não existia. Transposto aquele cordão de serras, ninguém mais pecava" (p. 538) ("Canudos was, appropriately enough, surrounded by a girdle of mountains. It was a parenthesis, a hiatus. It was a vacuum. It did not exist. Once having crossed that cordon of mountains, no one sinned any more" [p. 444]).

"Expressive blank" is, appropriately enough, an oxymoron, hence the space in which Canudos' teratology of tropes exists is itself contradictory and deformed. It is the space between the antagonic forces, the locus of violence, chance and change. It is a time and space before history, a prelapsarian opening, thus no sins have or could have occurred. It is a place before the law, before transgression, the fault before a sin. There is a haunting propriety to this gap being termed a hiatus, as if it were an interruption in the flow of verse, a stop to avoid the cacophony of contiguous vowels with similar sounds, itself a break from some superior law that is about to generate something anomalous. The conflictive hiatus where Canudos exists and the monstrous events take place is like a test-tube in the laboratory of some demented genius, a coop where the mutating time of the origin can come about in spurts of its own, prey to no predictable periodicities. This hiatus is the cave – the splendid isolation – the paleontologists searched for in their quest for a distinct origin. The peculiar expressivity of the blank contains that of nature as represented by the transcendental language of the text, for this is the place where the ultimate mutation occurs. That mutation is the absorption of error, the growth upon error, the building upon the fundamental fault of the beginning, like the subterranean tree, which can thrive in the drought and draw its exuberant, majestic shape from it. The hiatus is the eerie greenhouse in which the "traço superior à passividade da evolução vegetativa" (p. 122) ("a higher stroke in the evolution of vegetable passivity") is bred, the rarefied ambience in which one can read the "página perigosa" (p. 327) ("this dangerous page"), and understand the "lição eloqüente" (p. 374) ("the eloquent lesson").[52] This superior language to which Euclides often appeals is that capacious language – one that can scribble a problematic river on a map – which, like the *sertão*, can absorb it all, even its antagonists, like Conselheiro and his followers.

The last, or rather the ultimate, representation of this space is in the closing pages of the book, in which the exhumation of Conselheiro's body and the severing of his head are reported. The hiatus is clearly now Conselheiro's grave, and his rotting body, particularly the purulent head, is the monstrous language of the *sertão* and the book. Its sublime expression is stench, which represents putrefaction, the very image of an anomalous, matter-transfiguring time. The break in the ground, the pit, is very much like the one invoked to describe the uniqueness and isolation of the area. This is so also at a rhetorical level because the ending has been arbitrarily conjured; it is a violent cut in the flow of the narrative, a break: "Fechemos este livro" (p. 571) ("Let us bring this book to a close" [p. 475]). Since Canudos does not surrender, there is no "organic" way of ending the story; like Conselheiro's head, the story has to be cut. Only violence will represent violence. Every act performed in that closing parenthesis is a futile effort to represent Conselheiro's most expressive features – the photograph, the affidavits, the language of science. The passage reads:

Jazia [o cadáver] num dos casebres anexos à latada, e foi encontrado graças à indicação de um prisioneiro. Removida breve camada de terra, apareceu no triste sudário de um lençol imundo, em que mãos piedosas haviam desparzido algumas flores murchas, e repousando sobre uma esteira velha, de taboa, o corpo do "famigerado e bárbaro" agitador. Estava hediondo. Envolto no velho hábito azul de brim americano, mãos cruzadas ao peito, rosto tumefacto e esquálido, olhos fundos cheios de terra – mal o reconheceram os que mais de perto haviam tratado durante a vida.

Desenterraram-no cuidadosamente. Dádiva preciosa – único prêmio, únicos despojos opimos de tal guerra! – faziam-se mister os máximos resguardos para que se não desarticulasse ou deformasse, reduzindo-se a uma massa angulhenta de tecidos decompostos.

Fotografaram-no depois. E lavrou-se uma ata rigorosa firmando a su identidade: importava que o país se convencesse bem de que estava, afinal extinto, aquele terribilíssimo antagonista.

Restituíram-no à cova. Pensaram, porém, depois, em guardar a sua cabeça tantas vezes maldita – e como fora malbaratar o tempo exumando-o de novo, uma faca jeitosamente brandida, naquela mesma atitude, cortou-lha; e a face horrenda, empastada de escaras e de sânie, apareceu ainda uma vez ante aqueles triunfadores.

Trouxeram depois para o litoral, onde deliravam multidões em festa, aquele crânio. Que a ciência dissesse a última palavra. Ali estavam, no relevo de circunvoluções expressivas, as linhas essenciais do crime e da loucura ...   (p. 572)

It [Conselheiro's body] was lying in one of the huts next to the arbor [and was found thanks to the directions of a prisoner]. After a shallow layer of earth had been removed, the body appeared wrapped in a sorry shroud – a filthy sheet – over which pious hands had strewn a few withered flowers. There, resting upon a reed mat, were the last remains of the "notorious and barbarous agitator." They were in a fetid condition. Clothed in his old blue canvas tunic, his face swollen and hideous, the deep-sunken eyes filled with dirt, the Counselor would not have been recognizable to those who in the course of his life had known him almost intimately.

They carefully disinterred the body, precious relic that it was – the sole prize, the only spoils of war this conflict had to offer! – taking the greatest precautions to see that it did not fall apart, in which case they would have had nothing but a disgusting mass of rotting tissues on their hands. They photographed it afterward and drew up an affidavit in due form, certifying its identity; for the entire nation must be thoroughly convinced that at last this terrible foe had been done away with.

Then they put it back in its grave. Later, however, the thought occurred to them that they should have preserved the head on which so many maledictions had been heaped; and, since it was a waste of time to exhume the body once more, a knife cleverly wielded at the right point did the trick, the corpse was decapitated, and that horrible face, sticky with scars and pus, once more appeared before the victor's gaze.

After that they took it to the seaboard, where it was greeted by delirious multitudes with carnival joy. Let science have here the last word. Standing out in bold relief from all the significant circumvolutions were the essential outlines of crime and madness.   (p. 476)

Virtually fused with the earth, whose capricious mutability it expressed, Conselheiro's body occupies, literally, a hiatus, temporal and physical. He is now beyond all measure of normal time, yet remains, in death, a powerful expressive presence. Conselheiro may not be recognizable to those who knew him intimately, yet his body is the ultimate expression of the transcendental language of nature and of the book. His body as sign goes beyond nature, beyond life, annulling all contradictions; in the hiatus, as a hiatus, death does not here mean extinction, but an expansion into infinity of that special space in which the anomalous dwells. Because his body is now a relic, death has not stilled its capacity to be expressive; on the contrary, it has enlarged it. The detached head can provoke delirium in the crowds and unleash a carnivalesque celebration. Full of earth, the eyes are now literally the telos, his gaze is now that of the earth itself. With dirt staring out of his sunken sockets, Conselheiro's blank stare is that of the expressive blank itself. Beginning and end all in one, Conselheiro's body is that relic the paleontologists search for, the specimen that will unlock the secrets of an aberrant beginning.

Conselheiro's ultimate act of signification, which does not close the book, but leaves it open like his desecrated grave, is through those "circunvoluções expressivas, as linhas essenciais do crime e da loucura ..." – these are the tropes, the figures indelibly written upon his monstrous face, a last page that refuses to yield any secrets, and whose sublime expression is fear and the odor of decay. A hiatus within a hiatus, Conselheiro's body and wandering head never cancel Conselheiro's project. *Os Sertões* remains an open book, as the dots at the end of that last sentence reveal, and as the very last sentence of the book – a chapter unto itself – proclaims, still anxious for the certainties of science: "E que ainda não existe um Maudsley para as loucuras e os crimes das nacionalidades ..." (p. 573) ("The trouble is that we do not have today a Maudsley for acts of madness and crimes on the part of nations ..." [p. 476]).

Sarmiento's and Euclides' flight from the scientific model is to mimic it, and conversely to fuse with the object of that discourse. This is the fleeting point of their texts. In doing so, however, they have left monumental characters and a complex, contradictory language that points to a different source of narrative that is not in law, nor in science, but in logos: in language and myth. Facundo Quiroga and Antonio Conselheiro are tragic figures who anticipate the next masterstory, which is mediated by the discipline concerned with the madness of nations: anthropology.

4

The novel as myth and archive: ruins and relics of Tlön

Either that voice does not belong to that skin, or
that skin does not belong to that voice.
Pedro Calderón de la Barca, *En la vida todo es*
verdad y todo mentira, I, 901–2[1]

I

In the summer of 1947, the American Hispanist John E. Englekirk
flew from Caracas to San Fernando de Apure to research in the field
the genesis of *Doña Bárbara* (1929).[2] At approximately the same
time, Alejo Carpentier was traveling to the interior of Venezuela in
the first of two journeys that would lead him to write *Los pasos
perdidos*. In that summer of 1947 Rómulo Gallegos was in the midst
of the political campaign that would take him to the presidency of
Venezuela in December of that year. Gallegos was a politician
whose only baggage, according to campaign promotion, was a book
under his arm: that book was, needless to say, *Doña Bárbara*. The
novel had culled from the countryside, from the endless *llano*, the
essence of Venezuelan culture, which would now be transformed
into a political program to save the country.[3] Although Gallegos had
toured the Apure while preparing to write *Doña Bárbara*, the region
had entered the realm of writing long before. San Fernando had not
only been described by Alexander von Humboldt, but also by
Ramón Páez, the British-educated son of Venezuelan general José
Antonio Páez, in his *Wild Scenes in South America, or Life in the llanos of
Venezuela* (1862).[4] As *Escenas rústicas en Sur América o La vida en los llanos
de Venezuela*, the book had been one of the most important sources of
Doña Bárbara, furnishing Gallegos with much of the information on
the folklore of the Apure region. Another important source, as
Englekirk explains, was Daniel Mendoza's *El llanero venezolano*

142

(*Estudio de sociología venezolana*), a book published in 1922, whose descriptions of the plain are derived mostly from von Humboldt. It seems apparent that Englekirk would have done better had he stayed in Caracas and regularly visited the Biblioteca Nacional.

But Englekirk's trip and the article that he wrote about it are a remarkable novelistic coda to Gallegos' novel, almost as revealing as the one the other traveler in that summer of 1947, Alejo Carpentier, would publish a few years later: *Los pasos perdidos*. Englekirk intended to retrace Gallegos' steps in the author's own research journey to the *llano* prior to writing *Doña Bárbara*. What he found, however, was that the people of the Apure region had incorporated the novel into local lore. Englekirk found plainsmen whom Gallegos had used as models and who now, like characters in the second part of *Don Quijote*, knew that they had an added life in fiction. They had become experts in that fiction and were eager to act as guides and commentators. Englekirk's journey eventually brought him back to Caracas and to don Rómulo's study, a place obviously closer to the real sources of the book and the headquarters not only of a political campaign but also of the fictional world that enfolded the people of the Apure, and soon the whole of Venezuela. So thick was that fiction that Gallegos was unable to shed much light on the creation of the novel for Englekirk. The author too had been swallowed up by the novel's voracious fictionality. Gallegos' house, paid for with royalties from his famous book, bore the name of Marisela, one of the most memorable characters in *Doña Bárbara*, and his whole personal mythology, not to mention the program of Acción Demo-crática, was dominated by the irresistible power of the "devourer of men." Gallegos seemed to have been invented by *Doña Bárbara* and propelled into public life by its creed of cultural and national affirmation.

In spite of its obvious debt to *Facundo* and *Os Sertões*, *Doña Bárbara* is a turning point. Latin American fiction is no longer determined by the naturalists' conception of nature, but by myths of cultural beginnings, and authority itself – the possibility of being an author – is predicted on being able to generate a discourse capable of containing and expressing those myths. Such authority extends beyond the world of literature. From being the author of *Doña Bárbara* Gallegos can go on to become the "author" of Venezuela. This fiction turned out to be ephemeral compared to the lasting impact of the book. The military – descendants no doubt of Facundo

Quiroga, and also of the enchanters who plagued don Quijote – toppled don Rómulo less than a year after his election. Englekirk, an unwitting projection of Gallegos' authorial persona, will write his article as a kind of meta-end to *Doña Bárbara*, and anticipate the major figure in modern Latin American fiction: the Archive, or repository of stories and myths, one of which is the story about collecting those stories and myths. The inaugural archival fiction in that recent tradition would be the other text that issued from that summer of traveling through Venezuela, Carpentier's *Los pasos perdidos*.

This tale of two texts – *Doña Bárbara* and *Los pasos perdidos* – contains the story of Latin American fiction in the modern period, that is, from the 1920s to the present. It is a story that centers on anthropology as the hegemonic discourse that makes possible the Latin American narrative. Legitimacy is now obtained by mimicking the texts that constitute anthropological discourse, and the textual subplot of flight away from hegemony is from those anthropological texts. I shall first look at the sweep of that story and then at works by two very different authors who nevertheless strained the limits of the relationship between anthropology and narrative: Jorge Luis Borges and Miguel Barnet. This is a story that has no satisfactory ending because it brings us to archival fictions, which make up the current mode of Latin American narrative, the one to which my own discourse probably belongs.

2

As a discipline, anthropology becomes a hegemonic discourse in Latin American narrative in the twentieth century, but the discipline itself had some of its beginnings during the colonial period of what would become Latin America. This is so from the very moment of discovery. In 1494 Columbus left Fray Ramón Pané in Hispaniola with the charge of learning the language of the native *Taínos*, finding out about their beliefs, and writing a report about his discoveries. The Spanish Crown was interested in the natives' religion to gauge how difficult it would be to convert them to Christianity. Pané, a Catalan with an imperfect command of Spanish and no prior knowledge of the native population, dutifully went to the hills, lived among the *Taínos*, learned as much as he could of their language and religion, and by 1498 had written a truly extraordinary document, his *Relación acerca de las antigüedades de los indios*. Pané's *Relación* anticipates many of the issues debated today by anthropologists, issues that have also been significant in modern Latin American fiction until the very present; for instance, Mario Vargas Llosa's 1987 novel *El hablador*. Can one truly know the Other without doing violence to him or her and to his or her culture? Is contamination with Western culture desirable; will it not bring about destruction? Is it possible to write about one's knowledge of the Other without distorting his or her culture beyond recognition? Is it impossible to avoid making fiction out of any such attempt? The bizarre fate of Pané's report, a story that reads as if it had been written by Borges, makes it an even more compelling textual phenomenon. Not only was the *Relación* written, one presumes, in faulty Spanish, but the original was lost, not, however, before Columbus' son Hernando had copied it and included it verbatim in the biography of his father that he wrote. But the manuscript of Hernando's book on the Admiral also disappeared, not, however, before it was translated into Italian. The *Historie della vita, et de' fatti dell' ammiraglio D. Christoforo Colombo*, which appeared in Venice, in 1569, contained, of course, Pané's *Relación*, in Italian.

Contemporary scholars, most notably José J. Arrom, have sedulously translated Pané's text back into Spanish.[5] I carefully avoid saying "back to the original," because modern versions, using our refined philological methods and greater knowledge of Arawak culture, are more faithful in transcribing the names of *Taíno* gods than Pané could have been, and the Spanish is, needless to say, flawless. The delicate textual archaeology that yielded these versions involved cleansing of any trace of Italian the names of those gods and removing the vestiges of sixteenth-century Italian that adhered as the *Relación* passed through that language. Pané added further puzzlements to his premonitory text by writing in a very self-conscious manner. He complains a number of times that he is unsure of the story-line of *Taíno* theogony, because he has heard conflicting accounts from different informants, but adds that, even if he had had the time or certainty about alternatives to rewrite his report, he was, like the protagonist of *Los pasos perdidos*, short on paper and hence could not make several drafts. All of these difficulties, and no doubt his own good will, led Pané to assume a charming and in many ways exemplary humility before the *Taínos* and their beliefs, and his report, for all its faults, remains a fundamental source of information about the religion of that exterminated people. At the same time, the variegated history of the text, its existence in several languages none of which could be claimed either as the original or the definitive one, together with the uncertainties introduced by Pané himself, make the *Relación* a good example of the kind of literariness that current anthropologists are claiming for their writings and of the attendant crisis in anthropology as a discipline. There is no doubt, from the point of view of Latin American literature, that Pané's *Relación* uncannily anticipates many of the topics that are fundamental in modern novels like *Los pasos perdidos* and *El hablador*.

Pané's efforts and report are but the beginning of a wide-ranging and controversial campaign to acquire knowledge about the New World's native populations, carried out in the sixteenth and seventeenth centuries both by members of religious orders and by government officials such as the *cronista mayor*.[6] Works by Fray Bartolomé de las Casas and Fray Bernardino de Sahagún, to mention only the most prominent, were written to prevent the Spaniards from enslaving the Indians by documenting the richness of their civilizations, and hence their full-fledged membership in the human race. As is known, some friars, like Toribio de Motolinía, took the side of the natives to the point of becoming one with them, even taking an Aztec name.[7] Native writers like Alba Ixtlilxochitl, Garcilaso de la Vega, el Inca, and Guaman Poma de Ayala soon emerged to give characterizations of their own cultures. The polemic rages to this day because in some areas, such as Peru and Mexico, the destruction brought about by the conquest has not led to a viable cultural or political synthesis. The bases for the discourse about the Other have changed, but not the fissure that makes that discourse necessary or even possible, as *El hablador* makes amply clear.

The knowledge-gathering activities of the friars as well as the natives' own testimonies and pleas had a tremendous political and intellectual impact in Spain and the New World. The debates about the right to seize territories and peoples divided the Crown and its theological advisors, created turmoil in the colonies, and shook the ideological foundations of Western knowledge.[8] The work of the friars in particular is not only an invaluable source for, but a precursor of, modern anthropology, as much in method of research as in the manner of writing reports. (There are, of course, many other texts from the colonial period that offer as many premonitions as Pané's in terms of the future of anthropology and the Latin American narrative, most notably Alvar Núñez Cabeza de Vaca's *Naufragios*.)[9] For the narrative, the problem of describing American cultures in a Western discourse created an important topic: that of writing about an Other whose culture is radically different from the author's, yet who is in possession of a knowledge that appears to be whole and functioning on its own, in spite of the differences. In short, a story about an Other who can be other and human at the same time, a fact that threatens not only the right to hold power over him or her, but erodes any self-assurance about the universal validity of the culture pretending to exercise control over his or hers. Las Casas was quite explicit on this point in his many moments of despair. The Latin American narrative returns to this topic in the modern period, spurred on precisely by modern anthropology, whose source is perhaps, in the non-Hispanic world, Montaigne's essay "On Cannibals." Montaigne's well-known ironies were indictments in Las Casas, Sahagún, Motolinía, and Guaman Poma, clearly because they were closer to the destruction and genocide. These authors did not write ethnographic reports, given that such a rhetorical vehicle was non-existent in the sixteenth and seventeenth centuries. Their texts were, of necessity, part of the exchange of legal documents that prevailed in the colonial period. It was the only way of saying what they had to say, and the most effective way to give their writings an immediate political impact. Hence, as with the description of nature, what later became a masterstory is already latent in colonial times. What Pané lacked was the discourse of a discipline in which to see reflected the problematics of his own discourse. Modern anthropology would furnish that to Latin American writers.

The scientific travelers who swarmed over the New World from the eighteenth century on not only knew the writings of Las Casas and others, which had been widely disseminated to make up what is known today as the Black Legend, but were themselves interested both in the European-like culture of cities in the crumbling Spanish Empire, and in that of the non-European peoples who remained. Even though the natural world was the focus of the travelers' gaze, they provided a wealth of information about indigenous populations. Modern anthropology began as a branch of natural history, it grew out of the evolutionary conception of reality developed by nineteenth-century science. Human culture was perceived as a progression in which native American peoples stood somewhere in the early stages. Like nature in the New World, "contemporary savages" could furnish information about the ancestors of modern man; consequently American Indians were often the object of what George W. Stocking, Jr. has called "Victorian anthropology," in an important book of the same name.[10] This anthropology was ruled by a set of rhetorical guidelines whose function is comparable to the 1575 royal order the Spanish Crown sent to the Indies to regulate writing about "natives." Stocking writes: "At the same meeting, a committee was set up, with Lane Fox as secretary, to draw up brief forms of instruction 'for travelers, ethnologists and other anthropological observers.' By 1874, the committee, in which Tylor played a dominant intellectual role, had produced the first edition of *Notes and Queries on Anthropology, for the Use of Travellers and Residents in Uncivilized Lands*. Although the dropping of 'ethnologists' from the intended audience of *Notes and Queries* suggests a settling back into the armchair, the men who in that little volume proudly labeled themselves 'anthropologists' clearly anticipated a period of hard work and slow progress within an accepted framework, one that would be remembered as having established the new science on a solid empirical, theoretical and institutional footing" (p. 258). To describe the material culture and physical characteristics of these natives meant to follow the methods employed to analyze the flora and the fauna. Von Humboldt and his followers provided much knowledge about Indian and African cultures in the Americas, but not on the scale of the chroniclers and friars, although some travelers became particularly interested in one or another human group. Francis Bond Head, as we saw, wrote a detailed report on the gauchos.[11] Just as specimens of the flora and fauna were displayed in museums, "primitive cultures" became part of the entertainment of the *belle époque*, alongside circus freaks and other shows, such as the one in Brazil where Antonio Conselheiro's severed head was displayed to the delight of the multitudes.[12] Travelers often had pictures of the natives made, both for scientific and entertainment purposes, just as they had pictures made of specimens from the natural world.[13]

Latin American travelers like Lucio Mansilla in Argentina and Cirilo Villaverde in Cuba, to give but two examples, also wrote about non-Europeans in the New World; the first about Indians, the second about Blacks in Cuba's sugarmills. These reports, however, were not written in an effort to incorporate those populations into a more inclusive culture or polity. On the contrary, and as we saw in Sarmiento and Euclides da Cunha, these reports were often permeated by a "scientific racism" that decried the deleterious influence non-European races had on the moral, intellectual, cultural, and material progress of Latin America. Inferior races could play a role, even if a negative one, in natural history, but not in cultural history. The new republics, as is known, often engaged in campaigns to exterminate the Indians, now under the banner of modernization. It might be remembered here that Charles Darwin met the Argentine dictator Juan Manuel Rosas in the pampas while the latter was leading a raid against Indians, and that Mansilla's *Una escursión a los indios Ranqueles* was not a mere fact-finding expedition, but a military campaign, no matter how ironic and self-deprecating the Colonel was or how critical of "civilization."[14] The urge to modernize moved the republics away from the Indian past and against the Indian present. Romantic literature, particularly poetry, made idealized figures of the natives which had little in common with their current or past counterparts. These Indians came from Europe, mostly from Chateaubriand. In the Caribbean, where Blacks occupied a position somewhat but in reality not quite, analogous to that of Indians, the situation was similar, though the struggle against slavery generated some early studies of African cultures.[15] But no one thought, save in the most stylized and abstract romantic poems or novels which invoked "universal" feelings such as love or grief, that the Indian or the Black had anything to say that could be incorporated into Latin American culture, or that their history was anything but ancillary in the composition of the nascent independent states. They were not a source of stories that could express the innermost secrets of Latin American society, nor could their beliefs compete with the knowledge offered by "civilization" in general, or by scientific reportage in particular. As we saw in Esteban Echeverría's "El matadero" and Sarmiento's *Facundo*, the histories told by the Spanish chronicles were left behind. The new story had to be of the present. In the present Indians and Blacks appeared as part of nature, part of the violent becoming of the New World, but not its voice.

World War I , as we know, brought the nineteenth century to an end, tearing down the ideological certainties of the West. In Latin

America this meant the demise of Positivism, at the most visible level.[16] But it also meant disillusionment with nineteenth-century science. The crisis of the West, or the decline of the West to give it Spengler's widely known title, removed natural science as the mediating discourse in Latin American narrative, and made way for a new one, that of anthropology. But this was not an anthropology whose foundation was natural science anchored in the theory of evolution and its corollaries. The decline of Positivism in Europe itself had changed the foundations of Western anthropology. Stocking writes: "Although it reflected changes in the colonial situation and domestic ideological contexts of anthropology, this antievolutionary reaction was part of a more general 'revolt against Positivism' in European social thought. It involved both a reassertion of the role of 'irrational' factors in human life, and a critique of the methodological and epistemological grounding of prevailing scientific determinisms."[17] Such a reassertion also meant that European culture was no longer seen as the logical or even desirable goal of evolution; culture began to be conceived in a plural way, or rather, the idea that culture, not cultures, constituted the world, became a central tenet of the new anthropology. The shift is now precisely to what the native had to say. What the new discourse seeks is not so much knowledge about the Other as much as knowledge about the Other's knowledge. Anthropology appeared as a discipline capable of integrating into the polity as well as into Latin American consciousness the cultures of non-European peoples still very much present in the New World, that Other Within analyzed by Sarmiento and Euclides da Cunha. It was a totalizing discourse embracing all products of the human mind that promised to make whole political entities that were severely fragmented and often at war with themselves. Anthropology also offered those countries the possibility of claiming an origin different from that of the West; a fresh beginning that could lead away from the debacle of Western civilization. Anthropological knowledge could correct the errors of the conquest, atone for the crimes of the past, and make for a new history. Ironically this healing promise was a reflection of the role anthropology played in the West. Anthropology offered the West a mirror in which to look at its own battered culture to plot a new beginning, though, of course, in practice it was a legitimation of vast colonial enterprises that harked back to the nineteenth century.[18] Anthropology drew the veil of science over the violence of colonial occupation. It is this "prestige" of anthropology as a source of scientific knowledge about culture, as well as its complicity with modern art (particularly with the Surrealists), that made it a dominant form of discourse in Latin America.[19]

Anthropological knowledge provided the Latin American narrative with a source of stories, as well as a masterstory about Latin American history. In fiction, Latin American history will now be cast in the form of myth, a form derived from anthropological studies. The relationship of the Latin American novel to anthropological discourse is homologous to its relationship in earlier periods to law and science. Revealingly, anthropologically mediated Latin American narratives lead, through a process analogous to one that takes place within anthropology itself, to a crisis in anthropological knowledge. If in the novel we move from a Gallegos to a Borges, a Carpentier and a García Márquez; in anthropology we go from Bronislaw Malinowski and Marcel Griaule to Clifford Geertz, James Clifford, George Marcus, Talal Asad, Vincent Crapanzano, James Boon, Michael Taussig, and several others who are subjecting anthropological discourse to a radical critique.[20] Latin American narrative may well be the design on the reverse side of the picture, or the mirror-image of the crisis in anthropology as a discipline.

The historical scheme I offer here for anthropology is derived from James Clifford's influential work, now available in *The Predicament of Culture*. The parallel plots of anthropology and Latin American narrative are as follows: the period between the wars is one in which authoritative texts are produced both in anthropology and the anthropologically mediated Latin American novel; after World War II, and in the case of the Latin American novel, after *Los pasos perdidos* (1953), the authority of anthropological discourse is voided. The evolution of anthropological discourse took the following path, according to Clifford:

In the 1920's, the new field worker-theorist brought to completion a powerful new scientific and literary genre, the ethnography, a synthetic cultural description based on participant observation [which] may be briefly summarized [as follows] ... First, the persona of the field worker was validated, both publicly and professionally. In the popular domain, visible figures like Malinowsky, Mead, and Griaule communicated a vision of ethnography as both scientifically demanding and heroic. [...] the field worker was to live in the native village, use the vernacular, stay a sufficient

(but seldom specified) length of time, investigate certain classic subjects
[...] the new ethnography was marked by an increased emphasis on the
power of observation. Culture was construed as an ensemble of characteristic behaviours, ceremonies and gestures, susceptible to recording and
explanation by a trained onlooker. [...] certain powerful theoretical
abstractions promised to help academic ethnographers "get to the heart"
of a culture more rapidly [...] the new ethnographer tended to focus
thematically on particular institutions. [...] In the predominantly synech-
dochic rhetorical stance of the new ethnography, parts were assumed to be
microcosmos or analogies of wholes. This setting of institutional fore-
grounds against cultural backgrounds in the portrayal of a coherent world
lent itself to realist literary conventions.   (*The Predicament*, pp. 29–31)

These realist literary conventions in ethnography correspond to
those of the regionalist or telluric novel in Latin American fiction, a
kind of novel that prevails precisely between 1920 and 1950, cast
essentially in a nineteenth-century realist mold. *Doña Bárbara* is, of
course, the quintessential telluric novel. Around 1950 there is, then,
both in anthropology and in Latin American fiction a *crise de
conscience*, provoked by a political awakening on the part of the object
of anthropological study. The liberation of the post-colonial world,
and in Latin America events such as the Cuban Revolution,
undermined official stories such as the ones both literature and
anthropology provided about Latin American culture or cultures.
There was also an apparent complicity between anthropological
conceptions of culture, their application to Latin America, and
United States hegemony in the area that was vehemently
denounced in the 1960s. This is the subject of Vargas Llosa's *El
hablador*. In anthropology the crisis has generated a highly critical
metadiscourse. Clifford writes:

Henceforth, neither the experience nor the interpretive activity of the
scientific researcher can be considered innocent. It becomes necessary to
conceive ethnography, not as the experience and interpretation of a
circumscribed 'other' reality, but rather as a constructive negotiation
involving at least two, and usually more, conscious, politically significant
subjects. Paradigms of experience and interpretation are yielding to
paradigms of discourse, of dialogue and polyphony.   (p. 41)

In Latin American narrative there is a parallel evolution to highly
self-reflexive forms that turn back onto earlier narratives to reveal
their literariness, rather than the validity of their knowledge about
culture, annulling the anthropological mediation by showing it was

a literary conceit all along. More recent forms then turn onto the metadiscourse itself to reveal its literariness. These are the archival fictions: *Terra Nostra*, *Yo el Supremo*, *De donde son los cantantes*, *El arpa y la sombra*, *El libro de Manuel*, *Rayuela*, *Oppiano Licario*, to name but a few. Of course, in the case of most practitioners of the metadiscourse among recent anthropologists – victims of the "epistemological hypochondria" of which Geertz speaks – they gladly avow the literary quality of anthropology.[21] Literary means to these anthropologists a discourse that does not assume method to be a transparent medium, but that is embedded in rhetoric, and as such, partaking of the general circulation of texts in a given epoch. It also means a nonauthoritative discourse containing several voices, including, most importantly, that of the object of study. Finally, it means a text with multiple layered meanings which is never fixed, like Pané's *Relación*.

So there is in the present a coincidence in the urge to declare anthropology literary both in anthropology itself and in the Latin American narrative. In the latter this turn constitutes the escape from the constraint of the model discourse by means of the legitimizing act of mimesis. In recent fiction this move takes the form of a *re*turn to the Archive, the legal origin of the narrative in Latin America. The Archive does not privilege the voice of anthropological knowledge, nor does it abide by the discourse of anthropology in method or practice. The Archive questions authority by holding warring discourses in promiscuous and mutually contaminating contiguity, a contiguity that often erases the difference separating them. The Archive absorbs the authority of the anthropological mediation. Later, of course, in the archival fictions, the Archive is shown to be also a form of mythic discourse, not removed from the literary but a part of it. This swerve is, in turn, directed against the authority of the metadiscourse, by showing that the literary is not an independent category outside language, but language itself in its most vulnerable and self-revealing manifestation. Narrative invalidates the stance of the metadiscourse, showing that it is always part of the mythic.

3

Choses rares ou choses belles ici savamment assemblées, comme jamais encore vues. Toutes choses qui sont au monde.

On the façade of the Musée de l'Homme

During the 1920s, in the wake of World War I, institutions were created in many Latin American countries to gather information about the cultures of indigenous or African peoples present in their territories. A powerful agent in bringing about this reversal was the Mexican Revolution, one of whose central programs was a vindication of the Indian legacy, as well as a recognition of the presence of Indian cultures in the make-up of modern Mexico.[22] The state made a sustained effort in anthropology and related fields such as archaeology, founding museums, academies, schools, journals, and other institutions.[23] Although without undergoing a political upheaval as profound as Mexico's, in Peru and neighboring Andean countries the pre-Hispanic past was extolled and the study of present indigenous cultures was institutionalized. The foundation of Alianza Popular Revolucionaria Americana, the rekindling of *indigenismo* are all part and parcel of this movement.[24] In Argentina there was a rekindling of interest in *gauchesca* literature, while in the Caribbean attention was focused on Blacks. The Afro-Antillean movement was promoted by anthropologists such as Fernando Ortiz, who was the first president of the Sociedad de Folklore Cubano in 1923, and founded the Institución Hispano-Cubana de Cultura in 1925, and in 1937 the Sociedad de Estudios Afrocubanos, which published the journal *Estudios Afrocubanos*.[25] In Brazil, the Week of Modern Art in São Paulo (1922) celebrated the country's indigenous and African past, and attempted a mock vindication of cannibalism as a cultural practice. The influence of these self-proclaimed *antropófagos* was far-reaching. They exemplify the convergence of avant-garde movements and the more widely accepted and institutional search for national identities. Mario de Andrade's *Macunaíma* (1928) combines anthropology and avant-garde novelistic techniques to create a modern mythic hero. Both the institutions founded by the various governments and the avant-garde artists sought the discovery or creation of a national culture, a discourse, as it were, bespeaking the uniqueness of Latin America and of each individual subculture within it. The presence of anthropology in both as a mediating element, an authoritative method delimiting the possibilities of discourse, is shockingly evident, and the participation of writers, artists, and intellectuals in general in this enterprise is a very significant episode in modern Latin American history. Concepts, methods, and often knowledge itself was derived either from the work of European-based anthropologists, or from that of European-trained native anthropologists, such as Ortiz himself and his disciple Lydia Cabrera. Anthropology as a set of given discursive possibilities, as the very possibility of writing about Latin American culture, is a given within and against which much of Latin American narrative is written in the twentieth century. I have already mentioned in the first chapter a number of writers who combined literature and anthropological research, and one could add others like the Paraguayan Augusto Roa Bastos, the Brazilian Darcy Ribeiro, and the Mexican Juan Rulfo. But the point is that these writers make explicit a relationship between literature and anthropology that is implicit in the core of Latin American narrative in the modern period; in other words, Fernando Ortiz and Gilberto Freyre articulate in their scientific works what in the narrative is an inherent effort to represent culture that is ethnographic in its conception.[26]

The regionalist or telluric novel was conceived through this institutionalized anthropological grid. These novels are concerned with myth, religion, magic, language, genealogy, the impact of modern modes of production on traditional societies, retentions from earlier periods, in short, with the totality of a culture viewed and described from the outside, often through a narrator who follows a protagonist traveling to the jungle, the *llano* or the *pampa*. As novels, these books generally adhered to the practices of nineteenth-century realism. The anthropological mediation is evident as much in the stories about the creation of each novel as in the actual text. These ancillary stories or pretexts serve to legitimize the persona of the novelist as a knowledgeable individual, much in the same way that the public and professional figures of anthropologists were legitimized by stories of their voyages and sojourns in the wild. One could call these stories fables of validation or legitimation. For instance, it is part of the tale always told about the composition of novels such as *Don Segundo Sombra* (1926) and *Doña Bárbara* that both Ricardo Güiraldes and Rómulo Gallegos traveled to the *pampa* and the *llano*, respectively armed with notebook and pen to record unusual words, strange stories, customs regarding horsemanship and cattle-ranching, in fact, everything that any self-respecting anthropologist doing fieldwork would note. In the most advanced statement on the telluric novel, Carlos J. Alonso has convincingly argued that the project of novelists like Gallegos, Güiraldes, and Rivera was modern because of their critical perspective, which they sought to conceal, but was fundamental to their task: "The attempt to produce a text of autochthony places the writer in an eccentric perspective with respect to his or her own cultural circumstance; in the resulting displacement, the author necessarily becomes also a critic in spite of the unproblematic assumption of immediacy on which his project is predicated."[27] The critic that the novelist becomes is essentially an anthropologist, because anthropology furnishes the only discourse capable of authoritatively analyzing and narrating the autochthonous, hence the fable of legitimation, and the various information-gathering activities to which they devoted themselves once in the field. Alonso's most productive insight is to realize that the "quest for identity" project implicit in telluric novels is itself a myth, a reflection, I would add, of the very discourse on which it is based. He writes: "The Latin American quest for cultural identity could itself be regarded as a cultural myth of foundations; but a myth that narrates the story of an essential cultural schism, capable nonetheless of endowing the affairs of the collectivity with the requisite meaning and purpose. In the end, through this myth of permanent cultural crisis, Latin American intellectuals have paradoxically found an effective narrative of cultural identity" (p. 36). This reading is only possible from the perspective of the re-reading of the telluric novels that more recent fiction has made possible, from the point of view of the archival fictions to which, ultimately, Alonso's own book belongs.

In *Los de abajo* (1915; 1924), Mariano Azuela, with a stroke of genius, included the figure of the outside observer inside the novel: Dr. Cervantes (no less), who is forever frustrated in his efforts to understand the revolutionaries with whom he travels. A central concern of these so-called *novelas de la tierra* was to cull and record information about sectors of Latin American culture which, while contemporary and part of that culture, were outside modernity; more importantly, these were illiterate populations, possessing essentially oral cultures, thus fulfilling an important prerequisite to be the object of an anthropological study. In his position as outsider, the anthropologist-author searched for the secret of his own uniqueness, and the key to an originality that would be measured by its distance from the routines and commonplaces of the West. The insistence on *being there* – to use Clifford Geertz' formula – and being able to convince the reader of the authenticity of what is being written, takes a peculiar form in the case of the Latin American author because his conceit consists in affecting to have always been there, given that he is a native of the culture.[28] But, at the same time, he has to be outside to be able to record it, to inscribe it. Anthropology furnishes the novelists with the methodological instruments, the rhetoric or discourse to be both there and outside. On the most elementary level, as we saw, he or she carries a pad and pen to record what is out there. These efforts were not always as amateurish as they seem. If it is true that Güiraldes, Gallegos, and Rivera had really very little, if any training in ethnography, other writers, particularly those more closely associated with the avant-garde, did have some, or by their extended stays "in the field" developed methods close to those of professionally trained anthropologists. One should remember here two further fables of validation or legitimation. Carpentier has written in *La música en Cuba* (1946) about how he attended Afro-Cuban rituals with reverence, but also with notebook and pen to record the music as much as the story being acted out.[29] The results are found in his 1933 novel *¡Ecué-Yamba-O!*, which includes the quite reliable transcription of an initiation ceremony.[30] Another story is that of João Guimarães Rosa, who was not only a great Brazilian writer but also a medical doctor. Guimarães Rosa spent years caring for the dirt-poor people of the *sertão*. Since they could not pay him he would ask them to tell him stories in return for his services. From the stories that he collected he wrote many of his own short stories as well as his masterpiece *Grande sertão: veredas*.[31]

These novels are guided by a philological approach derived from nineteenth-century anthropology. The anthropologist-author aims to fix a text, containing a set of cultural practices and a group of stories. The study of this mythology is shrouded in the mystery of words, whose origin the anthropologist-author attempts to find, and whose meaning he discovers and sets. Novels like *Don Segundo Sombra* or *Canaima* are philological works in this sense. Often, as in *Doña Bárbara*, *La vorágine* and *¡Ecué-Yamba-O!* the books come equipped with glossaries, and Carpentier's novel even has illustrations. The narrative voice in these novels frequently contrasts a peculiar usage with the standard Spanish one. Gallegos, Güiraldes, and most regionalist novelists are experts in folklore and rural speech, and their novels show it. They are also at pains to reproduce through odd, presumably phonetic spelling, the peculiar pronunciation of their characters, creating an even stronger clash between their speech and the voice of the narrator. These books attempt to inscribe, to turn into writing, the oral culture or subculture in question, using the philological instruments of anthropology. Both in the actual creation of the novel and within the text, the trappings of method are present.

Anthropology as a form of hegemonic discourse is also evident in the regionalist novel because of the inordinate attention paid to matters of genealogy. Genealogy, as we know, is very much an element in conventional novelistic tradition, and could even be either a remnant of the epic or something willfully copied from the epic by novelists attempting to give their works an epic dimension. Be that as it may, genealogy is a fundamental element in modern Latin American fiction, not merely as a measure of time, nor as a reflection of myth, but also because the regionalist novel studies the family as a group, and how values are transmitted from generation to generation, as well as in social practices. The complex genealogical structure of *Doña Bárbara* has a mythic, theogonic dimension, but it is also a study of the clash between the conception of the family unit in rural Venezuela and urban Caracas. The apotheosis of genealogy one finds in *Cien años de soledad* is a parody of this aspect of the regionalist novel. The study of myth and the family commingle and give the regionalist novel a peculiar character, but only because myth and the family are aspects of that synechdochical rhetoric that ethnography finds suitable for a holistic study of society.

Another aspect of anthropological discourse evident in the regionalist novel is the comparative method, which appears in these books mainly in contrasts between the oral subcultures and the dominant culture, though comparisons between oral subcultures also abound. Chronological contrasts are also drawn, pitting the state of a given group before the arrival of the Europeans with their present condition, or chronicling the decline of a group as a result of a specific form of exploitation, as in the case of *La vorágine* and the rubber industry, *¡Ecué-Yamba-O!* and sugar production, or *Don Segundo Sombra* and *Doña Bárbara* and cattle-ranching. There is a sense of loss in these telluric novels, a nostalgia for a past when traditional values prevailed and non-European cultures were true to their nonhistorical "essence." The recuperation of that state is the mission of the novels, a mission that can be achieved by finding a modern, all-encompassing myth that will make whole the disparate fragments of the present: one Venezuela, one Argentina, or one Mexico, united in an apotheosis of cross-cultural communion.

The most interesting and enduring among these novels explode under the pressure of their internal contradictions. These novels are not ideal subjects for myth criticism as some have thought, but are themselves a form of myth criticism. The disparate mythic elements, the strands of various stories, plus the contemporary, historical plot involving the protagonists, cannot coalesce under the all-embracing allegory or metamyth. In regionalist novels the language of the narrator is about magic, but it is not magical. In these texts the literary element is found precisely in their inchoate nature, which reveals the trappings as well as the inadequacies of method. These novels are mock anthropology that unmasks the conventionality of ethnography, its being a willful imposition on the material studied as an act of appropriation. This revelation, when it occurs as in *Doña Bárbara*, constitutes the flight of these texts from the hegemonic discourse that mediates them – a flight into literariness.[32]

The solution to this dilemma, still under the mediating influence of anthropology, was to write novels whose inner coherence imitated that of sacred texts, even including numerological and symbolic correspondences, and leaving no fissures between the world of the characters and that of the narrator. This was the great achievement of the Carpentier of *El reino de este mundo* (1949) and of Miguel Angel Asturias' fiction in general. René Prieto has described Asturias' novelistic project in this way:

Like Joyce, who conceives *Ulysses* in terms of a complex narrative framework in which each chapter is linked with a section of the *Odyssey*, an hour of day, an organ of the body, an art, a color, and a musical instrument, Asturias builds his American idiom on the basis of layered relationships embracing elements, animals, colors and numbers [from Mayan lore] interlinked amongst themselves.[33]

In 1927 Asturias had translated, edited and published the *Popol Vuh* in Paris; better yet, and closer to Pané and Borges, Asturias translated into Spanish Georges Raynaud's French translation. His novels, particularly *Hombres de maíz*, which is the one being discussed above by Prieto, profited from the knowledge he acquired in that anthropologico-philological restoration. Asturias' novels also gained from the various textual siftings that the Mayan material went through, and from the traces that those siftings left in the final text. The Mayas had no writing and no books in the way the West conceives of them. They certainly had no novels. Their contemporary descendants write no novels either – unless they are called Miguel Angel Asturias – and probably read very few of them. Spanish versions of Mayan myth are always translations, and the concoction of a numerological system bonding the contemporary plot of the novel with the rigid language of sacred lore is a product of the literary imagination, not of ritual. *Hombres de maíz* is a novel in the measure in which it pretends to be myth, not because it is myth.

José María Arguedas' answer to these dilemmas in his autobiographical novel *Los ríos profundos* is to narrate in the first person the life of a boy who, like him, lived among Indians and learned Quechua before Spanish. Very much like *The Portrait of the Artist as a Young Man*, *Los ríos profundos* is a *Bildungsroman* in which the young protagonist is sent to a school where he is to learn to live in the society his parents have chosen for him. It is a deeply troubling experience because for Ernesto to learn from the Spanish-speaking priests and his classmates means to forget, or worse, to scorn the life of those who raised him. *Los ríos profundos* is almost an allegory about the conquest of Peru and the forced acculturation of the natives to Western civilization. It is not quite that because its most profound message is precisely that the wounds of the conquest have not healed, hence an overarching construct that will, as in Asturias, pretend to bind together the knowledge of the natives acquired by anthropological practice, and their own knowledge of themselves, is not possible. The disharmony at the core of Peruvian society is conveyed through the broken syntax of the narrator's discourse, which very often obeys the linguistic structures of Quechua. There are flashes of poetry in this fractured Spanish, catachreses created by the interference of another language. Moreover, as John Murra (an anthropologist) says about his colleague's fiction, for Arguedas the issue was "how to transmit to the reader of Spanish not only compassion for the oppressed, but a sense that the latter also had a perception, a world view of their own, in which people, mountains, animals, the rain, truth, all had dimensions of their own, powerful, revealing, and utterly unlike the Iberian ones."[34] *Los ríos profundos* represents through its very incompleteness and flaws the tense dialogue of cultures that makes up contemporary Peru, a dialogue in which the acquisition of knowledge about the other can still lead to genocide.

Given his unimpeachable credentials in anthropology, Arguedas' fable of legitimation is a much more dramatic one. By means of it, he clearly wanted to make a statement as much about his texts as about his life. When he killed himself in 1969, Arguedas was expressing not only a measure of his despair, but also perhaps of his guilt for having made use of anthropological knowledge to approach a part of himself, a process that was already a kind of partial suicide. Feeling, perhaps, that he had stilled through inscription one of the voices within him, he felt that the proper thing to do was to annihilate the Other. In Arguedas the anthropological mediation is not bypassed, as in Asturias, by exposing its literariness, but by denouncing its violent, repressive nature, and by stressing the limitations inherent in the kind of knowledge that it can generate. In Arguedas conquest and knowledge are still linked. Anthropology, which he practiced under the auspices of the sort of state organization to which I have alluded, was implicated in cultural genocide. He did not see a way out of the headlong rush to destruction that the arrival of the book and the cross in the Andes seemed to have started.

4

From early on, Borges has both profited from and offered a radical critique of anthropological discourse and its relationship to narrative. This is an aspect of Borges' work that can be easily overlooked because he wrote no novels and his fiction is considered to be inimical to the *novela de la tierra*. In "El jardín de senderos que se bifurcan" there is a passage that appears to be a critique of any kind of discourse that attempts to contain a country or a culture in the way that regionalist novels do. The protagonist says: "Pensé que un hombre puede ser enemigo de otros hombres, de otros momentos de otros hombres, pero no de un país: no de luciérnagas, palabras, jardines, cursos de agua, ponientes" ("I thought that a man might be an enemy of other men, of different moments of other men, but never an enemy of a country: not of fireflies, words, gardens, streams, or the West wind").[35] Yet in May of 1940, Borges published a story that is to my mind his regionalist novel, "Tlön, Uqbar, Orbis Tertius." Given Borges' distaste for the novel in general, and his disdain for realism and most forms of regionalism, it is not surprising that his *novela de la tierra* should be about a totally imaginary region. Borges was critical of regionalism and skeptical, if not mocking, of all efforts to define an independent Latin American consciousness or a unique Latin American literature. He was positively repelled by the link between such ideological enterprises and government programs. But he was hardly indifferent to these intellectual, cultural and political enterprises.[36] Borges himself began his literary career as a regionalist poet in *Fervor de Buenos Aires* (1923) and worked closely with Ricardo Güiraldes. He was also, fascinated by *gauchesca* literature, making quite a few valuable contributions himself in stories such as "El Sur" to a thematic that was essentially Argentine (in fact, "El Sur" is, in some ways, a story about a fable of legitimation like the ones just seen in relation to the telluric novel). In "El Aleph," furthermore, Carlos Argentino, who is bent on writing a national epic is the quintessential telluric writer, and no matter how ironically he is portrayed, his project is important enough to be a central concern of the story.

So, instead of reading one of the canonical *novelas de la tierra*, an enterprise admirably performed by Alonso, I will concern myself with the unwriting of the ideological and literary project behind such fictions in Borges' "Tlön, Uqbar, Orbis Tertius." Borges' story is in this respect a greater challenge, not only because of the caveats offered above, but because it has been read and re-read as a metaphysical fancy, outside the context of Latin American issues. The following analysis does not dispute other interpretations, but considers them too determined by the surface metaphysical tone of the story. As we shall see, "Tlön, Uqbar, Orbis Tertius" is corrosively aware of the mimetic pact between Latin American narrative and the anthropological mediation.

In "Tlön, Uqbar, Orbis Tertius" Borges reveals the artifice of the regionalist novel by creating an entirely imaginary country described with the methodological precision of an ethnographer's report. In a sense, what Borges does is to turn the regionalist novel inside out, performing in the process a severe ideological critique of the anthropological mediation. The style of the entry in the encyclopedia, where the narrator finds the information, is described as follows: "El pasaje recordado por Bioy era tal vez el único sorprendente. El resto parecía muy verosímil, muy ajustado al tono general de la obra y (como es natural) un poco aburrido. Releyéndolo, descubrimos bajo su rigurosa escritura una fundamental vaguedad" (p. 432) ("The passage remembered by Bioy was perhaps the only startling one. The rest seemed probable enough, very much in keeping with the general tone of the work and, naturally, a little dull. Reading it over we discovered, beneath the rigorous writing, a fundamental vagueness" [p. 19]). The key word here is the technical term *verosímil*, lost in the somewhat careless translation, which means realistic by virtue of the text's adherence to rhetorical norms for representing reality. The suggestion is clear: regionalist novels are fantastic, not realistic, the methodology that legitimizes them is no more than a pre-text to elaborate a cogent fictional world. Ethnography is always literature. The authoritative voice of method is as literary, as fantastic, as the stories that it uncovers.

Borges had anticipated this critique in a 1932 essay that is a direct answer to an anthropological treatise that had vast repercussions in Latin American literature, as well as many others, James G. Frazer's *The Golden Bough*.[37] In this essay, "El arte narrativo y la magia," Borges writes about novels and stories and their relation to the "primitive mind." He contends, as he will on several occasions, that novels are as chaotic as the real world, unless they are constructed like detective novels. Such stories, he says, are carefully constructed worlds in which there are secret connections between events. Borges is interested in the secret of those connections, which we accept without blinking. For Borges causality is the most important element in a story, but he asserts that causality in stories is as fantastic and as magical as the primitive cures described by Frazer, which depend on tropological relations between wound and cure, or between cure and and the weapon that inflicted the wound. Primitive medicine is based on belief in such a system of metaphors; magic would be the efficacy of such a system in affecting reality. In reading and writing stories, and in accepting detective stories as realistic, we indulge in the same kind of magic we assume to be typical of primitives. Hence our "study" of primitives by means of anthropology, and our writing about them using the literary conventions of ethnography, reveals much about us, much that is a mirror image of the object we purport to describe or analyze. The links that we establish between events, our own metatexts about the primitive, are cast in a rhetorical mold that is not radically unlike his. Given these propositions, Borges' Others in "Tlön, Uqbar, Orbis Tertius" are not going to be "contemporary savages," like those of Victorian anthropology, but imaginary beings that inhabit a kind of metatextual utopia.[38]

In "Tlön, Uqbar, Orbis Tertius" that metatext happens to be

about a non-existent realm, but the procedures and tropes that make it up are the same as those in ethnography; in fact, one could say that the story actualizes the metadiscourse of ethnography. The fable of validation or legitimation in Borges' story has, therefore, been internalized, has been made a part of the narrative. Legitimation is not granted here by a journey to the wild, by "being there," but by the discovery, in a pirated version of the *Britannica*, of an article about Uqbar, a country that the narrator and his friend Bioy cannot find in any atlas (Bioy is, of course, Adolfo Bioy Casares, an Argentine writer of fantastic fiction, a detail that vacuums into the fiction Borges' context at the time of writing). Uqbar is a very odd place indeed, but it is described by the encyclopedia, as we saw, in the flat tone characteristic of such reference works. A second fable of validation is provided by the appearance of another encyclopedia, produced by a character who is drawn out of the world of European expansion that generated modern anthropology. Legitimation in Borges does honor to the etymology of the word both as law and as reading. The textual space of the encyclopedia, which stands for all the knowledge in the West, a compendious and, at the same time, slightly frantic repository of information, is organized according to the most banal of conventions, the alphabet, yet can absorb anything, reducing to common knowledge the most distant and different cultural practices. Uqbar, knowledge of which the encyclopedia owes to the work of various German ethnographers and travelers, has a literature that is obsessively devoted to the description of two imaginary regions: Meljnas and Tlön. These are the telluric novels within the fictional telluric novel of Borges' story, the rest of which is about Tlön, one of those regions, which is as odd as Uqbar, if not more so. Information about Tlön is acquired from an *Encyclopedia of Tlön*, obtained from a blurry Englishman, appropriately named Herbert Ashe, who came to Argentina to work on the British-built railroads after some adventures in Brazil; he is obviously a figure of the European traveler, vaguely reminiscent of Francis Bond Head. Borges is notorious for the creation of this kind of *mise en abîme* to underline the textual nature of most phenomena. In this case, however, the presence of the encyclopedia in a remote neighborhood of Buenos Aires – as far as Borges would travel from the city – and the role played by the English engineer, clearly point not only to the literary nature of ethnographic writing, but also to the source of such discourse in institutions fostered by the British Empire. As we know, growth of the *Britannica* during the nineteenth century paralleled the expansion of the Empire, culminating in the tenth edition, published in 1902, the date given in Borges' story for the encyclopedia. Herbert Ashe merely heightens the atmosphere of Victorian colonial life that permeates "Tlön, Uqbar, Orbis Tertius."

But Ashe is significant in another way. He transmits the *Encyclopedia of Tlön* to the narrator through death, as it were; it is a posthumous gift, a partial key to the secrets of that elusive region. There is something funereal about Ashe anyway, beginning with his very name. He is, according to the story, one of those Englishmen who suffer from "unreality." The point is that, like the Buendía who manages to translate Melquíades' manuscript in *Cien años de soledad*, Ashe establishes a link between knowledge and death that will be one of the main components of archival fictions. Death is a metaphor for the impossibility of knowledge, or about the impossibility of there being any discourse about the Other that is not based on a potentially lethal power. Like Melquíades' manuscript and like all manuscripts found in the Archive, the *Encyclopedia of Tlön* is a partial or unfinished work; Ashe is only able to produce one volume. Like ethnography, according to Clifford, this encyclopedia is predicated on synecdoche, only that here, the part can hardly be expected to produce a whole. The sum total knowledge about Tlön is hopelessly incomplete and is in need of further invention or investigation. But while knowledge may be fragmentary and partial, the fiction is all-encompassing, as the reader discovers in the epilogue, where it is revealed that Tlön may be the fabrication of an international sect of Tlönists. The inversion has been completed. From a discourse designed to describe and discover the codes of a given culture, ethnography becomes a mastercode to invent a society. Tlön is to Borges as Venezuela is to Gallegos. Hence, Venezuela is like Tlön. But Tlön is a negative culture; in it things seems not to add up, but to "subtract down." While I am not unaware of the metaphysical implications of this, I am more taken by the way in which Borges has rewritten, or unwritten the rules that govern the production of discourse about another culture. Also by how he has anticipated that Macondo would be like a house of mirrors, and that the sources that Carpentier and Englekirk found in the Apure were always already stories.

5

Barnet has in no way pretended to have written literature, although he has produced one of the most accomplished Cuban literary works of this century.   Manuel Moreno Fraginals[39]

Biografía de un cimarrón was first published in 1966 by Cuba's Instituto de Etnología y Folklore, an entity whose origins are the Sociedad de Estudios Afrocubanos and other organizations founded by Fernando Ortiz. Barnet, once Ortiz' assistant, and who helped him pack and catalogue his library toward the end of the master's life, was among the original group of researchers when the Instituto de Etnología y Folklore opened its doors. He was on his way to becoming an anthropologist, perhaps Ortiz' successor. *Biografía de un cimarrón* which, as the institution that published it guaranteed, was intended as an ethnographic study, would change Barnet's life, perhaps as radically as *Doña Bárbara* changed Gallegos'. The enormous success of the book as a work of literature, both in Cuba and abroad, led Barnet to become an author both of various other testimonial narratives and of several books of poetry. Today he occupies a position at the Unión de Escritores, y Artistas de Cuba, not at the Instituto de Etnología y Folklore (which has in any case been disbanded). Barnet's procedures are rather conventional. He interviews his subjects, researches the social and historical contexts in libraries and archives, and then writes a first-person account in chronological order. *Biografía de un cimarrón* was, and continues to be, an important book because it reached to the core of the anthropological mediation and reopened issues that had been opened by Pané, Sahagún, Guaman Poma and other chroniclers of the discovery and conquest of America. Barnet's book, in addition, seemed to cut through the ritualistic arguments about socialist realism and modernism, which had been rehearsed once again in the Cuba of the 1960s, and answered Carpentier's challenge in *Los pasos perdidos*. Moreover, in a local context that had nevertheless international repercussions, *Biografía de un cimarrón* returned to the questions around which Cuban literature had begun as a self-conscious activity and an institution in the 1830s. Barnet established a link with anti-slavery narratives of that period such as Manzano's *Autobiografía*, and with a whole tradition that is, as William Luis has demonstrated, at the evolving center of Cuban narrative since the first half of the nineteenth century.[40] It was through anthropology that *Biografía de un cimarrón* tried to bypass the snares of the literary, but anthropology is so ingrained in Latin American narrative that it was hardly an escape, and escaping is a theme of paramount importance in the book. If one looks at *Biografía de un cimarrón* as an object one finds that outwardly it resembles as much a regionalist novel as an ethnographic monograph. There is a photograph of Manuel Montejo, an introduction, and a glossary at the end, very much like the ones found in novels such as *Doña Bárbara* and *¡Ecué-Yamba-O!*. It is true that the introduction and the first-person account have separated the voices of the narrator and the protagonist, but on the whole *Biografía de un cimarrón* appears as a logical sequel to the Latin American regionalist novel. But this is a sequel in which anthropological discourse is made evident to legitimize itself and the results of its research. What the book says is backed up by the Instituto de Etnología y Folklore.

Such legitimation is sought not only in the mimetic act of making the book an ethnographic monograph, but also by means of the introduction. There, young ethnographer Miguel Barnet dutifully explains how he went about his research, and later how he wrote *Biografía de un cimarrón*. The story of how Barnet discovered Montejo in a nursing home while doing research on Afro-Cuban religions, how he came to know him, the shared intimacies, the gifts offered to ease their relationship, the hours spent in conversation, has become as well-known as those about the regionalist novelists and their excursions to the *pampa* and the *llano* in preparation to write their novels. The difference is that Barnet is more professional in method. The story of how Barnet rearranges what Montejo tells him to give it a chronological order and to put it in a historical context harks back to Pané and to the narrator-protagonist of *Los pasos perdidos*. Here is where the productive conflicts begin. What is more authentic or legitimate, to retell the story as Montejo remembered it, or to put it in chronological order, as Barnet's anthropological training demands? Who is responsible for the historical context? Is history the sequence of epochs into which Barnet divides Montejo's life in accordance with the cant of official history, or is it Montejo's perception of the flow and significance of events from the perspective of his 106 years of age? Barnet writes in the introduction: "En todo el relato se podrá apreciar que hemos tenido que parafrasear mucho de lo que él nos contaba. De haber copiado fielmente los giros de su lenguaje, el libro se habría hecho difícil de comprender y en exceso

reiterante" (p. 10)[41] ("Throughout the story it will be obvious to
the reader that I have had to paraphrase much of what he told us. If
I had faithfully reproduced his way of speaking, the book would
have been difficult to understand and much too repetitive"). But
what if repetition is an essential part of Montejo's rhetoric, a
mnemonic device, a formula like those present in oral literature,
particularly in epic poems? Barnet's introduction opens as many
questions as it answers, and is thus an essential part of *Biografía de un
cimarrón*. Even when Barnet disavows any desire to write literature
he invokes the most fundamental novelistic topic, that of denying
that the book is a novel.

As opposed to the confidently knowledgeable introduction, the
first-person account begins with a defiant expression of the inability
to know, and an affirmation about the existence of things that
cannot be explained:

Hay cosas que yo no me explico de la vida. Todo eso que tiene que ver con
la Naturaleza para mí está muy oscuro, y lo de los dioses más. Ellos son los
llamados a originar todos esos fenómenos que uno ve, que yo *vide* y que es
positivo que han existido. Los dioses son caprichosos e inconformes. Por
eso aquí han pasado cosas tan raras.   (p. 15)

There are things about life I just don't get. Nature's a complete mystery to
me and the gods more so. They're supposed to be the ones who made all the
extraordinary things people see and that I *have* seen and which really do
exist. But the gods are moody and greedy. That's why there are such odd
goings-on here.

This clash between the authorial voices of Montejo and Barnet is
what constitutes the book. It is a clash in which the narrators and
their echoes and multiple reflections are often shuffled, shifted, and
exchanged. Because if in this inaugural utterance Montejo plays the
role of naive informant, in many others he plays that of knowledgeable, outside observer. One of Montejo's most remarkable traits is
that he assumes an ethnographer's perspective *vis-à-vis* the ethnic
groups that surround him, not only the Chinese and the Whites
(Galicians, natives of the Canary Islands, Turks – who are really
Lebanese – and Jews), but also with respect to the various Black
nationalities represented among the slaves and former slaves,
including his own. Montejo never marries and settles down. In his
years as a maroon (from *cimarrón*, a runaway slave) he is constantly
on the go. He is a perpetual traveler who is forced to join a slave

community only when he is captured. He is never at home in any of these groups, however. Constant movement gives him a comparative perspective, and trains him as a keen observer of others. This makes Montejo at once the best and the worst kind of informant. The best because of his powers of observation and his ability to establish a distance, the worst because he does not speak from inside any culture. In fact, Montejo cancels the possibility of there being a reliable inside informant. Like an ethnographer, Montejo travels; he is a shifting perspective, a moving point of view, observing the cultures that he passes through. He is also a shifting perspective on his own shifting, that is, on the movement of his own consciousness.

Montejo's most remarkable feature is not his penchant for communion with others but rather his yearning for solitude. He spends years in the wild alone, years in which he speaks to no one and retreats in to a paleolithic life-style. It is an existence he comes to like, one in which he learns the language of nature and develops a rich inner life. Montejo is escaping the horrors of slavery, but at the same time he is delving deep into himself to find freedom from humankind in general. His journeys into the Cuban *manigua* are like those of the narrator-protagonist of *Los pasos perdidos*, a flight from history, a voyage back in time to a prelinguistic world, free from the fetters of existence as much as from the chains of slavery. This mythic journey, this death and resurrection, make him wiser and stronger. Silence teaches him about the questionable value of words and makes him intolerant of garrulousness. In his opinion the Chinese in Sagua la Grande babble in their incomprehensible tongue just to be a bother ("para joder," as he puts it, p. 90). Montejo was evasive with other Blacks as he may have been with Barnet: "Muchos negros querían ser amigos míos. Y me preguntaban qué hacía yo de cimarrón. Y yo les decía: 'Nada.' A mí siempre me ha gustado la independencia. La salsa y la escandalera no sirven. Yo estuve años sin conversar con nadie" (p. 58) ("Many Blacks who wanted to be my friends asked me what I did when I was a maroon. And I would say 'Nothing.' I've always liked being independent. Dancing around and carrying on are no good. I spent years without talking to anyone"). Montejo rejects rituals of communal bonding, rituals in which the various African ethnic groups strengthened their bonds. The culture Montejo develops in the wild is as negative as Tlön's: it is almost a reduction to the mere structure of culture and being, a system emptied of content and wound up to function as a mechanism for analysis that precludes participation. It is a negativity like the language of Tlön that in Montejo is expressed by the significant negativity of silence. Montejo is as much the ethnographer as Barnet.

Yet in a curious way Montejo's detached perspective, his memory being a sort of archive of different narrative possibilities – he can speak of and about the Congo or the Lucumí – is a reflection of Neo-African culture in the Caribbean. Montejo moved among several ethnic groups who had different languages and religions, languages and religions that are still alive in Cuba today, as well as in New Jersey and Miami. It would be naive to think that these cultures and languages remained pure in Cuba, that they were not affected by their violent insertion into Western history. They were, indeed, profoundly affected, and Neo-African culture in the Caribbean tends to be synchretic, even absorbing Catholicism. The resilience of neo-African culture is one of the most remarkable factors of Caribbean life and history. Languages, religions, and all sorts of cultural practices survived the horrors of slavery and later the scorn of racial and class discrimination. Neo-African culture also survived being turned into an object of ethnographic study.

The institution created by slaves to oppose slavery was the maroon society or *palenque*, some of which became impregnable citadels. But there were *palenques* of many sizes. Their chief function was to provide refuge to maroon slaves and resist the attempts to return them to the plantations. They were societies under siege, made up of individuals whose origins could and often were very disparate. The *palenques* were as odd and as metadiscursive as Tlön. These were pluralistic societies harboring many languages and praying to many gods, with the one common purpose of survival.[42] Neo-African culture allowed gods from multiple theogonies to coexist, tacitly accepting a kind of religious pluralism and thus achieving a flexibility that may also go a long way to explain their survival. So, if one feature of Neo-African society was (and is) its clandestinity, the other was its capacity to absorb parallel or conflicting theogonies as well as a Babel of tongues. This, it seems to me, explains Montejo's relativistic wisdom, his being a storehouse of stories without giving pre-eminence to any of them. Montejo was a living Archive, and the text of his story as much an Archive as Melquíades' manuscript in *Cien años de soledad*.

In this regard Montejo and Barnet invoke a topic in Cuban literature, one that goes back to the anti-slavery narratives of the nineteenth century. When a slave became old and infirm, and therefore useless for productive work, he was often made into a *guardiero*. A *guardiero* was a keeper of the boundaries who lived on the frontiers between sugar plantations as a guard or gate-keeper. Because of their age and their commerce with many different people these *guardieros* also became keepers of the traditions. These wise old men could be consulted on many matters, ranging from social practices and religious lore to the medicinal quality of plants and the whereabouts of somebody. The *guardieros* sat on the fence, as it were, straddling the divisions between African cultures, and became ethnologists in their own right. I do not say this in a metaphorical sense, or as a *boutade*. Anti-slavery narratives like Anselmo Suárez y Romero's *Francisco* or Cirilo Villaverde's *Cecilia Valdés* incorporated the *guardieros* and some of their knowledge. Both these authors traveled to the provinces to witness slave society in the sugar mills. By an astonishing turn of fate those novels figure among the most important sources of information in Fernando Ortiz' early work on African religions in Cuba.[43] Ortiz, as we have seen, was Barnet's mentor and the knowledge and experience that he gathered from the *guardieros* is one of the voices in *Biografía de un cimarrón*, one that finds an echo in Montejo's own as well as in Barnet's.

Is there in Montejo's story about his life as a maroon not only a tale about attaining a plural perspective, but also an allegory of the text's escape from the mediation of the hegemonic discourse? Isn't his first-person account like that of the *pícaro* and other delinquents who live on the margins of the law and tell about their lives through the formulae of the notarial arts? Is Montejo's life not a return to the Archive, not only those in Carpentier, Fuentes, and García Márquez, but the original in the sixteenth century? Montejo's story takes the form of the picaresque autobiography being told to someone in authority, in this case Barnet, the representative of the Instituto de Etnología y Folklore. Like the *pícaros*, Montejo escapes the constraints of hegemonic discourse by mimicking it and therefore absorbing it. Montejo shows that Barnet's method is literary from the start. Unlike the *pícaro*, however, and also unlike Ernesto in *Los ríos profundos*, Montejo is old, incredibly old. The delusions of innocence are not his. There is no fresh start, his age is capacious like the Archive, it allows him to contain all the fresh starts, all the promises of a new beginning. Like Melquíades and Borges he is in possession of a knowledge that is at once all-inclusive and aware of the gaps and the unfinished stories.

6

On the other hand it is not possible for us to describe our own archive, since it is from within these rules that we speak, since it is that which gives to what we can say – and to itself, the object of our discourse – its modes of appearance, its forms of existence and coexistence, its system of accumulation, historicity, and disappearance.   Michel Foucault[44]

It is time to recapitulate and examine again archival fictions. Let us re-enter Melquíades' room.

The evolving nucleus of the Latin American narrative tradition is concerned with the uniqueness, difference, and autonomy of a cultural entity that defines itself within and yet against a powerful totality, real as well as invented, that could be called the discourse of the West. That tradition is generated in relation to three manifestations of Western hegemonic discourse: the law in the colonial period, the scientific writings of the many naturalists who ranged over the American continent in the nineteenth century, and anthropology, which supplies a dominant version of Latin American culture in the modern period both through the writings of Europeans and through the discourse of the State in the form of institutes of folklore, museums, and the like. The law in the colonial period sets the structure of the relationship between Latin American narrative and dominant discourses. Legal writings deal with legitimacy, enfranchisement, and self-definition in the context of a patrimonial–bureaucratic state that controls writing and hence knowledge, which it safeguards in great storehouses like the Archive at Simancas and the Escorial, both created by Philip II. Like the emerging modern novel in the Picaresque, Latin American narrative in the colonial period deals with delinquency and a general lack of legitimacy. These obstacles are circumvented through mimesis, the imitation of the forms of forensic rhetoric to gain freedom by showing the conventionality of legal language, its being a mere simulacrum to disguise arbitrary power. The performance of this mimetic act grants a momentary suspension of the censorious and punitive power of judicial language. This structure of constraint, imitation and release is the masterstory of Latin American narrative which prevails until the present, particularly in the other two major manifestations of hegemony.

The traveling naturalists furnished a version of American uniqueness by their representation of time and change as conceived by evolutionary nineteenth-century European science. The Latin American narrative imitates their representation of Latin American specimens, and takes advantage of their concept of mutation as well as of the exceptional time in which this process takes place to escape the dominant discourse by fusing with its transfiguring object. After the 1920s, ethnography, often aided by Latin American states, provided a way to represent the originality of Latin American stories, customs, speech, and other cultural phenomena. This is the discourse the Latin American narrative will imitate. The result was the *novela de la tierra* or telluric novel, a highly critical and hybrid product whose rhetorical model was furnished by anthropology, whose mastery it escaped also by fusing with its object of study, by showing the literariness of ethnography. A very self-conscious ethnography in the present is contemporaneous with a form of Latin American fiction that I call archival fictions, the most prominent manifestation of which is *Cien años de soledad*. It is a kind of novel that recovers the three previous mediations and hypostatizes their collecting function in the figure of the Archive, which harks back to the founding mediation. The quintessential Archive is Melquíades' room in the Buendía household, in which the gypsy writes the history of the family and Aureliano Babilonia later deciphers it with the aid of the Encyclopedia and *The Thousand and One Nights*. These archival fictions, which are my hermeneutical model, constitute in some ways a dialogue between Foucault and Bakhtin, a counterpoint of prison and carnival.[45]

Archival fictions are narratives that still attempt to find the cipher of Latin American culture and identity, hence they fall within the mediation provided by anthropological discourse. In the same manner as current ethnography, these books no longer accept the institutional discourse of method as a given, accepting the literariness of all representations of the Other, even, or perhaps especially, if it is an Other Within, as is the case with the Latin American narrative. Archival dictions have not given up on the promise of anthropology, but they probe into anthropology itself, becoming a kind of ethnography of anthropology, as in Mario Vargas Llosa's novel *El hablador*. At the same time that they undermine the bases of anthropology, archival fictions privilege the language of literature into which both the novel and anthropology take refuge. This is a literature that aspires to have a function similar to that of myth in primitive societies and that in fact imitates the forms of myth as provided by anthropological discourse. The mutual mirroring between the discourse of method and its object here is not seen as antagonistic or conflictual, but part and parcel of that category, the literary, into which all forms of storytelling are displaced. So the difference between archival fictions and their predecessors is that they pretend to be literature, not any other form of hegemonic discourse, yet in doing so they are in fact in a mimetic relationship with current anthropology. The obvious question, difficult to answer, is: is anthropology still a form of hegemonic discourse, or is it being replaced by another discourse not yet apparent?

Archival fictions also remain within the anthropological mediation because through it the narrative reaches back to the founding mediation, the discourse of the law. This is so because in anthropology the law stands for the primordial code of a given society, the master key to all of its codes. As the Law, legal discourse is the basic medium for the exchange of values, the metaphor of metaphors, the most archaic rule; both the ruling rule, as it were, and the most ancient. That rule of rules contains all previous mediations, all the guises of the law as hegemonic discourse. In archival fictions all the previous simulacra of the law parade as in a ghostly procession, like the dynasty of bodies that Philip II brings to El Escorial in Fuentes' *Terra Nostra*. Emptied of power, the phantoms of previous mediations appear as in a wake of fictions. Myths from various theogonies are also found in the Archive. As we saw, *Cien años de soledad* reflects, alludes, or remembers myths from several traditions. The Archive is a myth of myths.

How are archival fictions mythic, and how is the Archive a modern myth? First, they are mythic because archival fictions deal with the origin both in a thematic and in what could be called a semiotic way. By the origin I mean the beginning of history, or a commonly accepted source of culture. Figures endowed with founding significance like Columbus and Philip II appear frequently in archival fictions, as well as regions endowed with an originary aura, like the jungle or the village; activities like the founding of cities, the building of monuments, the redaction of histories occupy characters in archival fictions. Latin American history, as in *Cien años de soledad*, appears as being made up of a series of high points common to the whole continent and reducible to a single, shared story. These thematic origins are important in the mythic constitution of archival fictions, but more so are what I call semiotic ones. Here I refer to the functions of the Archive troped in these novels, like the gaps in the manuscripts, the floating texts, the storehouse function, in hoarding and accumulation. This accumulation function is semiotic in that it sorts the vestiges of previous mediations and displays them. Archival fictions are also mythic because, ultimately, they invest the figure of the Archive with an arcane power that is clearly originary and impossible to express, a secret that is lodged in the very expression of the Archive, not separate from it and hence impossible to render wholly discursive. This is why archival fictions incorporate death as a trope for the limits, for with death a sacralized, nondiscursive language becomes prevalent. This sacralized language cannot be sustained, however, for there is no hegemonic discourse to back it up, no authority to give it the proper intonation, or against which to establish a counterpoint. Nostalgia for this sacred language is evident in political doctrines that rewrite the past as teleological, apocalyptic, and leading to a single history. Such allegories remain outside the Archive. The Archive as myth is modern because it is multifarious, relativistic, and even thematizes relativism and pluralism as inherent qualities of literature, the language into which it escapes. Mythification is a version of the masterstory of escape from the strictures of the dominant discourse through fusion with one of the main objects of that discourse: myth. Heterogeneity of cultures, languages, sources, beginnings, is at the core of the Archive's founding negativity, a pluralism that is a subversion or sub-version of the masterstory. The Archive culls and looses, it cannot brand or determine. The Archive cannot coalesce as a national or cultural myth, though its make-up still reveals a longing for the creation of such a grandiose politico-cultural metastory.

Telluric novels were sustained by a pragmatic belief in the efficacy of literature as a political tool. Novelists like Gallegos had faith that once literature could express the essence of Latin American culture, a national or continental myth could lead to a kind of political anagnorisis, a blinding revelation that would in turn become the basis of a useful political program. The complicity of anthropology and Latin American states is a testament to this belief and evidence of the existence of a coalition of political, literary, and scientific discourses. The only pragmatic quality of archival fictions is to turn the gaze of a new, nonauthoritarian ethnology onto that coalition to display its inner springs, its ideological supports, as well as its constitutive idealizations. But in doing so archival fictions cannot escape their own mystifications which, as we saw, lead to their own mythification, one that renders them, no doubt, less efficacious as purveyors of political programs. In a way, this may be due to a loss of faith among writers about their anointment as political messiahs in their roles as writers, which has not stopped them, of course, from playing political roles as authors (that is, as public figures with a prestige and charisma that have political worth).

Archival fictions, then, return to the law as origin in order to delve into the structure of mediation as the constitutive structure of Latin American narrative, or perhaps of the Latin American imagination. These novels reach back to the legal origins of the narrative to pry into the relationship between power and knowledge, or better yet, the empowerment of knowledge through language in the legalistic, hence ritualistic, act of writing. This probe brings forth the violent, arbitrary nature of the act of empowerment and its link to punishment and incarceration. Narrative, be it novelistic or historical, often neutralizes this violence by thematizing the first escape from the strictures of hegemonic discourse, by fleeing the law, as in *Biografía de un cimarrón*. Archival fictions also deal with the accumulation of knowledge and the way in which knowledge is organized as culture. As storehouses of knowledge archival fictions are atavistic accumulations of the given. This is why archival fictions are often historical, and consist of a complex intertextual web that incorporates the chronicles of the discovery and conquest of America, other fictions, historical documents and characters, songs, poetry, scientific reports, literary figures, and myths, in short, a grab-bag of texts that have cultural significance. The organization of the Archive defies conventional classification because classification is at issue, but it does not abandon this basic function of the Archive to generate an inchoate, heteroglossic mass; a mass of documents and other texts that have not been totally, and sometimes not even partially absorbed, that retain their raw, undisturbed original existence as evidence of the non-assimilation of the Other. The

Archive, as is evident in *El arpa y la sombra*, also stands for loss, for emptiness, frequently hypostatized as old age and death. In *El arpa y la sombra* Columbus' bones, like the documents in the Archive, are dispersed, linked by gaps. Archival fictions are also crypts, like the Escorial itself, a figure of the very book we read, monumental repositories of death's debris and documents lacking currency. If the Archive's secret is that it has no secret other than this dialectic of gain and loss, this secret of secrets is uncovered through a set of figures and stories that characterize it like a subconscious of Latin American fiction.

Archival fictions are again concerned with the law because of their interest in the origins of the mediation process and the constitution of the narrative. The fact that the narrator-protagonist of *Los pasos perdidos*, the original archival fiction, writes his composition in notebooks destined to contain the first laws of Santa Mónica de los Venados suggests such a connection. So does the fact that the "case" on which *Crónica de una muerte anunciada* is based is culled from the brief drawn up many years before for the murder trial, and gathered by the narrator from the flooded Palace of Justice of Riohacha. This remarkable passage in García Márquez' novella is the most meaningful expression of the Archive in recent fiction. The passage recounts the narrator's search for the brief:

Todo lo que sabemos de su carácter [the lawyer's] es aprendido en el sumario, que numerosas personas me ayudaron a buscar veinte años después del crimen en el Palacio de Justicia de Riohacha. No existía clasificación alguna en los archivos, y más de un siglo de expedientes estaban amontonados en el suelo del decrépito edificio colonial que fuera por dos días el cuartel general de Francis Drake. La planta baja se inundaba con el mar de leva, y los volúmenes descosidos flotaban en las oficinas desiertas. Yo mismo exploré muchas veces con las aguas hasta los tobillos aquel estanque de causas perdidas, y sólo una casualidad me permitió rescatar al cabo de cinco años de búsqueda unos 322 pliegos salteados de los más de 500 que debió tener el sumario.

Everything that we know about his character has been learned from the brief, which several people helped me look for twenty years later in the Palace of Justice in Riohacha. There was no classification of files whatever, and more than a century of cases was piled up on the floor of the decrepit colonial building that had been Sir Francis Drake's headquarters for two days. The ground floor would be flooded by high tides, and the unbound volumes floated about the deserted offices. I searched many times with water up to my ankles in that lagoon of lost causes, and after five years of rummaging around only chance let me rescue some 322 pages filched from the more than 500 that the brief must have contained.[46]

The dilapidated Palace of Justice, dating from colonial times, obviously alludes to the constitutive presence of the law in that founding period. Its decay recalls the time of the naturalists – even the shaped stones that house the law will atrophy and become somewhat monstrous, as we shall see. The ruined palace stands, then, for the presence of the law as origin of the narrative, now hollowed out; it recalls the stage-set Palace of Justice in the first page of *Los pasos perdidos*, the Palacio de las Maravillas in *El arpa y la sombra*, and, of course, El Escorial in *Terra Nostra*. It even goes back to the ruined building cited by Cervantes in the last pages of the first part of *Don Quijote*, in which a manuscript containing the story of the mad hero is found, which I quoted in the first chapter ("This man had in his possession a leaden box which, so he said, he had found among the ruined foundations of an ancient hermitage, that was being rebuilt. In this box he had found some parchments written in the Gothic script but in Castilian verse, which contained many of the knight's exploits ..."). The construction of archives and the origins of the law are intricately connected, even etymologically. But here law as architexture, as arch-texture is a vestige. The fact that the Palace of Justice became the headquarters of a dashing and lawless Francis Drake suggests the reincarnation of the law as narrative. But there is more.

The volumes are unbound, unclassified and float through deserted offices because the power of the original Archive is suspended. A ruined palace of justice, the Archive functions as a sign, an allegory of the origin. Only the shell of the allegory remains, an empty form from which other meanings emanate; meanings that are unique to this specimen, which through change has evaded the uniformity of the law. *Descosidos* does not really mean unbound, in the sense that the documents are yet to be bound. In fact, *descosidos* could very well mean that these documents were once bound and have now literally fallen apart, become unsewn. If, indeed, the Archive is like Borges' study, it is like Borges' study after that master demolisher of fictions is through thrashing the books. They only become volumes again when they are rewritten as novels by Fuentes, Carpentier, García Márquez and others, simulacra of the original Archive. The absence of classification points to the importance of the unusual spaces between the documents. Here those gaps are filled with water. The documents float as opposed to being grounded, to being connected solidly to matter – to the earth – a condition that would provide them with a stable set of symbolic meanings, such as the ones in the *novela de la tierra*. (Earth, *tierra*, is, of course, a metaphor for the congealed ideology informing the surface project of telluric fiction.) The fact that the offices are now deserted, that the *letrados* have disappeared, further serves to withdraw authority from these papers. The *letrados* have left, leaving scattered traces of their foundational presence, as well as of their exit. They are a conspicuous and significant absence, like the ruined state of the Palace of Justice. Water could very well be the figure of time here, particularly since it is a water that ebbs and flows according to the laws of nature, to the tides. This *mar de leva* is a vestige of the naturalists' time machinery – in *Cien años de soledad* the most powerful vestige of the naturalists' time is the wind that razes the town at the end of the novel.[47] The Palace of Justice is very much like the trash bin of Bogotá's *audiencia* in Rodríguez Freyle's *El Carnero*, but it is a trash bin with a clock inside.

One cannot fail to notice that it was chance that allowed the narrator – a figure of the author – to find the documents that he did recover. It is chance, we might recall, that rules the life of Facundo Quiroga. The author re-covers scattered documents. Hence, the story based on them and its ensuing arrangement is due to chance, not to any given rule or law. But chance could also be a reflection of fortune, the force that naturally rules the tragedy recounted in *Crónica de una muerte anunciada*, the elusive law of destiny that in earlier stories shaped the lives of Facundo Quiroga and Antonio Conselheiro. The story and the text that contains it duplicate each other on the sheen of the water that floods the Palace of Justice, turning its floor into a mirror, a reversed and illusory dome; an inverted law overarching yet undermining the constitution of the text. It is the mirage of a roof that does not shelter, that only reflects, that does not house. The floor, the ground, on the other hand, is here a watery mirror that reflects, but cannot support anything.

The manuscript the narrator seeks to assemble is a *sumario*, technically a summary, but in any case a kind of adding up, or summing up, and merely 322 "pliegos *salteados*" (my emphasis; this important adjective was left out of the translation); that is to say, that the pages were not consecutive, that there were gaps between them. Actually, *sumario* conveys a sense of incompletion at the origin, since it is a gathering up of relevant documents leading up to an eventual summation, but not yet accomplished.[48] The pages were slapped together to form the story, but then the story contains those gaps, the "saltos" that make it a series of "pliegos salteados." Furthermore, the ideal number of pages, the round 500 that the brief is understood to have originally contained, is now replaced by the very incomplete 322. But incomplete does not mean insignificant. 322 is also a number that appears to open an infinite repetition of two's, the sign of the initial repetition, the one that denies the originary power to one. And three, the opening, is full of mythic and tragic resonances. Furthermore, 322 also suggests a winding down, a diminution; not two three, but three two. The Archive in its modern version does not add up, literally and figuratively; it is not a *suma*, but a *resta*, an intermittent series of subtractions. Archival fictions reveal the constitutive gaps that shine between the documents on the watery floor of the Palace of Justice. In them, the Archive is something between a ruin and a relic.

From the crumbling Palace of Justice in Riohacha we can move to national and even imperial archives in Asunción and El Escorial. The documents that Patiño supervises in *Yo el Supremo* are contained in the Paraguayan Archives of State, while in *Terra Nostra* the Escorial houses Philip II's papers, books and bodies – a genealogy of real corpses. As in *Crónica de una muerte anunciada*, these are literalizations of the figure of the Archive. One need not expect the figure always to be so legible. The manuscript that Consuelo keeps in a trunk and Felipe Montero restores and rewrites in Fuentes' *Aura* (Felipe Montero's name is etymologically a pleonasm, for *monteros* are lovers of horses, but may very well also be an allusion to the original archivist, Philip II) is another manifestation of the Archive. If Montero is a figure of the author of modern Latin American fiction, which I believe he is, his task is to rewrite the papers of the Archive, to write an archival fiction, which he does. To do it he must fill the gaps. This *arca* not only has a figural link to the Archive, but an etymological one as well. Like its distant predecessor in *Lazarillo de Tormes* it appears to be threatened by rats; the *arca* could leak, could lose some of its documents.[49] It is significant that Consuelo's diseased husband, the author of the manuscript, was an officer in Porfirio's army, hence, though not directly related to the State and the law, his manuscript has its fictive origin close to the source of political power. Like Patiño, the General is the underling of a dictator and a writer of sorts. As we shall see, it is significant that he is dead. Like the *letrados*, who have abandoned the Palace of Justice, the author here is also gone; all we have is his incomplete legacy.

The Archive is at once capacious and incomplete. Capaciousness, which is related to safe keeping and the atavistic enclosure function of the Archive, is a reflection of the totalizing force of the Law. The law of laws would contain all. Melquíades' manuscript supposedly encompasses the entire history of the Buendía family, that is, of Macondo and the novel's whole fictional world. García Márquez' project recalls that of the *cronista mayor* in the colonial period, particularly Herrera y Tordesillas'. The national archive in *Yo el Supremo* presumably safeguards all of the nation's documents: the record of each of the transactions that together make up the power of the state. The manuscript blown away by the hurricane in *Oppiano Licario* is a *summa*, the *Súmula nunca infusa de excepciones morfológicas*. The size and capacity of the Vatican Archive in *El arpa y la sombra* need not be belabored. The Archive's capacity, its totalization, is an emblem of its power. The Archive contains all knowledge; it is, therefore, the repository of all power. The crypt-like quality of the Archive and its association with death is partly derived from this sense of completion. But it is also a vestige of former mediations, that is to say, of law as legitimation, science as the expression of time, and anthropology as the metacode capable of containing all codes, or a synecdochical expression of all codes. The Archive is an image of the end of time. In *El arpa y la sombra* Carpentier places a figure of the Archive in the afterlife, in a circle of Dante's *Inferno*. The Archive is apolcalyptic, it is like a time capsule launched into infinity, but without hope of reaching eternity.

Capaciousness is sometimes reflected in the size of archival fictions, as in the case of the monumental *Terra Nostra*, but size is not always the measure of totalization, as is evident in the *Ur*-archival fiction "Tlön, Uqbar, Orbis Tertius," or in the relatively brief *El arpa y la sombra*. In some cases, in fact, as in *Cien años de soledad*, capaciousness is achieved through the reduction of all of history to a myth-like story, or, by centering, as in *El arpa y la sombra*, on a mythic figure of the origin, like Columbus, who would contain all *ab ovo*. This tendency in recent Latin American fiction has led some critics and novelists to speak of a "novela total." Vargas Llosa says the following about *Cien años de soledad* in his book on García Márquez:

"Fictitious reality is everything. It contains its own origin, he who creates and what is being created, he who narrates and what is being narrated. Thus, since the narrator's life is *all* of life, his death means the extinction of *everything*. The novel commits the same murder of god that the novelist wishes to perpetrate by exercising his vocation as writer. One ambition reflects the other."[50] Vargas Llosa and other critics are right in noticing the totalizing tendency, but they attribute it to the novel of the *boom*, when it is present since *Los pasos perdidos*. They fall prey to the illusion of totality, without noticing that so-called total novels underscore their own incompleteness through some of the devices seen before. They also fail to notice that the totalizing reduction of history to the language of myth is itself the reflection of an ethnographic discourse that still remains outside the totality, making its composition possible.

The Archive is incomplete as evidenced by the many unfinished or mutilated documents that it contains. This incompleteness generates the hoarding, the cumulative thrust of archival fictions. There are holes in Melquíades' manuscript that are not accounted for in the "final" version that we read. The lawyer in *Crónica* only recovers parts of the manuscript. The narrator-protagonist of *Los pasos perdidos* leaves his threnody unfinished. The *Súmula nunca infusa de excepciones morfológicas* is scattered by the hurricane. Felipe Montero must fill the gaps in order to rewrite General Llorente's manuscript in *Aura*. Consuelo tells him: "Son sus memorias inconclusas. Deben ser completadas. Antes de que yo muera" ("They're his unfinished memoirs. They have to be completed before I die"). The General's manuscript is not unfinished, but has holes burned in it by "el descuido de una ceniza de tabaco," and stains, "manchados por las moscas" ("some of them with holes where a careless ash had fallen"; "others heavily fly-specked").[51] Columbus' manuscripts, like his scattered skeleton, are incomplete and hence are rewritten in *El arpa y la sombra* (as they really were by Bartolomé de las Casas). This incompleteness appears as a blank, either at the end or elsewhere in the manuscript, and signals not only a lack of closure that works against the Archive's capaciousness and desire for totalization, but more importantly it underscores the facts that gaps are constitutive of the Archive as much as volume.

In addition to the unfinished or mutilated manuscripts, this fundamental discontinuity appears in other guises. The very notion of Archive is based more on contiguity than continuity, separation and difference as much as culling and adding up, safekeeping and bringing together. As with the encyclopedia, the principle of organization is not necessarily related to any intrinsic quality of the material in the Archive. An exogenous agent sifts, ranks and separates. The source of that agent's power is a secret the Archive does not comprise, yet it is the most important. Hence there is a radical and foundational fault in the Archive. That arbitrariness and incommensurateness are often represented in archival fictions by old age and death, as anticipated in the discussion of Borges and Barnet, that is, of Herbert Ashe and Manuel Montejo.

The presence of old, dying or dead characters in current Latin American fiction is remarkable and significant. We have already seen several: Melquíades, Columbus, Montejo, and Consuelo. But there are many others, like Anselmo in *La casa verde*, the aging dictator in *El otoño del patriarca*, Dr. Francia in *Yo el Supremo*, Florentino Daza in *El amor en los tiempos del cólera*, the Señora in *Colibrí* and Cobra in the novel of that name, and Empress Carlota in Fernando del Paso's *Noticias del Imperio* (1987). These oracular figures are links with the past and repositories of knowledge, like living archives. But their memories are faulty and selective. Senility is a figure for the gaps in these archival characters. Senility, curiously, here becomes a force for exuberant creativity, for originality. Senility is, in the context of my discussion, a metaphor for the incompleteness of the Archive, but also for the force, the glue by which texts are bound together. There is a whimsical creativity in these characters' recollections that is parallel to how selection takes place in the Archive in the creation of fiction, and which is found in their lapses of memory. These often decrepit characters (dilapidated like the Palace of Justice) stand in opposition to the figure of the Romantic child-like poet, whose presumably fresh vision shapes much of modern literature, yet share with him a creative *élan* born not of remembrance as much as of forgetfulness. Their age also approximates them to death, one of the founding tropes of archival fictions. Death stands for the gap of gaps, the mastergap of the Archive, both its opening and closing cipher. Consuelo's husband, author of the manuscript Felipe rewrites, is dead, so is Melquíades by the time his manuscript is read, and so are the narrators in *Pedro Páramo*.

Sometimes, as in *El otoño del patriarca* or *Noticias del Imperio*, one of these terrible and capricious oldsters is the narrator; while in others, as in *Biografía de un cimarrón*, the old, oracular figure absorbs the author, who stands for method, for discipline, for institutional discourse. Felipe Montero is also absorbed by Consuelo and in fact becomes her dead husband-author of the manuscript, and in *Yo el Supremo*, old and cantankerous Dr. Francia and Patiño merge as the secretary ages and joins the ranks of dying yet living archives. Melquíades, always the paradigm, is old beyond age, and the narrator as well as his readers and rewriters have to struggle with his apocalyptic vision. Narrative self-reflexiveness, as seen in the first chapter, is a figure of death. Self historicizing brings forth the gap wherein these dead or dying figures spin their web of writing. So, like Ashe, that timid and funereal author, all of these internal historians are touched by death because they narrate the blank and the gaps; like their faulty memories they create from the discontinuities, from the breaks. Their narrative issues from the lapses. They are ruins at the origin, like the various crumbling buildings in Carpentier's fiction and the Palace of Justice in *Crónica de una muerte anunciada*. Creators of fictions, these figures wind up entombed in their own fictions, in their own archives, like Philip II in El Escorial they lead the parade of ghostly forms voided in the Archive; they are the seat of theory.[52] This theory unveils the workings of the mediation process whereby fiction has been engendered. They are the mediation.

Perhaps the most significant of these figures is not so much Melquíades as Bustrófedon, the character in Guillermo Cabrera Infante's *Tres tristes tigres*. Bustrófedon is dead when the novel begins, yet he is the source of the language games that the other characters play; he is not only an oracular source, but the very source of language in the fiction. He inhabits the gap of gaps, having died of an aneurism of the brain, an interruption of his discursive powers that allowed him to break up language in his characteristic way. Bustrófedon's textual production is preserved in magnetic tapes, the sum total of which is the figure of the Archive in this novel. Silvestre, Cué, and the others replay these tapes and repeat Bustrófedon in a manner similar to the process of translation and decoding of Melquíades' manuscript by the Buendías. The characters in Cabrera Infante's novel engage in an interpretation and commentary of Bustrófedon's textual legacy, mindful that it may contain a dark and important secret. That secret is the peculiar breakdown of language enacted by Bustrófedon. Death as gap is most evident in *Tres tristes tigres* because it is at the source; it is the voided presence of the production of language. The gaps we intuit in Melquíades' manuscripts are displayed as the foundation of the manuscript within *Tres tristes tigres*, a manuscript that here is figured as a voicescript. *Tres tristes tigres* is founded upon an archive of voices, much in the same way as *Pedro Páramo*, another archival fiction. The same could be said of *Rayuela*, a novel that centers on the wake of Rocamadour, La Maga's child who brings together the figures of the romantic child creator and the dead archival source in modern Latin American fiction (in this novel, the figure of the Archive is the shifting number of dispensable chapters, which contain the theory on which the novel is based).[53] Bustrófedon, Melquíades, Rocamadour, the dead narrators in *Pedro Páramo*, Consuelo's dead husband, install death as the violent origin of discontinuity, the discontinuity that makes up the Archive.

These old, dying or dead figures share with the ruined Palace of Justice at Riohacha the mark of time, of time as change, as mutation. In this they are also a vestige of the naturalist's mediation. These figures are often not only old or dead but, like the manuscripts they sometimes hoard, they are mutilated, or monstrous in some other way. Time is written on their bodies as wrinkles, deformations, or disease. Much is made in *Terra Nostra* of Cervantes' mangled arm. In *Yo el supremo* Patiño drags around his swollen foot; the patriarch in *El otoño del patriarca* tows his enormous, herniated testicle; Consuelo, the very image of time, can transmute herself into a young Aura; Melquíades is a wizard. Bustrófedon, again, appears to be the most significant. His aneurism is literally an interruption of the natural flow of physical self, which is the source of the figurative deformations, the mutations of language in *Tres tristes tigres*. Through these physical ailments and deformations these characters reach back to Facundo Quiroga and Conselheiro, mutants of an earlier age that left an indelible imprint in archival fictions.

The lapse represented by death or by the faulty memory of old narrators does not signal an escape from the dominating discourse, but the opposite. The lapses and the Lapse stand for the gaps and cuts, the proscription of language, the origin of the law. Death is a trope for interdiction, and forgetfulness for the creativity from within interdiction, which is the mark of the Archive. This explains the seed-like function of Rocamadour and Bustrófedon, as well as of

Dr. Francia, the dead narrators in *Pedro Páramo*, and the death-like countenance of Ashe, and his posthumous production of the book. The gap is the mediation, the founding hole, the limit of limits. Archival fictions return to the gap at the core of the Archive, because it is the very source of fiction. This installment of death and old age as founding tropes to figure the Other, the power of hegemonic discourse, its originary and modelling force, is a mythification of the archive, of the Archive, the displacement of the language of method to the realm of myth and the sacred. Death tropes, mythifies the gap; its appearance in archival fictions is in no way a revelling in literal death, but a metaphor for the negativity of limit. Hence the Archive is not a Bakhtinian carnival but, if it is, it takes place within the confines of Foucault's prison.

Is there narrative beyond the Archive? Do archival fictions give way to new kinds of narrative that announce a new masterstory? What would the new hegemonic discourse be? Can narrative ever really break the mimetic bond sealed by the law in the sixteenth century? Obviously archival fictions continue to be produced in Latin America, if one considers that *Noticias del Imperio*, which exhibits all of the major features outlined above, was published as recently as 1987. But there seems to exist a desire to break out of the Archive, one that is no longer merely part of the economy of the Archive itself. Is a move beyond the Archive the end of narrative, or is it the beginning of another narrative? Could it be seen from within the Archive, or even from the subversions of the Archive? Most probably not, but if one form of discourse appears to be acquiring hegemonic power it is that of communication systems.[54] Perhaps a new masterstory will be determined by them, but it is difficult to tell with any degree of certainty from the Archive.

Notes

1 A clearing in the jungle: from Santa Mónica to Macondo

1 *The New York Times Book Review*, 6 April 1986, p. 34.
2 John G. Varner defines Adelantado as, "Title given a man who was sent out to explore and govern new lands." In the "Glossary of Spanish and Quechuan Words," appended to his *El Inca: The Life and Times of Garcilaso de la Vega* (Austin, University of Texas Press, 1968), p. 387.
3 All references are to Alejo Carpentier, *Los pasos perdidos*, ed. Roberto González Echevarría (Madrid, Cátedra, 1985), p. 252; *The Lost Steps*, tr. Harriet de Onís (New York, Alfred A. Knopf, 1956), pp. 189–90.
4 Although my debt to Michel Foucault's *Surveiller et punir* (Paris, Gallimard, 1975) should be obvious (more on this later in the text), my study of the relationship between the novel and the law has been enriched by the current movement in the U.S. academy generally called "the law-literature enterprise," which appears to have culminated with the foundation of *Yale Journal of Law and the Humanities* (on whose Editorial Advisory Board I am honored to serve). The first issue of that journal is recommended as an entryway into this already vast field of enquiry and debate. I have also learned much from the special issue "Law and Literature" of the *Texas Law Review*, 60, no. 3 (1982), which contains a lively exchange capped by a lucid piece by Stanley Fish ("Interpretation and the Pluralist Vision," pp. 495–505). A recent book by judge Richard Posner, *Law and Literature: A Misunderstood Relation* (Cambridge, Mass., Harvard University Press, 1988), though somewhat belligerent and short-sighted, contains a useful overview of the issues as well as ample bibliographical information in the footnotes.

The "law–literature enterprise" has been dominated, not surprisingly, by the issue of interpretation. Deconstruction and other schools of literary criticism, have invaded the law with their claims about the arbitrariness of the sign, hence questioning the validity of interpretations and the truth-value of monumental texts such as constitutions and legal codes. Fish shows that the pluralism that emerges is itself a position, allied to a conception of literature tied to a liberal ideology for the past two centuries. My position is that the shifting shapes of what is called narrative or the novel is determined by outside forces that determine it in a given moment, and that these changes take place initially in the rhetoric of the law. In the U.S. the issue of rhetoric and its relationship to the law, both as a matter of instituting power (persuasion) and as a historical phenomenon (the evolution of modern legal practices in Renaissance Bologna) has not been given enough attention.

5 I have studied in great detail this process in my *Alejo Carpentier. The Pilgrim at Home* (Ithaca, Cornell University Press, 1977).

6 *The Adventures of Don Quixote*, tr. J. M. Cohen (Baltimore, Penguin Books, 1968), pp. 457–8.

7 Of course, Menéndez Pidal's monumental enterprise is based on philology, so for him the *epopeya* is an origin that persists in Spanish literature. I would invert the perspective and say that, in many ways, the *epopeya* is an invented origin, as is the history of Latin America for Latin American literature.

8 *Tientos y diferencias* (Montevideo, Arca, 1967), p. 7.

9 Ralph Freedman, "The Possibility of a Theory of the Novel," in *The Disciplines of Criticism: Essays in Literary Interpretation and History*, eds. Peter Demetz, Thomas Greene and Lowry Nelson Jr. (New Haven, Yale University Press, 1968), p. 65. It is obvious now that Mikhail Bakhtin had made a similar proposal years earlier, but this was not known when Freedman wrote his piece.

10 *Rabelais and His World*, tr. Hélène Iswolsky (Bloomington, Indiana University Press, 1984), p. 8. Henceforth all quotes, indicated in the text, are taken from this edition.

11 The most reliable summary of Bakhtin's ideas on these issues is Tzevetan Todorov's *Michaïl Bakhtine. Le principe dialogique*, followed by Ecrits du Cercle de Bakhtine (Paris, Editions du Seuil, 1981). I have also profited from my friendship with my colleague and great Bakhtin scholar Michael Holquist.

12 See also Edward J. Goodman, *The Explorers of South America* (New York, The Macmillan Co., 1972). Jean Franco, "Un viaje poco romántico: viajeros británicos hacia Sudamérica, 1818–28)," *Escritura* (Caracas), Year 4, no. 7 (1979), pp. 129–41. Goodman's book contains an excellent bibliography on exploration in Latin America.

13 On the *novela de la tierra* the most advanced work is Carlos J. Alonso's *The Spanish American Regional Novel: Modernity and Autochthony* (Cambridge University Press, 1989).

14 John Freccero, "Reader's Report," Cornell University. *John M. Olin Library Bookmark Series*, no. 36 (April 1968); Eduardo G. González, *Alejo*

Carpentier: el tiempo del hombre (Caracas, Monte Avila, 1978). Clifford
Geertz, *Works and Lives: The Anthropologist as Author* (Stanford University
Press, 1988).

15 Carpentier corresponded with André Schaeffner, a musicologist who
participated in the Griaule expedition (see note 27, pp. 89–90, in my
edition of *Los pasos perdidos*). While in New York a group of anthropologists closely associated with the avant-garde and which included
Claude Lévi-Strauss, published a journal called *VVV*, the cypher giving
access to Santa Mónica de los Venados in *Los pasos perdidos*. It is quite
possible that the narrator-protagonist of the novel was modeled on
these anthropologists. See James Clifford, *The Predicament of Culture:
Twentieth-Century Ethnography, Literature, and Art* (Cambridge, Mass.,
Harvard University Press, 1988), pp. 117–85. Clifford's excellent book
is a must reading for anyone interested in Carpentier. The Cuban
novelist was in intimate intellectual contact with the world described
by Clifford, from the writings of Michel Leiris, a potential model for the
narrator-protagonist of *Los pasos perdidos*, to Lévi-Strauss. The relationship between this group and Carpentier deserves more detailed study
and reflection. Carpentier mentions the group of artists and anthropologists and the magazine *VVV* in one of his last novels, *La consagración de
la primavera* (Mexico: Siglo XXI, 1978), p. 273.

16 See René Lichy, *Yakú. Expedición Franco-Venezolana del Alto Orinoco*
(Caracas, Monte Avila, 1978). This expedition, which also included
Marc de Civrieux, took place in 1951.

17 All references are to Gabriel García Márquez, *Cien años de soledad*
(Buenos Aires, Editorial Sudamericana, 1967), and to *One Hundred
Years of Solitude*, tr. Gregory Rabassa (New York, Harper & Row, 1967).
I have also consulted the two critical editions extant by Joaquín Marco
(Madrid, Espasa Calpe, 1984) and Jacques Joset (Madrid, Cátedra,
1984).

18 I have had to change the translation, for this is one of the very few
places where Gregory Rabassa made a mistake.

19 See, for example, Ricardo Gullón, *García Márquez o el olvidado arte de
contar* (Madrid, Taurus, 1970) and Carmen Arnau, *El mundo mítico de
Gabriel García Márquez* (Barcelona, Ediciones Península, 1971). There
have been many studies since along these lines. The most convincing is
by Michael Palencia Roth, "Los pergaminos de Aureliano Babilonia,"
Revista Iberoamericana, nos. 123–4 (1983), pp. 403–17. Palencia Roth's
splendid piece argues in favor of the biblical myth of Apocalypse as the
principal one in the organization of the novel and insists on the
influence of Borges on García Márquez. As I will argue below,
however, no single myth controls the novel, and no transcendence is
allowed by the constantly undermined and undermining world of

writing, of the Archive. Only if we could escape the verbal, then the sort of simultaneity and atemporality of which Palencia Roth speaks so persuasively, and which are characteristic of myth, would be possible. On the influence of Borges on García Márquez see: Roberto González Echevarría, "With Borges in Macondo," *Diacritics*, 2, no. 1 (1972), pp. 57–60 and Emir Rodríguez Monegal *"One Hundred Years of Solitude: The Last Three Pages,"* *Books Abroad*, 47 (1973), pp. 485–9. I have learned a good deal from this article, in which the author singles out Melquíades' room as an important feature of the novel, and insists on the notion of the Book as key to an understanding of the text.

20 Lucila I. Mena, "La huelga de la compañía bananera como expresión de 'lo real maravilloso' americano en *Cien años de soledad*," *Bulletin Hispanique*, 74 (1972), 379–405.

21 Patricia Tobin has written an illuminating chapter on genealogy in *Cien años de soledad* in her *Time and the Novel: The Genealogical Imperative* (Princeton University Press, 1978). Another excellent study, written by someone trained in anthropology, is Mercedes López-Baralt's *"Cien años de soledad*: cultura e historia latinoamericanas replanteadas en el idioma del parentesco,"* *Revista de Estudios Hispánicos* (San Juan de Puerto Rico), Year 6 (1979), pp. 153–75.

22 Iris M. Zavala, *"Cien años de soledad*, crónica de Indias,"* *Insula*, no. 286 (1970), pp. 3, 11: Selma Calasans Rodrigues, *"Cien años de soledad* y las crónicas de la conquista,"* *Revista de la Universidad de México*, 38, no. 23 (1983), pp. 13–16. García Márquez' interest in the *crónicas de Indias*, established beyond doubt in Zavala's article, was made evident again in his speech accepting the Nobel Prize: "Los cronistas de Indias nos legaron otros incontables [testimonies of astonishing events and things in the New World]... En busca de la fuente de la eterna juventud, el mítico Alvar Núñez Cabeza de Vaca exploró durante ocho años el norte de México [*sic*], en una expedición venática cuyos miembros se comieron unos a otros, y sólo llegaron cinco de los 600 que la emprendieron," *El Mundo* (San Juan de Puerto Rico), Sunday, 12 December 1982, p. 21–C. An English translation of this address appears in *Gabriel García Márquez: New Readings* (Cambridge University Press, 1987), pp. 207–11. In a long interview published as a book García Márquez said: Yo había leído con mucho interés a Cristóbal Colón, a Pigafetta, y a los cronistas de Indias ...," *El olór de la guayaba. Conversación con Plinio Apuleyo Mendoza* (Bogotá, Editorial La Oveja Negra, 1982), p. 32. The early history of Macondo furnished in "Los funerales de la Mamá Grande" links the origins of the town to colonial Latin America through legal documents setting down the proprietary rights of the Matriarch: "Reducido a sus proporciones reales, el patrimonio físico [de la Mamá Grande] se reducía a tres encomiendas

adjudicadas por Cédula real durante la Colonia, y que con el transcurso del tiempo, en virtud de intrincados matrimonios de conveniencia, se habían acumulado bajo el domino de la Mamá Grande. En ese territorio ocioso, sin límites definidos, que abarcaba cinco municipios y en el cual no se sembró nunca un solo grano por cuarenta de los propietarios, vivían a título de arrendatarias 352 familias," *Los funerales de la Mamá Grande* (Buenos Aires, Editorial Sudamericana, 1967), pp. 134–5.

23 José María de la Peña y Cámara, *Archivo General de Indias de Sevilla. Guía del visitante.* (Valencia, Dirección General de Archivos y Bibliotecas–Tipografía Moderna, 1958), p. 35. For a thorough and official description and history of the Archive at Simancas, see: Francisco Romero de Castilla y Perosso, *Apuntes históricos sobre el Archivo General de Simancas* (Madrid, Imprenta y Estereotipía de Aribau y Co., 1873). In mid-October, 1785, 253 trunks full of documents arrived at Seville in two expeditions consisting of thirteen and eleven carts respectively. These papers, drawn from the Archive at Simancas, would constitute the Archivo de Indias in Seville, whose organization was due to the enlightened, Bourbon Spanish monarch Charles III.

24 Joan Corominas, *Breve diccionario etimológico de la lengua castellana* (Madrid, Gredos, 1961), p. 59.

25 *The Encyclopedia of Philosophy* (New York, Macmillan, 1967), I, p. 145.

26 I am referring to the box in chapter 2 of *Lazarillo* in which the priest hides the bread, and the trunk in *Aura* where Consuelo keeps the manuscripts left by her dead husband. There is a more thorough discussion of this in the last chapter.

27 Michel Foucault, *The Archaeology of Knowledge and The Discourse on Language*, tr. A. M. Sheridan Smith (New York, Pantheon Books, 1982), p. 129. Originally *L'Archéologie du savoir* (Paris, Gallimard, 1969).

28 *Ibid.*, pp. 130–1.

29 Alejo Carpentier, *El arpa y la sombra* (Mexico, Siglo XXI Editores, 1979), p. 112. My translation.

30 Georg Lukács, *The Theory of the Novel: A Historico-Philosophical Essay on the Forms of Great Epic Literature*, tr. Anna Bostock (Cambridge, Mass., The MIT Press, 1971; original German publication, 1920); M. M. Bakhtin, *The Dialogic Imagination*, ed. Michael Holquist (Austin, University of Texas Press, 1981).

2   The law of the letter: Garcilaso's *Comentarios*

1 Miguel de Cervantes, *The Adventures of Don Quixote*, tr. J. M. Cohen (Baltimore, Penguin Books, 1968), p. 280. I have changed "Lords of

the Privy Council" to "Lords of the Royal Council." Cervantes wrote "Concejo Real."

2 *European Americana: A Chronological Guide to Works Printed in Europe Relating to the Americas 1493–1750*, ed. John Alden, with the assistance of Dennis C. Landis, Providence, John Carter Brown Library (New York, Readex Books, A Division of the Readex Microprint Corporation, 1980), vol. 1. Also relevant are: *Europe Informed. An Exhibition of Early Books Which Acquainted Europe with the East* (Cambridge, Mass., Harvard College Library – Sixth International Colloquium on Luso-Brazilian Studies, 1966), of comparative interest; *Exotic Printing and the Expansion of Europe, 1492–1840, An Exhibit* (Bloomington, Indiana, Lilly Library–Indiana University, 1972); and the beautiful and informative catalogue of an exhibition at the John Carter Brown Library in Providence, Rhode Island, compiled by Julie Greer Johnson, *The Book in the Americas. The Role of Books and Printing in the Development of Culture and Society in Colonial Latin America* (Providence, The John Carter Brown Library, 1988).

3 I am using for the English the excellent *Royal Commentaries of the Incas and General History of Peru*, tr. with an introduction by Harold V. Livermore, foreword by Arnold J. Toynbee (Austin, University of Texas Press, 1966), 2 vols. References to the Spanish are to *Obras completas del Inca Garcilaso de la Vega*, edición y estudio preliminar del P. Carmelo Sáenz de Santa María, S.I. (Madrid, Biblioteca de Autores Españoles, 1963), 4 vols.

4 Biographical information, unless otherwise indicated, is drawn from John Grier Varner's superb *El Inca, The Life and Times of Garcilaso de la Vega* (Austin, University of Texas Press, 1968).

5 *English Literature in the Sixteenth Century Excluding Drama*, vol. II of *The Oxford History of English Literature*, ed. F. R. Wilson and Bonamy Dobrée (Oxford, Clarendon Press, 1954), p. 61.

6 *Pleitos colombinos*, ed. Antonio Muro Orejón (Seville, Escuela de Estudios Hispanoamericanos, 1964).

7 On the issue of centralization I am guided by, Juan Beneyto Pérez, "Los medios de cultura y la centralización bajo Felipe II," *Ciudad de Dios* (Valladolid), no. 150 (1927), pp. 184–99; J. H. Elliott, *Imperial Spain 1469–1716* (New York, St. Martin's Press, 1966); Charles Gibson, *Spain in America* (New York, Colophon Books, 1966); C. H. Haring, *The Spanish Empire in America* (New York, Harcourt, Brace and World 1963[1947]); C. H. Haring, *Las instituciones coloniales de Hispanoamérica siglos XVI a XVIII* (San Juan, P.R., Instituto de Cultura Puertorriqueña, 1957); H. G. Koenigsberger, *The Practice of Empire (Emended Edition of The Government of Sicily under Philip II of Spain)* (Ithaca, Cornell University Press, 1969); Ramón Menéndez Pidal, "Idea Imperial de

Carlos V," in his *Mis páginas Preferidas. Estudios lingüísticos e históricos* (Madrid, Gredos, 1957), pp. 232–53; J. M. Ots Capdequí, *El estado español en las Indias*, 2nd. ed. (Mexico, Fondo de Cultura Económica, 1946); J. H. Parry, *The Spanish Theory of Empire in the Sixteenth Century* (New York, Octagon Books, 1974[1940]); Claudio Véliz, *The Centralist Tradition of Latin America* (Princeton University Press, 1980).

8 Lesley Byrd Simpson, *The Encomienda in New Spain: The Beginning of Spanish Mexico* (Berkeley, University of California Press, 1966 [1929]). On the disputes over the rights of the Indians the reader may consult the classic works by Lewis Hanke.

9 Quoted in Luisa Cuesta and Jaime Delgado, "Pleitos cortesianos en la Biblioteca Nacional," *Revista de Indias*, Year 9 (1948), p. 262.

10 C. H. Cunningham, *The Audiencia in the Spanish Colonies* (Berkeley, University of California Publications in History, 1919); J. H. Parry, *The Audiencia of New Galicia: A Study in Spanish Colonial Government* (Cambridge University Press, 1948); Javier Malagón Barceló, *El distrito de la audiencia de Santo Domingo en los siglos XVI a XIX* (Santo Domingo, Editora Montalvo, 1942); Silvio Zavala, *Las instituciones jurídicas en la Conquista de América*, 2nd ed (Mexico, Porrúa 1971[1935]).

11 Américo Castro, *De la edad conflictiva* (Madrid, Taurus, 1961).

12 "The Role of the *Letrado* in the Colonization of America," *The Americas*, 18, no. 1 (1961), p. 7. I owe much to this fine article as well as to Francisco Márquez Villanueva's "Letrados, consejeros y justicias (artículo–reseña)," *Hispanic Review*, 53 (1985), pp. 201–27. The most thorough study of the letrado is in Richard L. Kagan's *Students and Society in Early Modern Spain* (Baltimore, The Johns Hopkins University Press, 1974), who links the rise of this figure with developments in educational policy. Kagan writes: "Previously, the letrado was a marginal figure in Castilian society, a learned specialist, represented in a few small universities and a handful of places in the cathedral chapters, monasteries and courts of law. But thanks to Ferdinand and Isabel and the Habsburgs, he acquired a central position in Castile, and as his numbers increased, so did his political influence and social prestige" (p. 85). On the "reconquest" of America by the *letrados* see J. M. Ots Capdequí, *El estado español en las Indias*, p. 55. An indispensable source of information concerning the relationship between the New World and the Spanish Crown is Ernst Schafer's *El Consejo Real y Supremo de las Indias. Su historia, organización y labor administrativa hasta la terminación de la Casa de Austria* (Seville, Publicaciones del Centro de Estudios de Historia de América, 1933–47).

13 Haring, *The Spanish Empire in America*, p. 25.

14 Angel Rama made valuable observations about the *letrados* in his posthumous book, *La ciudad letrada* (Hanover, New Hampshire, Edi-

ciones del Norte, 1984). It is known that Rama did not have a chance to review this book, which promised to be a coherent theory of the evolution of Latin American elites and their intellectual production. As it stands, however, *La ciudad letrada* is based on what appears to be a very scanty knowledge of the sixteenth century. For instance, Rama makes the shocking claim that the *traza* of colonial cities, which took the form of a chessboard, was influenced by Neoplatonism and the codification of abstract forms by mathematics in Descartes: "La traslación [de un orden social a una realidad física] fue facilitada por el vigoroso desarrollo alcanzado en la época por el sistema más abstracto de que eran capaces aquellos lenguajes: las matemáticas, con su aplicación en la geometría analítica, cuyos métodos habían sido ya extendidos por Descartes a todos los campos del conocimiento humano, por entenderlos los únicos válidos, los únicos seguros e incontaminados. El resultado en América fue el diseño en damero ..." (p. 6). But Descartes (1596–1650) did not publish his *Discours* until 1637, when most colonial Latin American cities had been founded for over a century. The model for Latin American cities was Santa Fe, the encampment from which the Catholic Kings laid siege to Granada. Rama's conception of the *letrado* is too vague, because it is not based – among other things – on knowledge of Derecho Indiano, nor even familiarity with the questions of writing and reading discussed by Américo Castro (see the article by Francisco Márquez Villanueva). He is also wrong when he claims that the *letrados*, in his very general conception of the type, wished to keep others illiterate. The religious orders and the Crown were interested in creating at least a class of lettered Indians to inculcate both religious dogma and the very legitimation of power, hence the *abecedarios* and other devices used for this purpose. We cannot, of course, judge such efforts by modern standards since they now seem paltry in number, but they were significant at the time.

15 Parry, *The Spanish Theory of Empire*, p. 2.
16 Vittorio Salvadorini, "Las 'relaciones' de Hernán Cortés," *Thesaurus (Boletín del Instituto Caro y Cuervo)*, 18, no. 1 (1963), pp. 77–97. Vittorini gives ample evidence concerning Cortés' background in law and makes important observations about the *relación* as a form of writing. On Cortés' education, J. H. Elliott writes, in a crucial article on the conquistador: "But there is no doubt that his two years in Salamanca, followed by a long period of training and experience as a notary, first in Seville and then in Hispaniola, gave him a working knowledge of Latin and a close acquaintance with the methods and technicalities of Castilian laws" (p. 43), "The Mental World of Hernán Cortés," *Transactions of the Royal Historical Society*, 5th series, 17 (1967), pp. 41–58.

André Saint-Lu makes a similar point about Bartolomé de las Casas' legal training in the introduction to his edition of the *Brevísima relación de la destrucción de las Indias* (Madrid, Cátedra, 1982), p. 49.

17 There are two informative books on American pillories, both by Constantino Bernaldo de Quirós, *La picota en América* (Havana, Jesús Montero, 1948), and *Nuevas noticias sobre picotas americanas* (Havana, Jesús Montero, 1952).

18 Pármeno's mother spent half a day on a picota-like structure as punishment for being a witch. See Fernando de Rojas, *La Celestina*, ed. Dorothy Severin (Madrid, Alianza, 1969), p. 124.

19 "The *Recopilación* contains 6,377 laws taken from among a total of more than 200,000 – an enormous number and yet only part of the total for a century of life (it means an average of one law per day, granting that the Sunday was sanctified)," Malagón Barceló, "The Role of the *Letrado*," p. 11. See also *Recopilación de las leyes de los reynos de las Indias* (Madrid, Consejo de la Hispanidad, 1943), 3 vols. There is a useful anthology containing, among other documents, the "Capitulaciones de Santa Fe," edited by Francisco Morales Padrón, *Teoría y leyes de la Conquista* (Madrid, Ediciones Cultura Hispánica, 1979).

20 *Spain and its World 1500–1700. Selected Essays* (New Haven, Yale University Press, 1989), p. xi.

21 There is a marvellous book on the Archivo de Indias that includes a good deal on Simancas and archival practices from the Catholic Kings to the eighteenth century by José María de la Peña y Cámara, *Archivo General de Indias de Sevilla. Guía del visitante* (Valencia, Dirección General de Archivos y Bibliotecas–Tipografía Moderna, 1958). The enthusiastic Peña y Cámara, who was Director of the Archivo de Indias when he wrote the book, refers to the archives from the chancelleries of Valladolid and Granada brought to Simancas as "potosíes genealógicos" (p. 9).

22 Ivo Domínguez, *El derecho como recurso literario en las novelas ejemplares de Cervantes* (Montevido, Publicaciones y Lingüísticas Literarias del Instituto de Estudios Superiores de Montevideo, 1972). The importance of the law in the origins of Spanish literature seems to be greater than one might have suspected, particularly if one accepts Colin Smith's theories about the author of the *Poema de Mío Cid*. Making a great deal of the court scene at the end of the poem, Smith writes, "In my view the author cannot have been other than a lawyer, or at least a person who had been trained in the law and had considerable technical knowledge of it," Colin Smith, ed., *Poema de Mío Cid* (Oxford, Clarendon Press, 1972), p. xxxiv.

23 On the writing–reading situation in the Picaresque, see Roberto González Echevarría, "The Life and Adventures of Cipión, Cervantes

and the Picaresque," *Diacritics*, 10, no. 3 (1980), pp. 15–26. A "real life" example of picaresque dialogue is found in a document by, precisely, the author of the most famous picaresque novel, Mateo Alemán. In it, the author of *Guzmán de Alfarache* questions a number of *galeotes* working in the mines of Almadén. The text, with ample commentary, has been published by Germán Bleiberg in "El 'Informe Secreto' de Mateo Alemán sobre el trabajo forzoso en las minas de Almadén," *Estudios de Historia Social* (Madrid), Year 1, nos. 2–3 (1977), pp. 357–443. Márquez Villanueva writes: "La verdad es que los españoles vivían bajo el terror obsesivo de algún tropiezo judicial" ("Letrados, consejeros y justicias," p. 214).

24 "El letrado en la sátira de Quevedo," *Hispanic Review*, 54 (1986), p. 45.

25 Koenigsberger's is the most succinct account I have found. The most vivid picture of how this centralized bureaucracy worked can be gleaned from the many instructions found in the *Recopilación de leyes de los reynos de las Indias* about how to channel the paper flow to the Council of the Indies.

26 Haring, *The Spanish Empire in America*, p. 3.

27 Magali Sarfatti, *Spanish Bureaucratic Patrimonialism in America* (Berkeley, Institute of International Studies, 1966). Sarfatti charts in minute detail how the Spanish bureaucracy functioned.

28 Richard M. Morse, "Political Foundations" in *Man, State and Society in Latin American History*, eds. Sheldon B. Liss and Peggy K. Liss (New York, Praeger Publishers, 1972), pp. 72–8. The article appeared originally in *The Founding of the New Societies*, ed. Louis Hartz (1964).

29 *Ibid.* p. 75.

30 Sarfatti, *Spanish Bureaucratic Patrimonialism in America*, p. 76.

31 *Ibid.* p. 19.

32 *Ibid.* p. 7.

33 Morse, "Political Foundations," p. 75.

34 *Ibid.* p. 76.

35 Quoted by Charles B. Faulhaber in "The *Summa* of Guido Faba" in *Medieval Eloquence: Studies in the Theory and Practice of Medieval Rhetoric*, ed. James J. Murphy (Berkeley, University of California Press, 1978), p. 94.

36 "Verdad es que muchos no escriven sino trasladan, otros vierten y las más vezes pervierten."

37 Lewis Hanke, "The *Requerimiento* and Its Interpreters," *Revista de Historia de América*, no. 1 (1938), pp. 25–34. Hanke writes, "Having promulgated the *Requerimiento* in due form, the Spanish captain sent the official report back to Spain with the necessary signatures and his conscience was clear" (p. 28). Concerning the issue of compliance and authority in the Spanish legal system, John Leddy Phelan writes,

discussing specifically the formula *se acata pero no se cumple*: "The formula's origins go back to the Roman law concept that the prince can will no injustice. The 'I obey' clause signifies the recognition by subordinates of the legitimacy of the sovereign's power who, if properly informed of all circumstances, would will no wrong. The 'I do not execute' clause is the subordinate's assumption of the responsibility of postponing the execution of an order until the sovereign is informed of those conditions of which he may be ignorant and without a knowledge of which an injustice may be committed." "Authority and Flexibility in the Spanish Imperial Bureaucracy," *Administrative Science Quarterly* (Cornell University), 5, no. 1 (1960), p. 59.

38 On Nebrija's famous dictum that language is the handmaiden of Empire Eugenio Asensio writes, "Antonio de Nebrija colocó la lengua en la vía central de la historia. La lengua acompaña al proceso orgánico de la suprema creación del hombre, el Estado, con el que florece y se marchita," "La lengua compañera del Imperio(a)," *Nueva Revista de Filología Española*, 43, cuadernos 3–4 (1960), p. 407. Asensio gives the Humanistic background of Nebrija's ideas. On the debates on language during the sixteenth century, see Mary Lee Cozad, "A Platonic–Aristotelian Linguistic Controversy of the Spanish Golden Age, Dámaso de Frías' *Diálogo de las lenguas* (1579)" in *Florilegium Hispanicum; Medieval and Golden Age Studies Presented to Dorothy Clotelle Clarke*, ed. John S. Geary (Madison, Wis., Seminary of Medieval Studies, 1983), pp. 203–27. On Erasmianism and the debates concerning the translation of Holy Scripture the classic continues to be Marcel Bataillon's *Erasme et l'Espagne*, which I have read in the augmented Spanish edition *Erasmo y España. Estudios sobre la historia espiritual del siglo XVI*, 2nd edn. (Mexico, Fondo de Cultura Económica, 1966).

39 Juan Durán Luzio, *Creación y utopía, letras de hispanoamérica* (San José, Costa Rica, Editorial de la Universidad Nacional, 1979). The most elegant and influential consideration of the topic is, of course, Alfonso Reyes' *Ultima Tule*, in which the great Mexican essayist discusses the premonitions of a new world in European literature as a desire to recover a lost paradise. As Durán Luzio amply shows, the topic persists in Latin American literature to the present.

40 *Colección de documentos inéditos relativos al descubrimiento, conquista y colonización de las posesiones españolas en América y Oceanía, sacados en su mayor parte, del Real Archivo de Indias* (Madrid, Imprenta de Manuel B. Quirós, 1864–84).

41 *Recopilación de leyes de los reynos de las Indias*, 1, p. 653 (3, título 16).

42 There are three excellent articles by Antonia M. Heredia Herrera on the style of letters and other legal documents from which I have learned much: "Los cedularios de oficio y de partes del Consejo de Indias: sus

tipos documentales (s. XVII)," *Anuario de Estudios Americanos* (Seville), 29 (1972), pp. 1–60; "Las cartas de los virreyes de Nueva España a la corona española, en el siglo XVI (características diplomáticas, índices cronológico y de materias)," *Ibid.*, 31 (1974), pp. 441–596; "La carta como tipo diplomático indiano," *ibid.* 34 (1977), pp. 65–95. The last is the most important for my purposes here.

43 For more details see Diego Luis Molinari, "Naturalidad y connaturalización en el derecho de Indias," *Revista Jurídica y de Ciencias Sociales* (Buenos Aires), Year 32 (1915), pp. 698–714. Marriage and legitimacy were poignant questions in Colonial Latin America, particularly in regard to the relationships between conquistadors and Indian women and their issue. Varner discusses the problem as well as the legislation that tried to solve it (*El Inca*, pp. 101–10).

44 Bernal's commentary of López de Gómara's *Historia* is a clear case where the text's existence depends on its polemical relation with another. López de Gómara's text, though criticized, serves as *aide mémoire* for Bernal, and in a very real sense structures it.

45 Bakhtin, of course, is in the back of my mind here. My departure from him lies in my including in this intertextual dialogue a host of texts from outside the literary realm.

46 Santiago Montero Díaz, "La doctrina de la historia en los tratadistas españoles del Siglo de Oro," *Hispania. Revista Española de Historia*, 4 (1941), pp. 3–39. I have also learned a good deal about the relationship between historiography and the *relaciones* from Lewis Hanke's discussion of *La relación de Potosí* in his "La villa imperial de Potosí," *Revista Shell*, no. 42 (1962), pp. 4–10.

47 My information on the *cronista mayor* comes from the documents quoted later and also from Rómulo D. Carbia, *La crónica oficial de las Indias Occidentales. Estudio histórico y crítico de la historiografía mayor de Hispano-América en los siglos XVI a XVIII* (Buenos Aires, Biblioteca de Humanidades, 1934).

48 Marcel Bataillon, "Historiografía oficial de Colón, de Pedro Mártir a Oviedo y Gómara," *Imago Mundi* (Buenos Aires), Year 1, no. 5 (1954), pp. 23–39.

49 Erich Auerbach, "Figura," *Scenes from the Drama of European Literature*, foreword by Paolo Valesio (Minneapolis, University of Minnesota Press, 1984 [1959]), pp. 11–76.

50 Carbia, *La crónica oficial.*

51 Secretaries were not only in charge of correspondence, but were also the keepers of Archives. On the role of secretaries in the Renaissance, see Gary Sanziti, "A Humanist Historian and His Documents: Giovanni Simonetta, Secretary to the Sforzas," *Renaissance Quarterly*, 34, no. 4 (1981), pp. 491–516. In reference to Spain, there is Hayward Kenis-

ton's masterful study *Francisco de los Cobos: Secretary of the Emperor Charles V* (University of Pittsburgh Press, 1958), which gives an excellent account of the role of secretaries within the highest spheres of the Spanish bureaucracy. The *leyes de Indias* were explicit and even prolix in outlining the duties of secretaries, particularly those of the Council of the Indies. The entire *título seis* of Book II is devoted to "los secretarios del Concejo Real," *ibid.*, pp. 277–95.

52 "Códice de leyes y ordenanzas para la gobernación de las Indias, y buen tratamiento y conservación de los indios (año de 1571)," in *Colección de documentos inéditos*, vol. XVI, p. 458.

53 "Real cédula," issued at San Lorenzo el Leal on 5 August 1572, printed in Antonio Caulin, *Historia corográfica, natural y evangélica de la Nueva Andalucía, Provincias de Cumaná, Nueva Barcelona, Guayana y vertientes del río Orinoco* (Caracas, George Corser, 1841[1779]), pp. 3–4.

54 Antonio de Herrera y Tordesillas, *Historia general de los hechos de los castellanos en las islas i tierra firme del mar Océano* (Madrid, Imprenta Real–Juan Flamenco, 1601). Herrera y Tordesillas states in the front matter that, in addition to reading "Los autores impresos y de mano que han escrito cosas particulares de las Indias Occidentales," he has "seguido en esta historia los papeles de la cámara real y reales archivos, los libros, registros y relaciones y otros papeles del Real y Supremo Concejo de las Indias, dejando aparte muchas cosas por no poderse verificar con escrituras auténticas."

55 Carbia, *La crónica oficial*, p. 121.

56 Asensio, "La lengua compañera". Nebrija's work made its way to the New World very soon: "Al año siguiente – 1513 – se entregan al bachiller Suárez, que se trasladaba a la Isla Española 'a mostrar gramática a los hijos de caciques,' veinte ejemplares del *Arte de la langua castellana* de Antonio de Nebrixa ...," José Torre Revello, "Las cartillas para enseñar a leer a los niños en América española," *Thesaurus*, 15 (1960), p. 215. C. Bermúdez Plata prints the *cédula* authorizing the sale of Nebrija's books in the New World in "las obras de Antonio de Nebrija en América," *Anuario de Estudios Americanos*, 3 (1946), pp. 1029–1032.

57 On printing in colonial Latin America see Stephen C. Mohler's "Publishing in Colonial Spanish America; An Overview," *Revista Interamericana de Bibliografía/Inter-American Review of Bibliography*, 28 (1978), pp. 259–73 and Antonio Rodríguez-Buckingham's "The Establishment, Production and Equipment of the First Printing Press in South America," *Harvard Library Bulletin*, 26, no. 3 (1978), pp. 342–54. These are useful updates, but the classic works by José Toribio Medina continue to be the main source of information on the matter. Mohler is particularly useful on laws restricting the printing and circulation of books.

58 The first figure is from Richard L. Kagan, *Students and Society*, p. 21, the second from José Torre Revello, "La enseñanza de las lenguas a los naturales de América," *Thesaurus*, 17 (1962), p. 501. See also by the same author, "Las cartillas . . ." The most recent update of this topic is by Gertrui van Acker, "The Creed in a Nahuatl Schoolbook of 1569," *LIAS* (Amsterdam), 11, no. 1 (1984), pp. 117–36. Van Acker details the teaching methods of the missionaries. Other useful books on education in colonial times are: Francisco Borgia Steck, O.F.M., *El primer colegio de América, Santa Cruz de Tlatelolco. Con un estudio del Códice de Tlatelolco, por R. H. Barlow* (Mexico, Centro de Estudios Franciscanos, 1944); Pedro Henríquez Ureña, "La cultura y las letras coloniales en Santo Domingo" in his *Obra crítica*, ed. Emma Susana Speratti Piñero, prologue by Jorge Luis Borges (Mexico, Fondo de Cultura Económica, 1960), pp. 331–444; Robert Ricard, *La Conquête spirituelle du Méxique. Essai sur l'apostolat et les missionaires des Ordres Mendiants en Nouvelle-Espagne de 1523–24 a 1572* (Paris, Institut d'Ethnologie, 1933). On the teaching of Latin and the classics during the colonial period, see Ignacio Osorio Romero, *Floresta de gramática, política y retórica en Nueva España (1521–1767)* (Mexico, Universidad Nacional Autónoma de Mexico, 1980). There are, of course, numerous works on education in colonial Latin America, particularly those by John Tate Lanning.

59 *Royal Commentaries*, II, p. 1430; *Obras completas*, IV, p. 137.

60 Margarita Zamora, *Language, Authority, and Indigenous History in the Comentarios reales de los incas* (Cambridge University Press, 1988).

61 "Medieval Italian rhetoric was quite a different thing from Ciceronian humanism in the Renaissance. For the most part it was quite mundane and practical activity, called *ars dictaminis* or *ars notaria*. *Ars dictaminis* had to do primarily with letter-writing; its practitioners, called *dictatores*, wrote about the principles of epistolary composition, applied them to specific situations, and made formularies of letters for use on various occasions both by individuals and by town governments or princes. *Ars notaria* was the craft of the *notaio* or notary, whose chief tasks revolved around drawing up documents and contracts; his clients might also be either private individuals or public officials. While the two arts were distinct, they were very closely related. Often the *notaio* and the *dictator* were the same person; writers on *notaria* included precepts of composition in their works, and manuals of *dictamen* sometimes contained notarial forms," Jerrold E. Seigel, *Rhetoric and Philosophy in Renaissance Humanism: The Union of Eloquence and Wisdom: Petrarch to Valla* (Princeton University Press, 1968), pp. 205–6. With the advent of the Renaissance, humanism and notarial rhetoric at the service of the law drew closer, beginning in Bologna. In this and other matters concerning rhetoric and humanism I am guided by Seigel's

excellent account. For the history of notarial arts from Bologna to Castille I am indebted to Juan Antonio Alejandre García, "El arte de la notaría y los formularios del derecho común hasta la ley del notariado," *Revista de Historia del Derecho* (Universidad de Granada), 2, no. 1 (1977–8), Volumen Homenaje al Profesor M. Torres López, pp. 189–220. This article is good on the transition from the *ars dictandi* to the *ars notariae*. Alejandre García says that the latter were late in arriving in Castille, which leads one to suspect that it was Ferdinand's side of the union that brought, from Catalonia, more developed notarial arts. See Z. García Villada, "Formularios de las bibliotecas y archivos de Barcelona siglos x–xv," *Anuari de l'Institut de Estudis Catalans*, 4 (1911–12), pp. 533–52. Alejandre García believes that there were many formularies in Castille during the sixteenth century. A broader and, for my purposes, excessively detailed study of the notarial arts in Spain is found in José Bono, *Historia del derecho notarial español* (Madrid, Junta de Decanos de los Colegios Notariales de España, 1982), 2 vols. Further information and polemics can be found in the papers collected in *Centenario de la Ley del Notariado. Sección Primera. Estudios Históricos*, vol. 1 (Madrid, Junta de Decanos de los Colegios Notariales de España, 1964). About the medieval sources in Castille, I have consulted the classic study by my admired friend Charles B. Faulhaber, *Latin Rhetorical Theory in Thirteenth Century Castille* (Berkeley, University of California Publications in Modern Philology No. 103, 1972). The most remarkable and useful book on rhetoric in colonial Spanish America is Ignacio Osorio Romero's *Floresta de gramática, poética y retórica en Nueva España (1521–1767)*. Examples of formulae may be found in Ludwig Rockinger, ed. *Briefsteller und Formelbucher des elften bis vierzehnten Jahrhunderts* (New York, B. Franklin, 1961 [1863–4]), 2 vols. On Passaggeri, see Rolandino Passaggieri, *Aurora, con las adiciones de Pedro de Unzola*, versión al castellano del Illmo. Señor Don Víctor Vicente Vela, y del Excmo Señor Don Rafael Núñez Lagos (Madrid, Ilustre Colegio Notarial de Madrid – Imprenta Góngora, 1950). The introduction to this beautiful edition has been published separately by its author, Rafael Núñez Lagos, as *El documento medieval y Rolandino (notas de historia)* (Madrid, Imprenta Góngora, 1951).

62 Erich Auerbach, *Mimesis: The Representation of Reality in Western Literature*, tr. Willard R. Trask (Princeton University Press, 1953), pp. 152ff.

63 Julián Calvo, "El primer formulario jurídico publicado en la Nueva España, la *Política de escrituras* de Nicolás de Irolo (1605)," *Revista de la Facultad de Derecho en México*, 1, nos. 3–4 (1951), p. 58. Calvo writes in the introduction: "Con los descubridores llegaron los primeros escribanos a dar fe de los primeros actos de aquéllos. Escribanos de nao, de

armadas, de minas y registros, de concejo trajeron consigo su propia formación jurídica y sus hábitos profesionales, de los que eran parte integrante los antiguos formularios españoles. Virreyes, Audiencias y Cabildos dieron lugar a su vez a nuevas especializaciones del oficio de escribano. Los formularios judiciales y extrajudiciales fueron así no sólo recibidos, sino que llegaron a constituir una pieza fundamental en la vida jurídica de la Nueva España. [...] El repertorio de antiguos formularios españoles [...] fue íntegramente conocido en la Nueva España y usado por notarios y escribanos de todas clases en el ejercicio de su oficio [...] Todos ellos forman parte de la cultura jurídica de la Colonia y en sus bibliotecas y librerías hallaron obligado acomodo" (p. 48). He adds, "Junto a los formularios propiamente dichos – colecciones de fórmulas redactadas para servir como arquetipos o modelos, mas no para su aplicación directa – encontramos en la Nueva España numerosos esqueletos, formas o machotes cuyas cláusulas esenciales se hallan redactadas siguiendo los formularios conocidos y en los que se intercalan los blancos o espacios necesarios para ser rellenados en cada caso de aplicación" (p. 49). In his indispensable "La literatura notarial en España e Hispanoamérica, 1500–1820," *Anuario de Estudios Americanos* (Seville), 18 (1981), Jorge Luján Núñez writes: "La formación de los escribanos era fundamentalmente práctica. Luego de terminada la educación elemental, hacia los catorce años, el aspirante a escribano era colocado como aprendiz en la oficina de un escribano. No había una duración fija, pero generalmente terminaba esta etapa antes de los veinte años" (p. 101). Luján Núñez provides a fairly long list of *formularios* which is known to have circulated in the Indies. He asserts that "las obras sobre práctica notarial tenían una gran venta," to judge by the frequency with which they appeared in ship manifestoes. He draws this information from Irving Leonard's classic *Books of the Brave*. I have also consulted Núñez Luján's more compendious *Los escribanos en las Indias Occidentales y en particular en el Reino de Guatemala* (Guatemala City, Instituto Guatemalteco de Derecho Notarial, 1977).

64 "Y pues vuestra merced escribe se le escriba y relate el caso muy por extenso, pareciome no tomarle por el medio, sino del principio, porque se tenga entera noticia de mi persona."

65 William D. Ilgen was the first to refer to this part as the paternal one in his "La configuración mítica de la historia en los *Comentarios reales* del Inca Garcilaso de la Vega," *Estudios de literatura hispanoamericana en honor de José J. Arrom*, eds. Andrew P. Debicki and Enrique Pupo-Walker (Chapel Hill, North Carolina Studies in the Romance Languages and Literatures, 1974), pp. 37–46.

66 According to Harold V. Livermore, in his Introduction to the trans-

lation of the *Comentarios* being used here the title was changed by the Royal Council, (p. xxvi).

67 *Comentarios*, IV, 66–7; *Commentaries*, II, p. 1,317. Ramón Iglesia writes, concerning Hernando Colón's biography of his father: "El libro de Hernando, en el que se propone refutar todas estas afirmaciones [critical of the Admiral], es, pues, básicamente un alegato en defensa de su padre, escrito de ocasión, obra polémica." *Vida del Almirante don Cristóbal Colón escrita por su hijo don Hernando*, edited with a prologue and notes by Ramón Iglesia (México, Fondo de Cultura Económica, 1947), p. 13.

68 Varner, *El Inca*, is my source here. Daniel G. Castanien's *El Inca Garcilaso de la Vega* (New York, Twayne, 1969) is also a reliable source. It is a curious fact that Garcilaso was also related to the great baroque poet, don Luis de Góngora.

69 "No pude en el Perù escrivir ordenadamente esta Relacion (que no importàra poco para su perfección) porque solo averla allà começado, me huviera de poner en peligro de la vida, con Maestre de Campo de Gonçalo Piçarro, que amenaçaba de matar à qualquiera que escriviese sus hechos, porque ententió que eran mas dignos de la lei de olvido (que los Athenienses llaman Amnistia) que no de memoria, ni perpetuidad." *Historia del descubrimiento y conquista de la provincia del Peru, y de las guerras, y cosas señaladas en ella, acaecidas hasta el vencimiento de Gonzalo Pizarro, y de sus sequaces, que en ella se rebelaron, contra su Magestad*, in *Historiadores primitivos de las Indias Occidentales, que juntó, tradujo en parte, y sacó a la luz, ilustrados con eruditas notas, y copiosos indices, el ilustrisimo señor D. Andrés González Barcia (Madrid, Imprenta de Francisco Martínez Abad, 1749), I, dedicatoria.

70 On the issue of succession regarding *encomiendas* and the legitimacy of claimants there is a fine account in Lesley Byrd Simpson, *The Encomienda in New Spain*, pp. 114–15.

71 Chapter 7 of Varner's book gives an excellent account of the problems of marriage and succession in colonial Peru (see especially pp. 156–7).

72 Technically, however, Sebastián was not among the first conquistadors. On the status of the Incas under Spanish rule see John Howland Rowe, "The Incas Under Spanish Colonial Institutions," *Hispanic American Historical Review*, 37, no. 2 (1957), p. 157, and George Kubler, "The Neo-Inca State (1537–1572)," *Hispanic American Historical Review*, 27, no. 2 (1947), pp. 189–203.

73 Varner, *The Encomienda in New Spain*, pp. 225–6. Max Hernández and Fernando Saba have attempted a psychoanalytic interpretation of the name changes in their "Garcilaso Inca de la Vega, historia de un patronímico" in *Perú: identidad nacional* (Lima, Centro de Estudios para el Desarrollo y la Participación, 1979), pp. 109–21.

74 *Comentarios*, IV, pp. 173–4; *Commentaries*, II, pp. 1485–6.

75 *Comentarios*, IV, p. 173; *Commentaries*, II, p. 1485.

76 The best treatment of rhetoric in Spanish historiography continues to be Santiago Montero Díaz', "La doctrina de la historia en los tratadistas españoles del Siglo de Oro," pp. 3–39. A useful update is Francisco J. Cevallos' "La retórica historiográfica y la aculturación en tres cronistas peruanos," *Revista de Estudios Hispánicos*, 20, no. 3 (1986), pp. 55–66. Cevallos is good on the providentialist design in Garcilaso. But on Garcilaso's debt to Renaissance historiography, the indispensable source is Enrique Pupo-Walker's *Historia, creación y profecía en los textos del Inca Garcilaso de la Vega* (Madrid, José Porrúa Turanzas, 1982).

77 Father Carmelo Sáenz de Santa María notes in the introduction to the Biblioteca de Autores Españoles edition that in the *Historia* Garcilaso makes reference to four dates as the time in which he writes, all between 1611 and 1613. Garcilaso died in 1616.

78 The trial and execution of Tupac Amaru, last of the Inca emperors, is narrated in the last book of the *Comentarios*.

79 I have counted over a hundred instances. The index of the English edition has a half-column entry for Sebastián. That is, of course, a very rough indication of his importance in the book, since there are whole chapters devoted to him.

80 See Enrique Pupo-Walker, *Historia, creación y profecía* and also his *La vocación literaria del pensamiento histórico en América. Desarollo de la prosa de ficción: siglos XVI, XVII, XVIII y XIX* (Madrid, Gredos, 1982).

81 Varner writes the following about Silvestre in the introduction to his superb translation of this book: "But the bulk of his [Garcilaso's] facts came to him orally from the aforementioned noble Spaniard, whom he eventually cornered in Las Posadas. The identity of this man he for some reason leaves shrouded in mystery; nevertheless there is sufficient evidence for speculation, and historians in general have concluded that he was none other than Gonzalo Silvestre, a native of Herrera de Alcántara, whose fine horsemanship and exceptional boldness displayed as he gallops through the pages of *The Florida* threatened at times to eclipse the glory of the Adelantado [Hernando de Soto] himself." *The Florida of the Inca*, tr. John Grier Varner and Jeannette Johnson Varner (Austin, University of Texas Press, 1980), p. xxiii.

82 Of these the most dramatic is the account of Carvajal's life and death, but there are many others, just as anthological as the story of Pedro Serrano, so much discussed by criticism, which appears in the *primera parte*.

83 See Fernando Díaz de Toledo, *Las notas del relator con otras muchas añadidas. Agora nuevamente impresas y de nuevo añadidas las cosas siguientes primeramente. Las notas breves para examinar los escrivanos. Carta de afletar*

navíos. Carta o poliza de seguros. Nuevamente Impressos en Burgos, año 1531. *Relación* in this sense means both a reading of a case to note what is relevent and a summary. Covarrubias in his *Tesoro* describes the *relator* as: "oficio en los consejos o audiencias, el que refiere una causa bien, y fielmente, sin daño de ninguna de las partes," p. 138.

84   Al principio fue el notario,
      polvoriento y sin prisa,
      que inventó el inventario.

From *El diario que a diario*. Translation from *The Daily Daily*, tr. Vera M. Kutzinski (Berkeley, University of California Press, 1989), p. 3.

85 *Comentarios*, III, p. 360; *Commentaries*, II, 1153–4.

86 Francisco López de Gómara, *La historia general de las Indias, con todos los descubrimientos, y cosas notables que han acaescido en ellas dende que se genaron hasta agora* (Antwerp, Casa de Juan Steelsio, 1553). Garcilaso's quotations from López de Gómara, though certainly selective, are accurate.

87 Augustín de Zárate, *Historia del descubrimianto y conquista.*

88 Diego Fernández, *Primera y segunda parte de la historia del Perú*, in Biblioteca de Autores Españoles, vols. 164–5, ed. Juan Pérez de Tudela Bueso (Madrid, Ediciones Atlas, 1963).

89 *Comentarios*, III, p. 360; *Commentaries*, II, 1154.

90 I am using the edition published by Bolsilibros Bedout (Bogota, 1973). There is an English translation by William C. Atkinson: *The Conquest of New Granada* (London, Folio Society, 1961).

91 Susan Herman, "The *Conquista y descubrimiento del Nuevo Reino de Granada*, Otherwise Known as *El Carnero*: the *Corónica*, the *historia*, and the *novela*," unpublished Ph.D dissertation, Yale University, 1978. It was not, in all likelihood, Rodríguez Freyle himself who gave the title *Carnero* to the book, but later commentators. It does not matter, of course; what is important is his conception of the scrap paper of the Bogotá Audiencia as the fictive origin of his manuscript. For an update of the issue the reader should consult Herman's "Toward Solving the Mystery of the Name *Carnero* Placed on Juan Rodríguez Freyle's History," which I have been able to read in manuscript thanks to the generosity of the author.

92 Harry Sieber, *Language and Society in La vida de Lazarillo de Tormes* (Baltimore, The Johns Hopkins University Press, 1978); Javier Herrero, "The Great Icons of the *Lazarillo*: the Bull, the Wine, the Sausage and the Turnip," *Ideologies and Literatures*, I, no. 5 (1978), pp. 3–18; Roberto González Echevarría, "The Life and Adventures of Cipión."

3   A lost world re-discovered: Sarmiento's *Facundo* and E. da Cunha's
                          Os Sertões

1 *Love in the Time of Cholera*, tr. Edith Grossman (New York, Alfred A.
   Knopf, 1988), p. 337.
2 Esteban Echeverría, "El matadero" in *El cuento hispanoamericano. Antolo-
   gía crítico-histórica*, ed. Seymour Menton. 3rd edn (Mexico, Fondo de
   Cultura Económica, 1986), p. 13; "The Slaughterhouse," in *The Borzoi
   Anthology of Latin American Literature*, ed. Emir Rodríguez Monegal (New
   York, Alfred A. Knopf, 1977), vol. I, p. 210. The story was probably
   written about 1838.
3 C. H. Haring, *The Spanish Empire in America* (New York, Harcourt,
   Brace, and World, 1963 [1947]); Jorge I. Domínguez, *Insurrection or
   Loyalty. The Breakdown of the Spanish Empire* (Cambridge, Mass., Harvard
   University Press, 1980); T. Halperin Donghi, *Politics, Economics, and
   Society in Argentina in the Revolutionary Period* (Cambridge University
   Press, 1975).
4 Manuel Moreno Fraginals, *El ingenio: complejo económico-social del azúcar*
   (Havana, Ciencias Sociales, 1978). Translated as *The Sugarmill* (New
   York, Monthly Press, 1976).
5 Karen Anne Stolley, "*El Lazarillo de ciegos caminantes*: un itinerario
   crítico," unpublished Ph.D. dissertation, Yale University, 1985.
6 See "The Case of the Speaking Statue: *Ariel* and the Magisterial
   Rhetoric of the Latin American Essay," in my *The Voice of the Masters:
   Writing and Authority in Modern Latin American Literature* (Austin, University of Texas Press, 1985), pp. 8–32.
7 I have written about the dictator novel in terms that may be relevant to
   the discussion here in "The Dictatorship of Rhetoric/The Rhetoric of
   Dictatorship," *The Voice of the Masters*, pp. 64–85.
8 "Such are all great historical men – whose own particular aims involve
   those large issues which are the will of the World-Spirit. [...] Such
   individuals had no consciousness of the general Idea they were
   unfolding, while prosecuting those aims of theirs; on the contrary, they
   were practical, political men, who had an insight into the requirements
   of the time – *what was ripe for development*. [...] When their object is
   attained they fall like empty hulls from the kernel. They die early, like
   Alexander; they are murdered, like Caesar; transported to St. Helena,
   like Napoleon." G. H. F. Hegel, *The Philosophy of History*, introduction
   by C. J. Friedrich (New York, Dover Publications, 1956), pp. 30–1.
   Napoleon is one of Sarmiento's most frequent references.
9 For the poetic, legal and narrative versions of Quiroga's death see
   Armando Zárate, *Facundo Quiroga, Barranca Yaco: juicios y testimonios*
   (Buenos Aires, Editorial Plus Ultra, 1985).

10 *La Nación*, 3 August 1941.

11 Percy G. Adams, *Travel Literature and the Evolution of the Novel* (Lexington, University of Kentucky Press, 1983), p. 275.

12 Edward J. Goodman, *The Explorers of South America* (New York, The Macmillan Co., 1972). See also his *The Exploration of South America: An Annotated Bibliography* (New York, Garland Publishing Co., 1983). Another charming and entertaining book on the subject is Victor Wolfgang von Hagen's *South America Called Them: Explorations of the Great Naturalists La Condamine, Humboldt, Darwin, Spruce* (New York, Alfred A. Knopf, 1945).

13 Carlos J. Cordero, *Los relatos de los viajeros extranjeros posteriores a la Revolución de Mayo como fuentes de historia argentina. Ensayo de sistematización bibliográfica* (Buenos Aires, Imprenta y Casa Editora "Coni", 1936). Cordero provides reliable bibliographical information on each book, a biographical sketch of the author, and a table at the end with information about the professional expertise, purposes of the trip and nationality of each author. His book gives ample evidence of the importance of these travel books at the time they were written. Their translations were sometimes commissioned by the Argentine government.

14 Mariano Picón Salas, *A Cultural History of Spanish America: From Conquest to Independence*, tr. Irving A. Leonard (Berkeley, University of California Press, 1962 [original edition 1944]), pp. 155–6. There are also the following works on travel literature: Lincoln Bates, "En pos de una civilización perdida: dos audaces viajeros del siglo XIX exploran la América Central," *Américas* (OAS), vol. 38, no. 1 (1986), pp. 34–9; Chester C. Christian Jr., "Hispanic Literature of Exploration," *Exploration* (Journal of the MLA Special Session on the Literature of Exploration and Travel), 1 (1973), pp. 42–6; Evelio A. Echeverría, "La conquista del Chimborazo," *Américas* (OAS), vol. 35, no. 5 (1983), pp. 22–31; Iris H. W. Engstrand, *Spanish Scientists in the New World: The Eighteenth-Century Expeditions* (Seattle, University of Washington Press, 1981). Engstrand's superb book should be read in conjunction with María de los Angeles Calatayud Arinero's *Catálogo de las expediciones y viajes científicos españoles siglos XVIII y XIX* (Madrid, Consejo Superior de Investigaciones Científicas, 1984). Continuing the list: Jean Franco, "Un viaje poco romántico: viajeros británicos hacia [*sic*] Sudamérica: 1818–1828," *Escritura* (Caracas), year 4, no. 7 (1979), pp. 129–41. (This article is one of the few, and perhaps the first in recent times, to notice the importance of travel-accounts as writing; there was no contradiction, however, as Franco assumes, between the economic motivation of the journeys and the romanticism of the writers); C. Harvey Gardiner, "Foreign Travelers' Accounts of Mexico, 1810–

1910," *Américas* (OAS), vol. 8 (1952), pp. 321–51; Gardiner was the editor of a series of travel books called Latin American Travel. His introductions to the following two volumes are important: Francis Bond Head, *Journeys Across the Pampas and Among the Andes* (Carbondale, Southern Illinois University Press, 1967), pp. vii–xxi, and Friedrich Hassaurek, *Four Years Among the Ecuadorians* (Carbondale, Southern Illinois University Press, 1967), pp. vii–xxi; Ronald Hilton, "The Significance of Travel Literature With Special Reference to the Spanish and Portuguese Speaking World," *Hispania* (AATSP), 49 (1966), pp. 836–45; Sonja Karsen, "Charles Marie de la Condamine's Travels in Latin America," *Revista Interamericana de Bibliografía/Inter-American Review of Bibliography*, vol. 36, no. 3 (1986), pp. 315–23; Josefina Palop, "El Brasil visto por los viajeros alemanes," *Revista de Indias*, year 21, no. 83 (1961), pp. 107–27; Mary Louise Pratt, "Scratches on the Face of the Country; What Mr. Barrow Saw in the Land of the Bushmen," *Critical Inquiry*, 12, no. 1 (1985), pp. 119–43, and her "Fieldwork in Common Places" in *Writing Culture. The Poetics and Politics of Ethnography*, ed. James Clifford and George E. Marcus (Berkeley, University of California Press, 1986), pp. 27–50. Though these articles are essentially about Africa, there are useful observations about Latin America. Arthur Robert Steele, *Flowers for the King. The Expedition of Ruiz and Pavón and the Flora of Peru* (Durham, Duke University Press, 1964); Samuel Trifilo, "Nineteenth-century English Travel Books on Argentina: A Revival in Spanish Translation," *Hispania* (AATSP), 41 (1958), pp. 491–6. See also Clifford Geertz, *Works and Lives: The Anthropologist as Author* (Stanford University Press, 1988), pp. 35ff.

None of these works approach the depth and beauty of Paul Carter's *The Road to Botany Bay: An Exploration of Landscape and History* (New York, Alfred A. Knopf, 1988), which is about the founding of Australia. Marshall Sahlins' superb *Islands of History* (University of Chicago Press, 1985), though more relevant to my next chapter, centers on Captain Cook's travels through the South Pacific.

15 There were, in fact, quite a few Spanish travelers also, particularly in the first years of the Bourbon dynasty. See the books by Calatayud, Engstrand, and Steele. At the same time, Spain had been the object of travel accounts since the seventeenth century. The latest update on the topic is by R. Merrit Cox, "Foreign Travelers in Eighteenth-Century Spain," *Studies in Eighteenth-Century Literature and Romanticism in Honor of John Clarkson Dowling*, ed. Douglas and Linda Jane Barnette (Newark, Delaware, Juan de la Cuesta, 1985), pp. 17–26.

16 There were also U.S. travelers who explored what would become, or was already a part of, their country, as is the case of William Bartram (1739–1823). His *Travels Through North & South Carolina, Georgia, East &*

West Florida, The Cherokee Country, The Extensive Territories of the Muscoulges, or Creek Confederacy, and the Country of the Chactaws (1791) "caught the imagination of the Romantics and influenced, among others, Chateaubriand, Coleridge, Emerson, and Wordsworth," according to Edward Hoagland, the General Editor of the Penguin Nature Library, to whom I owe this information, as well as a copy of the 1988 edition of Bartram's *Travels*, with an introduction by James Dickey (New York, Penguin). See also A. Curtis Wilgus, "Viajeros del siglo XIX: Henry Marie Brackenridge," *Américas* (OAS), vol. 24, no. 4 (1972), pp. 31–6. Melville, of course, not only traveled to Latin America, but left in *Benito Cereno* a literary record of that experience. See Estuardo Núñez, "Herman Melville en la América Latina," *Cuadernos Americanos* (Mexico City), 12, no. 9 (1953), pp. 209–21.

17 *El Plantel*, 2nd series (October 1838). On the foundation of the Royal Botanical Garden in Mexico City, see Engstrand, pp. 19–21.

18 The literary tendency known in conventional literary history as *costumbrismo* is not free from the traveler's influential gaze. *Costumbrismo*, or the description of the quaint and unique, often the vestiges of colonial times, is in a way a description from the outside. That outside is the one furnished by a point of view that feels superior because of its knowledge of something else. That something else, if not always science, was at least a method, a way of looking.

19 Trifilo, "Nineteenth-century English Travel Books on Argentina," pp. 491–2.

20 Miguel Rojas-Mix, "Las ideas artístico-científicas de Humboldt y su influencia en los artistas naturalistas que pasan a América a mediados del siglo XIX" in *Nouveau monde et renouveau de l'histoire naturelle*, présentation M. C. Bénassy-Berling (Paris, Service des Publications Université de la Sorbonne Nouvelle, Paris III, 1986), pp. 85–114. Rojas-Mix studies the influence of von Humboldt on painters like the ones mentioned in the next note. Von Humboldt himself was an artist, as Rojas-Mix reports, and even wrote one volume of poetry, *Die Lebenskraft oder der rhodische Genius*, which has been studied, in conjunction with his scientific ideas, by Cedric Hentschel, "Zur Synthese von Literatur und Naturwissenschaft bein Alexander von Humboldt" in *Alexander von Humboldt: Werk und Weltgeltung*, ed. Heinrich Pfeiffer (Munich, Piper, 1969), pp. 31–95.

21 I am guided here by Verlyn Klinkenborg's description of the manuscript in the exquisite catalogue of the exhibition *Sir Francis Drake and the Age of Discovery* (New York, The Pierpont Morgan Library, 1988). It seems that Drake was not only accompanied by artists in his travels, but was himself a deft painter of natural phenomena. On the artists, see Donald C. Cutter and Mercedes Palau de Iglesias, "Malaspina's

Artists," *The Malaspina Expedition* (Santa Fe, Museum of New Mexico Press, 1963); Donald C. Cutter, "Early Spanish Artists on the Northwest Coast," *Pacific Northwest Quarterly*, 54 (1963), pp. 150–7; Iris H. W. Engstrand, *Spanish Scientists in the New World*; Barbara Stafford, "Rude Sublime: The Taste for Nature's Colossi ..." *Gazette des Beaux Arts* (April 1976), pp. 113–26; José Torre Revello, *Los artistas pintores de la expedición Malaspina* (Buenos Aires, Universidad de Buenos Aires – Instituto de Investigaciones Históricas de la Facultad de Filosofía y Letras, 1944). There is an anonymous note on an exhibition of prints from travel books in *Americas* (OAS), 5, no. 10 (1953), pp. 24–6. In Cuba the books by La Plante and Irene Wright became classics. It is quite possible that a book such as Neruda's *Arte de pájaros* was inspired by some of the works of artists contained in travel books. Nicolás Guillén's *El gran Zoo* also appears to follow the same format. Though not normally considered as part of art history, the work produced by these artists was often of superb quality and should occupy the place they deserve in shaping an artistic vision of the New World. Gabriel García Márquez avers that he looked at drawings from travel books when writing *El amor en los tiempos del cólera*, see Raymond Leslie Williams, "The Visual Arts, the Poetization of Space and Writing: An Interview with Gabriel García Márquez," *Publications of the Modern Language Association of America*, 104 (1989), pp. 131–41.

22 Rob Rachowiecki writes, in an article relating a journey to Mount Roraima, in the area of Guayana visited by Carpentier when he was writing *Los pasos perdidos*: "The plateau summits of the *tepuís* are separated from their surroundings by almost impenetrable cliffs, and they harbor a flora and fauna that is not only distinct from the lowlands, but is different from mountain to mountain. Indeed, so remote are the summits that 19th century scientists debated the possibility of prehistoric dinosaurs surviving atop the isolated massifs. This idea was popularized by Sir Arthur Conan Doyle's science fiction novel, *The Lost World*, published in 1912. The book is said to have been based on Roraima and the 'lost world' tag has stuck to this day." "The Lost World of Venezuela," *Américas* (OAS) 4, no. 5 (1988), p. 46.

23 I am guided here, above all, by Michel Foucault's *Les Mots et les choses* (Paris, Gallimard, 1966) and Arthur O. Lovejoy, *The Great Chain of Being* (Cambridge, Mass., Harvard University Press, 1936).

24 Antonello Gerbi, *Nature in the New World from Christopher Columbus to Gonzalo Fernández de Oviedo*, tr. Jeremy Moyle (University of Pittsburgh Press, 1985 [original 1975]).

25 "Überhaupt ist mit dem neuen Leben, das einem nachdenkenden Menschen die Betrachtung eines neuen Landes gewärt, nichts zu vergleichen. Ob ich gleich noch immer derselbe bin, so mein'ich, bis

aufs innerste Knochenmark verändert zu sein." In *Italienische Reise, Goethes Werke* (Hamburg, Christian Wegner Verlag, 1950 [1967]), vol. XII, p. 146. I have learned much about this "grand tour" from a paper by my dear friend Giuseppe Mazzotta, which centers on W. H. Auden's poem "Good-bye to the Mezzogiorno," and reviews the works of travelers through Calabria in the nineteenth century. The paper is entitled "Travelling South" and is unpublished.

26 Larra casts a critical view on his own country in his famous essay "La diligencia," which is a kind of travel-account of his journeys through the provinces of Spain. He had spent a good deal of time in France and looked upon Spain from the perspective of a foreigner. Fernán Caballero, in her novel *La gaviota* (Madrid, Espasa Calpe, 1960 [first edition 1849]), includes a footnote to justify a lengthy description of a convent. Her reason is that such a description "tendría interés para los extranjeros que no conocen nuestros bellos y magnos edificios religiosos" (p. 33). In a sense her book, along with much of *costumbrismo* in both Spain and Spanish America, appears as a travelogue for foreigners and city dwellers.

27 Villaverde's book is modeled after those of the European travelers and narrates an experience that in some ways anticipates the plot of Carpentier's *Los pasos perdidos*. See Antonio Benítez Rojo's chapter in *La isla que se repite* (Hanover, New Hampshire, Ediciones del Norte, 1989). There is a modern edition of Villaverde's book (Havana, Editorial Letras Cubanas, 1981).

The most advanced work on the Countess is Adriana Méndez Rodenas' "A Journey to the (Literary) Source: The Invention of Origins in Merlín's *Viaje a La Habana*," which I have read in manuscript thanks to the kindness of the author.

28 Thomas Belt, *The Naturalist in Nicaragua*, with a foreword by Daniel H. Janzen (University of Chicago Press, 1985), p. 147. The first edition is from 1874. Belt was an English engineer whose work was much admired by Darwin.

29 Goodman, *The Explorers of South America*, p. 191.

30 George Gaylord Sympson, *Splendid Isolation: The Curious History of South American Mammals* (New Haven, Yale University Press, 1980) and *Discoverers of the Lost World: An Account of Some of Those Who Brought Back to Life South American Mammals Long Buried in the Abyss of Time* (New Haven, Yale University Press, 1984). Sarmiento, who seems to have had time to read everything, knew the work of some of these paleontologists well, above all that of Argentine Francisco J. Muñiz, whose biography he wrote. It is now collected in volume XLIII of *Obras de Domingo F. Sarmiento* (Buenos Aires, Imprenta y Litografía Mariano Moreno, 1900).

31 *Voyage aux régions équinoxiales Nouveau Continent, fait en 1799, 1800, 1801,*

1802, 1803 et 1804, par Al. de Humbold et A. Bonpland (Paris, Librarie Grecque-Latine-Allemande, 1816), II, p. 303.

32 I quote from *Facundo o civilización y barbarie en las pampas argentinas* fijación del texto, prólogo y apéndices de Raúl Moglia, xilografías de Nicasio (Buenos Aires, Ediciones Peuser, 1955). The translation in this case is mine. Unless otherwise indicated translations are from *Life in the Argentine Republic in the Days of the Tyrants; or Civilization and Barbarism,* with a biographical sketch of the author by Mrs. Horace Mann. First American from the third Spanish edition, New York, 1868 [Reprint 1960 Hafner Library of Classics].

33 I have used C. Harvey Gardiner's edition, (Carbondale, Southern Illinois University Press, 1967). The original is from 1826.

34 Edward W. Said, *Orientalism* (New York, Vintage Books, 1979).

35 I take the information and the quote from Mary Sayre Haverstock, "The Cosmos Recaptured," *Américas* (OAS), vol. 35, no. 1 (1983), p. 41.

36 Amado Alonso, *Estudios lingüísticos: temas hispanoamericanos,* 3rd edn (Madrid, Gredos, 1976), p. 55.

37 "Porque las estirpes condenadas a cien años de soledad no tenían una segunda oportunidad sobre la tierra." (Buenos Aires, Sudamericana, 1967), p. 351; *One Hundred Years of Solitude,* tr. Gregory Rabassa (New York, Harper and Row, 1970), p. 422.

38 Euclides da Cunha, *Os Sertões,* edição crítica por Walnice Nogueira Galvão (São Paulo, Editora Brasiliense, S.A., 1985), p. 85; *Rebellion in the Backlands,* tr. Samuel Putnam (University of Chicago Press, 1944), p. xxix.

39 Following the custom of Brazilian critics, I will refer to Euclides da Cunha always as Euclides.

40 I have learned much from Leopoldo Bernucci's authoritative "Além do real, aquém do imaginário: D. F. Sarmiento e E. da Cunha," unpublished manuscript. I wish to thank my dear colleague for allowing me to read this piece, and for all his expert advice on Euclides da Cunha.

41 Carpentier devoted one of his columns in *El Nacional* (Caracas), to Euclides' book, calling it "un gran libro americano." "*Los sertones,*" 8 September 1951, p. 12. Borges alludes to *Os Sertões* in "Tres versiones de Judas," *Ficciones, Obras completas* (Buenos Aires, Emecé, 1974), p. 516n. Some of the success Euclides has had in Latin America was in part due to the rewritings of his book in the works of the Brazilian novelists of the Northeast, who were widely translated into Spanish, and, lately, needless to say, in the brilliant counterpoint offered by João Guimarães Rosa's *Grande sertão, veredas.* But, in general terms, his impact on Latin America comes from the fact that he furthered the

tradition of Sarmiento, which was taken up later by writers like Rómulo Gallegos and others, and continues to the present with critics of Sarmiento and Rodó like Roberto Fernández Retamar. Pedro Henríquez Ureña writes, in his influential *Las corrientes literarias en la América hispánica*, that *Os Sertões* is, in the opinion of many, "la más grande obra escrita hasta la fecha en el Brasil" (Mexico, Fondo de Cultura Económica, 1949). Published in the original English in 1944, the book contains the Eliot Norton lectures at Harvard for the academic year 1940–1. Guimarães Rosa's superb novel would today compete for the honor of the best work ever written in Brazil.

On the relationship between Euclides and Vargas Llosa see Sara Castro-Klarén's two articles, "Locura y dolor: la elaboración de la historia en *Os Sertões* y *La guerra del fin del mundo*," *Revista de Crítica Literaria Latinoamericana*, year 10, no. 20 (1984), pp. 207–31; "*Santos* and *Cangaçeiros*: Inscription Without Discourse in *Os Sertões* and *La guerra del fin del mundo*," *Modern Language Notes*, 101, no. 2 (1986), pp. 366–88. The most reliable and illuminating work on the topic, however, is Leopoldo Bernucci's *Historia de un malentendido (un estudio transtextual de La guerra del fin del mundo de Mario Vargas Llosa)*, University of Texas Studies in Contemporary Spanish-American Fiction, vol. 5 (New York, Peter Lang, 1989).

42 This aberrancy explains Euclides' stylistic "bad taste and errors." Antonio Candido refers to Euclides' style as "brillante, difuso, no pocas veces del mal gusto, pero personal." *Introducción a la literatura de Brasil* (Caracas, Monte Avila, 1968), p. 56.

43 For biographical information I am relying on the material furnished by Putnam in his translation as well as that provided by Galvão in her critical edition.

44 Nancy Stepan, *Beginnings of Brazilian Science: Oswaldo Cruz, Medical Research and Policy, 1890–1920* (New York, Science History Publications, 1976), pp. 26–7.

45 I am not saying that Brazil was a leader in the advancement of scientific research, but merely stating that there was a commitment to science that was stronger than in other Latin American countries. Stepan (*ibid.*) emphasizes that Brazil was in a dependent situation *vis-à-vis* European countries in terms of scientific development.

46 Euclides da Cunha, *Canudos (diario de uma expedição)*, introduction by Gilberto Freyre (Rio de Janeiro, José Olympio, 1939).

47 Unfortunately Galvão's otherwise excellent edition does not provide footnotes detailing Euclides' debt to science, nor an index of names. Putnam's translation, however, does have such an index, and some notes on the naturalists.

48 *Historia de un malentendido*, p. 209.

49 On this topic see Daniel R. Headrick's illuminating *The Tools of Empire: Technology and European Imperialism in the Nineteenth Century* (New York, Oxford University Press, 1981).

50 In his Glossary Putnam writes: "this word, originally meaning a ruffian, in Cunha comes to be practically synonymous with *sertanejo*, or inhabitant of the backlands."

51 Putnam often translates *expressivos* as "significant," which, I suppose, is admissible, though it undermines Euclides' effort to "translate" the rhetoric of nature into tropes and figures.

52 I have considerably changed the translations, which were off the mark in Putnam's version.

4 The novel as myth and archive: ruins and relics of Tlön

1   O esa voz no es de esa piel
    o esa piel no es de esa voz.

2 John E. Englekirk, "Doña Bárbara, Legend of the Llano," *Hispania*, 31 (1948), pp. 259–70.

3 The best account of the elections is found in John D. Martz, *Acción democrática: Evolution of a Modern Political Party in Venezuela* (Princeton University Press, 1966), pp. 49–106. Gallegos' speeches and articles from the period are contained in his *Una posición en la vida, 1909–1947* (Caracas, Ediciones Centauro, 1977). A remarkable account of the festivities at Gallegos' inauguration, which consisted mainly of a Pan-Venezuelan display of folklore (mainly music and dance), has recently been reissued. See Juan Marinello, "Días de Venezuela," *Casa de las Américas*, no. 170 (1988), pp. 55–63.

4 Englekirk, "Doña Bárbara," pp. 264–5.

5 Ramón Pané, *Relación acerca de las antigüedades de los indios: el primer tratado escrito en América*, nueva versión con notas, mapa y apéndices por José Juan Arrom (Mexico, Siglo XXI Editores, 1974).

6 *Colección de documentos inéditos, relativos al descubrimiento, conquista y organización de las antiguas posesiones españolas, de América y Oceanía sacados de los archivos del reino, y muy especialmente del de las Indias* (Madrid, Imprenta de José María Pérez, 1881), p. 458. For more details on the *cronista mayor* see chapter two of this book.

7 Fray Toribio de Motolinía, *Historia de los indios de la Nueva España*, ed. Georges Baudot (Madrid, Castalia, 1985). The best general work on this subject continues to be Robert Ricard, *The Spiritual Conquest of Mexico. An Essay on the Apostolate and Evangelizing Methods of the Mendicant Orders in New Spain: 1523–1572*, tr. Lesley Byrd Simpson (Berkeley, University of California Press, 1966 [original French edition 1933]). See chapter two in particular, "Ethnographic and Linguistic Training of the Missionaries," pp. 39–60.

8 Lewis Hanke, *The Spanish Struggle for Justice in the Conquest of America* (Philadelphia, University of Pennsylvania Press, 1949). On the turmoil caused in the New World by the New Laws, see Lesley Byrd Simpson, *The Encomienda in New Spain. The Beginnings of Spanish Mexico* (Berkeley, University of California Press, 1966 [1929]), and, of course, Garcilaso de la Vega el Inca's *Comentarios reales*, Part two.

9 On Cabeza de Vaca, see the new, forthcoming edition by Enrique Pupo-Walker. The *Naufragios*, of course, have been claimed by both anthropology and literature. Claire Martin has written important pages on the relationship between Cabeza de Vaca's report and Alejo Carpentier's *Los pasos perdidos* in her "Alejo Carpentier y las crónicas de Indias: orígenes de una escritura americana," unpublished Ph.D. dissertation, Yale University 1988.

10 George W. Stocking, Jr., *Victorian Anthropology* (New York, The Free Press, 1987).

11 *Journeys Across the Pampas and Among the Andes*, ed. C. Harvey Gardiner (Carbondale, Southern Illinois University Press, 1967 [1826 original]). Expeditions like the one led by Malaspina discussed in the previous chapter also described the natives.

12 Charles Rearick, *Pleasures of the Belle Epoque: Entertainment and Festivity in Turn-of-the-Century France* (New Haven, Yale University Press, 1985), p. 138.

13 Paintings and drawings of non-European peoples abounded in both European and Latin American books. Some foreign and domestic painters began to pay attention to Indians and Blacks, though often their images are heavily influenced by classical conceptions of the body, apparel, and gestures. For a good collection of such images see *México ilustrado por Europa del Renacimiento al Romanticismo*, the catalogue of an exhibition presented at the Palacio de Iturbide, Mexico City, from 24 March to 30 June 1983.

14 Nancy Stepan, *The Idea of Race in Science: Great Britain 1800–1960* (New Haven, Archon Books, 1982), and, by the same author, *Beginnings of Brazilian Science: Oswaldo Cruz, Medical Research and Policy, 1890–1920* (New York, Science History Publications, 1976). See also D. F. Sarmiento's *Conflicto y armonías de las razas en América* (Buenos Aires, 1883), and Martin S. Stabb's "El continente enfermo y sus diagnosticadores" in his *América Latina en busca de una identidad* (Caracas, Monte Avila, 1969). Racism in various guises was part and parcel of "Victorian Anthropology" (see Stocking, *Victorian Anthropology*).

15 For instance, José Antonio Saco's *Historia de la esclavitud* and Richard Madden's report on slavery in Cuba, which contained some literary works by the members of Domingo del Monte's literary cenacle.

16 See Stabb's "La rebelión contra el cientificismo" in his *América Latina en busca de una identidad*, pp. 55–90.

17 Stocking, *Victorian Anthropology*, p. 287.

18 Talal Asad, ed. *Anthropology and the Colonial Encounter* (New York, Humanities Press, 1973).

19 It is a well-known fact that André Breton had in his Paris apartment many artifacts from Africa and other regions studied by anthropologists. The relationship of modern painting, particularly Picasso's, to ethnography is also common knowledge. *Les Demoiselles d'Avignon* was based on some African masks that Picasso saw at the Trocadero Museum. The best account of this commingling of anthropology and the avant-garde is Roger Shattuck's *The Banquet Years: The Origins of the Avant-Garde in France, 1885 to World War I*, rev. ed. (New York, Vintage Books, 1968).

20 Clifford Geertz, *Works and Lives. The Anthropologist as Author* (Stanford University Press, 1988); James Clifford and George E. Marcus, *Writing Culture: The Poetics and Politics of Ethnography* (Berkeley, University of California Press, 1982); James Clifford, *The Predicament of Culture: Twentieth-Century Ethnography, Literature and Art* (Cambridge, Mass., Harvard University Press, 1988). For an excellent article about anthropology and literature in Africa, with many insights relevant to Latin America, see Christopher L. Miller, "Theories of Africans: The Question of Literary Anthropology," *Critical Inquiry*, 13, no. 1 (1986), pp. 120–39. Miller develops more fully these ideas in his *Blank Darkness: Africanist Discourse in French* (University of Chicago Press, 1985). Here Miller sees an escape from Western ethnological discourse in African literature through a process of assimilation and distortion that is similar to my version of Latin American narrative. There is a keen review of Miller in Manthia Diawara's "The Other('s) Archivist," *Diacritics* 18, no. 1 (1988), pp. 66–74. For an insightful critique of relativism in anthropology in the context of current debates, see S. P. Mohanty's "Us and Them: On the Philosophical Bases of Political Criticism," *The Yale Journal of Criticism*, 2, no. 2 (1989), pp. 1–31.
    A fruitful polemic has arisen between the group of revisionist anthropologists mentioned above, and one of their precursors, Edward W. Said, whose *Orientalism* is a landmark study of imperial representations of the other. James Clifford writes that what Said opposes to the reifying glance of the anthropologist is a form of "old-fashioned existential realism" (p. 259). Said replies in his wide-ranging "Representing the Colonized: Anthropology's Interlocutors," *Critical Inquiry*, 15, no. 2 (1989), pp. 205–25. His somewhat predictable charge is that essentially the revisionists' projects are an aesthetic response to the crisis. There is a certain anachronism in Said's perception of the "Third World," both in concept and terminology (which sounds very much a product of the U.S. 1960s), but more alarmingly an ahistorical

approach to imperialism, which he appears to view as being the same everywhere and at any time. Aside from the distortions this constitutive idealization may produce, by moving far beyond his areas of competence Said falls into reifying clichés and misrepresentations of his own, such as referring to "Central and Latin America" (p. 215). But, beyond these quibbles, the problem with Said, which Clifford identifies with his comment about existentialism (one should say Sartreanism), is to assume that an "aesthetic" response cannot be subversive, or that Said's own constructs are more effectual as actual agents of change. His call to do away with anthropology is one that could be considered – and has been in Latin America, as I explain here – but I would hesitate to encourage anyone to dispense with Borges, García Márquez, Carpentier, Vargas Llosa and others. I doubt that many in Latin America would.

21 *Works and Lives*, p. 71.
22 Jesús Silva Herzog, *Breve historia de la Revolución Mexicana*, 2nd edn. (Mexico, Fondo de Cultura Económica, 1962). See also Alejandro D. Marroquín, *Balance del indigenismo. Informe sobre la política indigenista en América* (Mexico, Instituto Indigenista Interamericano, 1972). The most remarkable monument to this movement is, of course, the splendid Museo Nacional de Antropología, in whose entrance one reads the following inscription, which leads to a visual display of the history of anthropology and of pre-Hispanic Mexican cultures: "El hombre creador de la cultura ha dejado sus huellas en todos los lugares por donde ha pasado. La antropología, ciencia del hombre que investiga e interpreta esas huellas y a los grupos humanos contemporáneos, nos enseña la evolución biológica del hombre, sus características y su lucha por el dominio de la naturaleza. Las cuatro ramas de esa ciencia única; antropología física, lingüística, arqueología y etnología nos dicen que de diferentes modos, todos los hombres tienen la misma capacidad para enfrentarse a la naturaleza, que todas las razas son iguales, que todas las culturas son respetables y que todos los pueblos pueden vivir en paz." It is worthwhile reading the *Guía oficial* of the Museum to understand how deeply ingrained anthropology is in contemporary Mexican official culture.
23 In a chapter entitled "El momento presente, 1920–1945," Pedro Henríquez Ureña writes: "Después de planteles de excepcional importancia, como el Museo Nacional de México, el Instituto de Filología de Buenos Aires y el Instituto Histórico y Geográfico del Brasil, se establecen muchos nuevos; tales, el Museo de Antropología en Lima; el Instituto Nacional de Antropología, en México; el Laboratorio de Ciencias Biológicas, en Montevideo." *Historia de la cultura en la América Hispánica* (Mexico, Fondo de Cultura Económica, 1964 [1967]),

pp. 133-4. The very concept of culture in the title of this book is a reflection of the impact of anthropology on Latin American literature in general. On the Museum of Anthropology in Mexico, see Ignacio Bernal, Román Piña-Chan and Fernando Cámara Barbachano, *The Mexican National Museum of Anthropology* (London, Thames and Hudson, 1968). Another important institution was the Instituto Panamericano de Geografía e Historia, founded in Havana in 1929, as reported in Pánfilo D. Camacho, "Cuba y la creación del Instituto Panamericano de Geografía e Historia," *Revista Bimestre Cubana* (Havana), 63, nos. 1, 2, 3 (1949), pp. 223-30.

24 The most recent update on the history of *Mexican indigenismo* is found in Frances R. Dorward, "The Evolution of Mexican *indigenista* Literature in the Twentieth Century," *Revista Interamericana de Bibliografía/Inter-American Review of Bibliography*, 37, no. 2 (1987), pp. 145-59. For Peru, the best work is Efraín Kristal's sedulous *The Andes Viewed from the City: Literary and Political Discourse on the Indian in Peru 1848-1930* (New York, Peter Lang, 1987). Kristal lucidly plots the relationship of political movements to the representation of the Indian in Peruvian literature, discarding accuracy as a criterion for success, and underlining the ideological nature of each construct.

25 See Ortiz's speech inaugurating the Sociedad in *Estudios Afrocubanos* (Havana), 1, no. 1 (1937), pp. 3-6.

26 A whole essayistic tradition concerned with the issue of cultural identity and profoundly influenced by anthropology began in the Latin America of the twenties and lasted until the fifties, roughly from Mariátegui to Paz and Fernández Retamar. Some of these writers, like Paz, wrote about anthropology, as his *Lévi-Strauss o el festín de Esopo* (Mexico, Joaquin Mortiz, 1968) attests. Others, like Arguedas and Roa Bastos wrote anthropology. I have dealt with the essay in my *The Voice of the Masters: Writing and Authority in Modern Latin American Literature* (Austin, The University of Texas Press, 1985).

27 Carlos J. Alonso, *The Spanish American Regional Novel: Modernity and Autochthony* (Cambridge University Press, 1989), p. 6. Alonso holds that the *novela de la tierra* issues out of a sense of crisis, a crisis about the status of Latin American culture and modernity. He centers that crisis on two events, the Spanish American War and the Centenary celebrations around 1910, which made Latin Americans take stock of the predicament of their countries. He also underlines the importance of Pan-Americanism as a policy, which forced Latin Americans to compare their cultures to that of the United States. The desire to posit the autochthonous issues from these stimuli.

28 "Ethnographers need to convince us [...] not merely that they themselves have truly 'been there,' but that had we been there we should

have seen what they saw, felt what they felt, concluded what they concluded," *Works and Lives*, p. 16.

29 *La música en Cuba* (Mexico, Fondo de Cultura Económica, 1946), p. 236.

30 *¡Ecué-Yamba-O!* (Madrid, Editorial España, 1933), pp. 173–90.

31 "Guimarães Rosa, born in Codisburgo in 1908, belonged to an old patrician family. He studied medicine in Belo Horizonte, and after graduation, set up his practice in a rural area. It has been said that quite frequently he would ask for a story in lieu of payment." Emir Rodríguez Monegal, *The Borzoi Anthology of Latin American Literature* (New York, Alfred A. Knopf, 1977), II, p. 677.

32 See my "*Doña Bárbara* writes the Plain" in *The Voice of the Masters: Writing and Authority in Modern Latin American Literature* (Austin, University of Texas Press, 1985), pp. 33–63.

33 René Prieto, "The New American Idiom of Miguel Angel Asturias," *Hispanic Review*, 567 (1988), pp. 191–2. This is, of course, the so-called "magical realism" or "lo real maravilloso americano," of which I have written in *Alejo Carpentier: The Pilgrim at Home* (Ithaca, Cornell University Press). Michael Taussing has also noted to what degree "magical realism" was a mediated version of the Other's – that is the Indian or the Black – cultural practices. *Shamanism: A Study in Colonialism, and Terror and the Wild Man Healing* (University of Chicago Press, 1987), p. 201.

34 John V. Murra, "Introduction," José María Arguedas, *Deep Rivers*, tr. Frances Horning Barraclough, Afterword by Mario Vargas Llosa (Austin, University of Texas Press, 1978), p. xi. Fernando Alegría writes, perceptively, about *Los ríos profundos*: "Una impresión inicial pudiera confundir su lenguaje [Arguedas'] con el de un reconcentrado etnólogo y arqueólogo. Y, de pronto, eso que podría ser un catálogo de iglesias, plazas, muros, artesanos y ruinas, se pone a vivir independientemente ..." *Nueva historia de la novela hispanoamericana* (Hanover, New Hampshire, Ediciones del Norte, 1986), p. 263.

35 Jorge Luis Borges, *Ficciones* (Buenos Aires, Emecé, 1966 [1944]), p. 103. The translation is from *Ficciones*, ed. Anthony Kerrigan (New York, Grove Press, 1962), p. 94. It was probably Borges himself who gave a Wordsworthian turn to the English version.

36 See Emir Rodríguez Monegal, "Borges and Politics," *Diacritics*, 8, no. 4 (1978), pp. 55–69.

37 Borges also wrote a review of Frazer's *The Fear of the Dead in Primitive Religion*, now collected in *Textos cautivos: ensayos y reseñas en "El hogar" (1936-1939)*, ed. Enrique Sacerio Garí and Emir Rodríguez Monegal (Barcelona, Tusquets, 1986), pp. 60–1. Another reader of Frazer was José Lezama Lima, *Las eras imaginarias* (Madrid, Fundamentos, 1971), p. 26.

38 James E. Irby, "Borges and the Idea of Utopia," *Books Abroad*, 45, no. 3 (1971), pp. 411–19.

39 "Barnet no ha pretendido en forma alguna hacer literatura, aunque haya logrado una de las más acabadas obras literarias cubanas de este siglo." Review of *Biografía de un cimarrón*, in *Casa de las Américas*, no. 40 (1967), p. 132.

40 William Luis, *Literary Bondage: Slavery in Cuban Narrative* (Austin, University of Texas Press, 1990).

41 Miguel Barnet, *Biografía de un cimarrón* (Havana, Instituto de Etnología y Folklore, 1966). The book has been translated into English as *The Autobiography of a Runaway Slave* (London, The Bodley Head, 1969), but the translation is so poor that I have decided to furnish my own.

42 See the excellent collection of essays edited by Richard Price, *Maroon Societies: Rebel Communities in the Americas* (New York, Anchor Books, 1973).

43 Fernando Ortiz, *Hampa Afro-cubana. Los negros brujos. Apuntes para un estudio de etnología criminal*, prologue by Alberto N. Pamies (Miami, Ediciones Universal, 1973 [1906]).

44 *The Archaeology of Knowledge and the Discourse on Language*, tr. A. M. Sheridan Smith (New York, Pantheon Books, 1972), p. 130.

45 Of Bakhtin I am referring, of course, to both *The Dialogic Imagination*, ed. Michael Holquist (Austin, University of Texas Press, 1981) and *Rabelais and His World*, tr. Hélène Iswolsky (Bloomington, Indiana University Press, 1984). In the case of Foucault I have in mind both *The Archaeology of Knowledge and the Discourse on Language* and *Language, Countermemory, Practice*, ed. Donald F. Bouchard (Ithaca, Cornell University Press, 1977).

46 Gabriel García Márquez, *Crónica de una muerte anunciada* (Bogotá, Editorial La Oveja Negra, 1981), p. 129: *Chronicle of a Death Foretold*, tr. Gregory Rabassa (New York, Alfred A. Knopf, 1983), pp. 98–9.

47 Actually, *mar de leva* can also be interpreted as the opposite of periodicity; that is, it can mean, also significantly, accident, since it really means a swelling up of the sea caused by a storm that took place far away. It seems to me that the interpretation can hover between these two poles, both furnished by the naturalists' discourse, because in Spanish the meaning of the phrase is changing from its original sense of unique upheaval to refer to the tides.

48 The *Diccionario* of the Real Academia says: "For. [forense] Conjunto de actuaciones encaminadas a preparar el juicio criminal, haciendo constar la perpetración de los delitos con las circunstancias que puedan influir en su calificación, determinar la culpabilidad y prevenir el castigo de los delincuentes."

49 The *arca* appears in the second chapter of *Lazarillo de Tormes*.

50 Mario Vargas Llosa, *García Márquez: historia de un deicidio* (Barcelona, Barral Editores, 1971), p. 542. Emir Rodríguez Monegal attributes to the influence of James Joyce's *Ulysses* the totalizing desire of what he calls the new Latin American novel, *El Boom de la novela latinoamericana* (Caracas, Editorial Tiempo Nuevo, 1972), p. 88. It would be foolish to deny the powerful influence of Joyce on Latin American novelists who, like the Irish master, wrote from a strategic marginal position, but from our point of view Joyce also falls within the anthropological mediation. Carlos Fuentes, writing about Vargas Llosa's *La casa verde* finds that the totalization occurs when language in the present re-activates all of language in the past, the *parole* rearranges *langue*, in his Saussurian terminology. *La nueva novela hispanoamericana* (Mexico, Joaquín Mortiz, 1969), pp. 35–48. See also: Robert Brody, "Mario Vargas Llosa and the Totalizing Impulse," *Texas Studies in Literature and Language*, 19, no. 4 (1977), pp. 514–21, and Luis Alfonso Díez, *Mario Vargas Llosa's Pursuit of the Total Novel* (Cuernavaca, CIODC, Serie Cuadernos, No. 2, 1970).

51 I quote from the bilingual edition, tr. Lysander Kemp (New York, Farrar, Strauss and Giroux, 1975), pp. 20–21 and 54–55.

52 This ghostly parade is what links archival fictions to the Neo-baroque. See my *La ruta de Severo Sarduy* (Hanover, New Hampshire, Ediciones del Norte, 1987).

53 Another archival fiction is Cortázar's *Libro de Manuel*, in which an album of newspaper clippings is being composed for when the child – Manuel – grows up.

54 I have written elsewhere about what is being called the post-Boom, suggesting that there is a novel beyond those by the masters here discussed that would not be determined by the nostalgia of origins or by the longing for uniqueness and identity. I (and others) have suggested that this kind of novel would be more plot-oriented and hence more conventional in narrative structure. Only Sarduy, Manuel Puig, the remaining Boom authors García Márquez, Vargas Llosa and very few others appear to be writing this kind of fiction, however, while others have taken advantage of the situation to return to a kind of naive realism that plunges them back into problematic of the *novela de la tierra* without the powerful, layered, critical apparatus that the great novels of the 1930s displayed. See my *La ruta de Severo Sarduy*, and Donald Shaw's lucid "Toward a Description of the Post-Boom," *Bulletin of Hispanic Studies*, 66 (1989), pp. 87–94.

Bibliography

This bibliography contains works that I consider crucial to the book's central theme and to the major topics discussed. It includes works that are cited or mentioned in the text and notes as well as others that are not. The bibliography attempts to give the range of my reading and research. For more detailed information the reader is invited to consult the notes and index.

Abrams, M. H. *Natural Supernaturalism: Tradition and Revolution in Romantic Literature*. New York, W. W. Norton, 1971.

Adams, Percy G. *Travel Literature and the Evolution of the Novel*. Lexington, Ky., University of Kentucky Press, 1983.

Adorno, Rolena. *Guaman Poma. Writing and Resistance in Colonial Peru*. Austin, University of Texas Press, 1986.

Alden, John, ed., with the assistance of Dennis C. Landis. *European Americana: A Chronological Guide to Works Printed in Europe Relating to the Americas 1493–1750*. Providence, John Carter Brown Library. New York, Readex Books, A Division of the Readex Microprint Corporation, 1980, vol. 1.

Alegría, Fernando. *Nueva historia de la novela hispanoamericana*. Hanover, New Hampshire, Ediciones del Norte, 1986.

Alejandre García, Juan Antonio. "El arte de la notaría y los formularios del derecho común hasta la ley del notariado," *Revista de Historia del Derecho* (Universidad de Granada), 2, no. 1 (1977–8), Volumen Homenaje al Profesor M. Torres López, pp. 189–220.

Alonso, Amado. *Estudios lingüísticos: temas hispanoamericanos*. 3rd edn. Madrid, Gredos, 1976.

Alonso, Carlos J. *The Spanish American Regional Novel: Modernity and Autochthony*. Cambridge University Press, 1989.

Arguedas, José María. *Los ríos profundos*. Santiago, Chile, Editorial Universitaria, 1967 [1958]; *Deep Rivers*, tr. Frances Horning Barraclough, "Introduction" by John V. Murra, "Afterword" by Mario Vargas Llosa. Austin, University of Texas Press, 1978.

Asad, Talal, ed. *Anthropology and the Colonial Encounter*. New York, Humanities Press, 1973.

Asensio, Eugenio. "La lengua compañera del Imperio (a): historia de una idea de Nebrija en España y Portugal," *Nueva Revista de Filología Española*, 43, cuadernos 3–4 (1960), pp. 399–413.

Auerbach, Erich. *Mimesis: The Representation of Reality in Western Literature*, tr. Willard R. Trask. Princeton University Press, 1953.

"Figura," *Scenes from the Drama of European Literature*, foreword by Paolo Valesio. Minneapolis, University of Minnesota Press, 1984 [1959], pp. 11–76.

Bakhtin, M. M. *The Dialogic Imagination*, ed. Michael Holquist. Austin, University of Texas Press, 1981.

Rabelais and His World, tr. Hélène Iswolsky, prologue, Michal Holquist. Bloomington, Indiana University Press, 1984.

Barnet, Miguel. *Biografía de un cimarrón*. Havana, Instituto de Etnología y Folklore, 1966.

Bartram, William. *Travels Through North & South Carolina, Georgia, East & West Florida, The Cherokee Country, The Extensive Territories of the Muscoulges, or Creek Confederacy, and the Country of the Chactaws*, with an introduction by James Dickey. New York, Penguin, 1988.

Bataillon, Marcel. "Historiografía oficial de Colón de Pedro Mártir a Oviedo y Gómara," *Imago Mundi* (Buenos Aires), Year 1, no. 5 (1954), pp. 23–39.

Erasmo y España. Estudios sobre la historia espiritual del siglo XVI, 2nd edn. Mexico, Fondo de Cultura Económica, 1966.

Bates, Lincoln. "En pos de una civilización perdida: dos audaces viajeros del siglo XIX exploran la América Central," *Américas* (OAS), vol. 38, no. 1 (1986), pp. 34–9.

Belt, Thomas. *The Naturalist in Nicaragua*, with a foreword by Daniel H. Janzen. The University of Chicago Press, 1985.

Beneyto Pérez, Juan. "Los medios de cultura y la centralización bajo Felipe II," *Ciudad de Dios* (Valladolid), no. 150 (1927), pp. 184–99.

Benítez Rojo, Antonio. *El mar de las lentejas*. Havana, Editorial Letras Cubanas, 1979.

Bermúdez Plata, C. "Las obras de Antonio de Nebrija en América," *Anuario de Estudios Americanos*, 3 (1946), pp. 1029–32.

Bernaldo de Quirós, Constantino. *La picota en América*. Havana, Jesús Montero, 1948.

Nuevas noticias sobre picotas americanas. Havana, Jesús Montero, 1952.

Bernucci, Leopoldo. *Historia de un malentendido (un estudio transtextual de La guerra del fin del mundo de Mario Vargas Llosa)*. University of Texas Studies in Contemporary Spanish-American Fiction, vol. v. New York, Peter Lang, 1989.

"Além do real, aquém do imaginário: D. F. Sarmiento e E. da Cunha." Unpublished manuscript.

Bleiberg, Germán. "El 'Informe Secreto' de Mateo Alemán sobre el trabajo forzoso en las minas de Almadén," *Estudios de Historia Social* (Madrid), Year 1, nos. 2–3 (1977), pp. 357–443.

Bono, José. *Historia del derecho notarial español.* Madrid, Junta de Decanos de los Colegios Notariales de España, 1982, 2 vols.

Borges, Jorge Luis. *Ficciones.* Buenos Aires, Emecé, 1966 [1944]; *Ficciones*, several translators, ed. Anthony Kerrigan. New York, Grove Press, 1962.

Borgia Steck, Francisco, O.F.M. *El primer colegio de América, Santa Cruz de Tlatelolco. Con un estudio del Códice de Tlatelolco, por R. H. Barlow.* Mexico, Centro de Estudios Franciscanos, 1944.

Brody, Robert. "Mario Vargas Llosa and the Totalizing Impulse," *Texas Studies in Literature and Language,* 19, no. 4 (1977), pp. 514–21.

Cabrera Infante, Guillermo. *Tres tristes tigres.* Barcelona, Seix Barral, 1968.

Calatayud Arinero, María de los Angeles. *Catálogo de las expediciones y viajes científicos españoles siglos XVIII y XIX.* Madrid, Consejo Superior de Investigaciones Científicas, 1984.

Calvo, Julian. "El primer formulario jurídico publicado en la Nueva España, la *Política de escrituras* de Nicolás de Irolo. (1605)," *Revista de la Facultad de Derecho en México,* 1, nos. 3–4 (1951), pp. 41–102.

Candido, Antonio. *Introducción a la literatura de Brasil.* Caracas, Monte Avila, 1968.

Carbia, Rómulo D. *La crónica oficial de las Indias Occidentales. Estudio histórico y crítico de la historiografía mayor de Hispano-América en los siglos XVI a XVIII.* Buenos Aires, Biblioteca de Humanidades, 1934.

Carpentier, Alejo. *¡Ecué-Yamba-O!.* Madrid, Editorial España, 1933.
   La música en Cuba. Mexico, Fondo de Cultura Económica, 1946.
   "Los sertones," *El Nacional* (Caracas), 8 September (1951), p. 12.
   Tientos y diferencias. Montevideo, Arca, 1967 [1964].
   El arpa y la sombra. Mexico, Siglo XXI Editores, 1979.
   Los pasos perdidos, ed. Roberto González Echevarría. Madrid, Ediciones Cátedra, 1985 [1953]; *The Lost Steps,* tr. Harriet de Onís. New York, Alfred A. Knopf, 1956.

Carter, Paul. *The Road to Botany Bay: An Exploration of Landscape and History.* New York, Alfred A. Knopf, 1988.

Casas, Bartolomé de las. *Brevísima relación de la destrucción de las Indias,* ed. André Saint-Lu. Madrid, Cátedra, 1982.

Castanien, Daniel G. *El Inca Garcilaso de la Vega.* New York, Twayne, 1969.

Castro, Américo. *De la edad conflictiva.* Madrid, Taurus, 1961.

Castro-Klarén, Sara. "Locura y dolor: la elaboración de la historia en *Os Sertões* y *La guerra del fin del mundo*," *Revista de Crítica Literaria Latinoamericana* (Lima), Year 10, no. 20. (1984), pp. 207–31.

"*Santos* and *Cangaçeiros*: Inscription Without Discourse in *Os Sertões* and *La guerra del fin del mundo*," *Modern Language Notes*, 101, no. 2. (1986), pp. 366–88.

Caulin, Antonio. *Historia corográfica, natural y evangélica de la Nueva Andalucía, Provincias de Cumaná, Nueva Barcelona, Guayana y vertientes del río Orinoco.* Caracas, George Corser, 1841 [1779].

Centenario de la Ley del Notariado. Sección Primera. Estudios Históricos, vol. 1, Madrid, Junta de Decános de los Colegios Notariales de España, 1964.

Cevallos, Francisco J. "La retórica historiográfica y la aculturación en tres cronistas peruanos," *Revista de Estudios Hispánicos* (Vassar College, Poughkeepsie), 20, no. 3 (1986), pp. 55–66.

Christian, Chester C., Jr. "Hispanic Literature of Exploration," *Exploration* (Journal of the MLA Special Session on the Literature of Exploration and Travel), 1 (1973), pp. 42–6.

Clifford, James. *The Predicament of Culture: Twentieth-Century Ethnography, Literature, and Art.* Cambridge, Mass., Harvard University Press, 1988.

and George E. Marcus, eds., *Writing Culture: The Poetics and Politics of Ethnography.* Berkeley, University of California Press, 1982.

"Códice de leyes y ordenanzas para la gobernación de las Indias, y buen tratamiento y conservación de los indios (año de 1571)," *Colección de documentos inéditos, relativos al descubrimiento, conquista y organización de las antiguas posesiones españolas, de América y Oceanía sacados de los archivos del reino, y muy especialmente del de las Indias.* Madrid, Imprenta de José María Pérez, 1881, p. 458.

Colección de documentos inéditos relativos al descubrimiento, conquista y colonización de las posesiones españolas en América y Oceanía, sacados en su mayor parte, del Real Archivo de Indias. Madrid, Imprenta de Manuel B. Quirós, 1864–84.

Cordero, Carlos J. *Los relatos de los viajeros extranjeros posteriores a la Revolución de Mayo como fuentes de historia argentina. Ensayo de sistematización bibliográfica.* Buenos Aires, Imprenta y Casa Editora "Coni", 1936.

Cortázar, Julio. *Rayuela.* Buenos Aires, Editorial Sudamericana, 1966.

El libro de Manuel. Buenos Aires, Editorial Sudamericana, 1973.

Cox, R. Merrit. "Foreign Travelers in Eighteenth-Century Spain," *Studies in Eighteenth-Century Literature and Romanticism in Honor of John Clarkson Dowling*, ed. Douglas and Linda Jane Barnette. Newark, Delaware, Juan de la Cuesta, 1985, pp. 17–26.

Cozad, Mary Lee. "A Platonic–Aristotelian Linguistic Controversy of the Spanish Golden Age, Dámaso de Frías's *Diálogo de las lenguas* (1579)" in *Florilegium Hispanicum: Medieval and Golden Age Studies Presented to Dorothy Clotelle Clarke*, ed. John S. Geary. Madison, Wis., Seminary of Medieval Studies, 1983, pp. 203–27.

Cuesta, Luisa and Jaime Delgado. "Pleitos cortesianos en la Biblioteca Nacional," *Revista de Indias*, Year 9 (1948), pp. 247–95.

Cunha, Euclides da. *Canudos (diario de uma expedição)*, introduction by Gilberto Freyre. Rio de Janeiro, José Olympio, 1939.

    Os Sertões, edição crítica por Walnice Nogueira Galvão. São Paulo, Editora Brasiliense, S.A., 1985 [1902]. *Rebellion in the Backlands*, tr. Samuel Putnam. University of Chicago Press, 1944.

Cunningham, C. H. *The Audiencia in the Spanish Colonies*. Berkeley, University of California Publications in History, 1919.

Cutter, Donald C. "Early Spanish Artists on the Northwest Coast," *Pacific Northwest Quarterly*, 54 (1963), pp. 150–7.

    and Mercedes Palau de Iglesias. "Malaspina's Artists," *The Malaspina Expedition*. Santa Fe, Museum of New Mexico Press, 1963.

Darwin, Charles. *Charles Darwin's Diary of the Voyage of H.M.S. "Beagle"*, ed. Nora Barlow, Cambridge University Press, 1933.

    The Illustrated Origin of Species, abridged and introduced by Richard E. Leakey. New York, Hill and Wang, 1982 [1859].

    The Voyage of the Beagle, with introduction and notes. New York: The Harvard Classics, vol. XXIX, P. F. Collier and Son, Co., 1909.

Davis, Natalie Zemon. *Fiction in the Archives: Pardon Tales and Their Tellers in Sixteenth-Century France*. Stanford University Press, 1987.

De Man, Paul. "Dialogue and Dialogism" in his *The Resistance to Theory*. Minneapolis, University of Minnesota Press, 1986, pp. 106–14.

Diawara, Manthia. "The Other('s) Archivist," *Diacritics*, 18, no. 1 (1988), pp. 66–74.

Díaz de Toledo, Fernando. *Las notas del relator con otras muchas añadidas. Agora nuevamente impresas y de nuevo añadidas las cosas siguientes primeramente. Las notas breves para examinar los escrivanos. Carta de afletar navíos. Carta o poliza de seguros.* Nuevamente Impressos en Burgos, año 1531.

Domínguez, Ivo. *El derecho como recurso literario en las novelas ejemplares de Cervantes*. Montevideo, Publicaciones Lingüísticas y Literarias del Instituto de Estudios Superiores de Montevideo, 1972.

Domínguez, Jorge I. *Insurrection or Loyalty: The Breakdown of the Spanish Empire*. Cambridge, Mass., Harvard University Press, 1980.

Dorward, Frances R. "The Evolution of Mexican *indigenista* Literature in the Twentieth Century," *Revista interamericana de bibliografía/Inter-American Review of Bibliography*, 37, no. 2 (1987), pp. 145–59.

Durán Luzio, Juan. *Creación y utopía, letras de hispanoamérica*. San José, Costa Rica, Editorial de la Universidad Nacional, 1979.

Echeverría, Esteban. "El matadero" in *El cuento hispanoamericano. Antología crítico-histórica*, ed., Seymour Menton, 3rd edn. Mexico, Fondo de Cultura Económica, 1986, pp. 13–33; "The Slaughterhouse" in *The Borzoi Anthology of Latin American Literature*, ed. Emir Rodríguez Monegal. New York, Alfred A. Knopf, 1977, vol. 1, pp. 209–22.

Echevarría, Evelio A. "La conquista del Chimborazo," *Américas* (OAS), vol. 35, no. 5 (1983), pp. 22–31.

Elliott, J. H. *Imperial Spain 1469–1716*. New York, St. Martin's Press, 1966.

"The Mental World of Hernán Cortés," *Transactions of the Royal Historical Society*, 5th series, 17 (1967), pp. 41–58.

Spain and its World 1500–1700. Selected Essays. New Haven, Yale University Press, 1989.

Englekirk, John E. "Doña Bárbara, Legend of the Llano," *Hispania* (AATSP), 31 (1948), pp. 259–70.

Engstrand, Iris H. W. *Spanish Scientists in the New World: The Eighteenth-Century Expeditions*. Seattle, University of Washington Press, 1981.

Europe Informed. An Exhibition of Early Books Which Acquainted Europe with the East. Cambridge, Mass., Harvard College Library – Sixth International Colloquium on Luso-Brasilian Studies, 1966.

Exotic Printing and the Expansion of Europe, 1492–1840, An Exhibit. Bloomington, Lilly Library–Indiana University, 1972.

Faulhaber, Charles B. *Latin Rhetorical Theory in Thirteenth Century Castile*. Berkeley, University of California Publications in Modern Philology No. 103, 1972.

"The *Summa* of Guido Faba" in *Medieval Eloquence: Studies in the Theory and Practice of Medieval Rhetoric*, ed. James J. Murphy. Berkeley, University of California Press, 1978, pp. 85–111.

Fernández, Diego. *Primera y segunda parte de la historia del Perú* in Biblioteca de Autores Españoles, vols. 164–5, ed. Juan Pérez de Tudela Bueso. Madrid, Ediciones Atlas, 1963.

Fish, Stanley. "Interpretation and the Pluralist Vision," *Texas Law Review*, 60, no. 3 (1982), pp. 495–505.

Foucault, Michel. *Les Mots et les choses*. Paris, Gallimard, 1966.

L'Archéologie du savoir. Paris, Gallimard, 1969; *The Archaeology of Knowledge and The Discourse on Language*, tr. A. M. Sheridan Smith. New York, Pantheon Books, 1972.

Surveiller et punir. Paris, Gallimard, 1975.

Language, Countermemory, Practice, ed. Donald F. Bouchard. Ithaca, Cornell University Press, 1977.

Franco, Jean. "Un viaje poco romántico: viajeros británicos hacia Sudamérica, 1818–28," *Escritura* (Caracas), Year 4, no. 7 (1979), pp. 129–41.

Frazer, James G. *The Golden Bough: The Roots of Religion and Folklore*. New York, Avenel Books, 1981 [1890].

Freedman, Ralph. "The Possibility of a Theory of the Novel" in *The Disciplines of Criticism: Essays in Literary Interpretation and History*, eds. Peter Demetz, Thomas Greene and Lowry Nelson Jr. New Haven, Yale University Press, 1968, pp. 57–77.

Fuentes, Carlos. *La nueva novela hispanoamericana*. Mexico, Joaquín Mortiz, 1969.

    Aura, bilingual edition, tr. Lysander Kemp. New York, Farrar, Strauss and Giroux, 1975 [1962].

    Terra Nostra. Mexico, Joaquín Mortiz, 1975.

Gallegos, Rómulo. *Doña Bárbara*. Mexico, Fondo de Cultura Económica, 1975 [1929].

    Una posición en la vida, 1909–1947. Caracas, Ediciones Centauro, 1977.

García Márquez, Gabriel. *Crónica de una muerte anunciada*. Bogotá, Editorial La Oveja Negra, 1981; *Chronicle of a Death Foretold*, tr. Gregory Rabassa. New York, Alfred A. Knopf, 1983.

    El olor de la guayaba. Conversación con Plinio Apuleyo Mendoza. Bogotá, Editorial La Oveja Negra, 1982.

Speech accepting the Nobel Prize. *El Mundo*. San Juan de Puerto Rico, Sunday, 12 December 1982, p. 21-c. An English translation of this address appears in *Gabriel García Márquez. New Readings*, ed. Bernard McGuirk and Richard Cardwell. Cambridge University Press, 1987, pp. 207–11.

    Cien años de soledad, ed. Jacques Joset. Madrid, Cátedra, 1984 [1967]; *One Hundred Years of Solitude*, tr. Gregory Rabassa. New York, Harper & Row, 1970.

    El amor en los tiempos del cólera. Barcelona, Brugera, 1985; *Love in the Time of Cholera*, tr. Edith Grossman. New York, Alfred A. Knopf, 1988.

García Villada, Z. "Formularios de las bibliotecas y archivos de Barcelona siglos x–xv," *Anuari de l'Institut de Estudis Catalans*, 4 (1911–12), pp. 533–52.

Gardiner, C. Harvey. "Foreign Traveler's Accounts of Mexico, 1810–1910," *Américas* (OAS), vol. 8 (1952), pp. 321–51.

Geertz, Clifford. *Works and Lives: The Anthropologist as Author*. Stanford University Press, 1988.

Gerbi, Antonello. *Nature in the New World from Christopher Columbus to Gonzalo Fernandez de Oviedo*, tr. Jeremy Moyle. University of Pittsburgh Press, 1985 [original 1975].

Gibson, Charles. *Spain in America*. New York, Colophon Books, 1966.

Goethe, Johann Wolfgang. *Italienische Reise, Goethes Werke*. Hamburg, Christian Wegner Verlag, 1950 [1967], vol. 11.

Gómara, Francisco López de. *La historia general de las Indias, con todos los descubrimientos, y cosas notables que han acaescido en ellas dende que se ganaron hasta agora*. Antwerp, Casa de Juan Steelsio, 1553.

González, Eduardo G. *Alejo Carpentier: el tiempo del hombre*. Caracas, Monte Avila, 1978.

González Echevarría, Roberto. "With Borges in Macondo." *Diacritics*, 2, no. 1 (1972), pp. 57–60.

Alejo Carpentier: The Pilgrim at Home. Ithaca, Cornell University Press, 1977.

"The Life and Adventures of Cipión, Cervantes and the Picaresque," *Diacritics*, 10, no. 3 (1980), pp. 15–26.

The Voice of the Masters: Writing and Authority in Modern Latin American Literature. Austin, University of Texas Press, 1985.

La ruta de Severo Sarduy. Hanover, New Hampshire, Ediciones del Norte, 1987.

Goodman, Edward J. *The Explorers of South America*. New York, The Macmillan Co., 1972.

The Exploration of South America: An Annotated Bibliography. New York, Garland Publishing Co., 1983.

Guaman Poma de Ayala, Felipe. *El primer Corónica y buen gobierno*, eds. John V. Murra and Rolena Adorno, translations and textual analysis of the Quechua by Jorge L. Urioste. Mexico, Siglo XXI Editores, 1980. 3 vols.

Hagen, Victor Wolfgang von. *South America Called Them. Explorations of the Great Naturalists La Condamine, Humbold, Darwin, Spruce*. New York, Alfred A. Knopf, 1945.

Halperin Donghi, T. *Politics, Economics, and Society in Argentina in the Revolutionary Period*. Cambridge University Press, 1975.

Hanke, Lewis. "The *Requerimiento* and Its Interpreters," *Revista de Historia de América*, no. 1 (1938), pp. 25–34.

The Spanish Struggle for Justice in the Conquest of America. Philadelphia, University of Pennsylvania Press, 1949.

"La villa imperial de Potosí," *Revista Shell*, no. 42 (1962), pp. 4–10.

Haring, C. H. *Las instituciones coloniales de Hispanoamérica siglos XVI a XVIII*. San Juan, Puerto Rico, Instituto de Cultura Puertorriqueña, 1957.

The Spanish Empire in America. New York, Harcourt, Brace, and World, 1963 [1947].

Hassaurek, Friedrich. *Four Years Among the Ecuadorians*, ed. C. Harvey Gardiner. Carbondale, Southern Illinois University Press, 1967 [1867].

Haverstock, Mary Sayre. "The Cosmos Recaptured," *Americas* (OAS), vol. 35, no. 1 (1983), pp. 37–41.

Head, Francis Bond. *Journeys Across the Pampas and Among the Andes*, ed. C. Harvey Gardiner. Carbondale, Southern Illinois University Press, 1967 [1826].

Headrick, Daniel R. *The Tools of Empire: Technology and European Imperialism in the Nineteenth Century*. New York, Oxford University Press, 1981.

Hegel, G. H. F. *The Philosophy of History*, intr. C. J. Friedrich. New York, Dover Publications, 1956.

Henríquez Ureña, Pedro. *Las corrientes literarias en la América hispánica*. Mexico, Fondo de Cultura Económica, 1949.

"La cultura y las letras coloniales en Santo Domingo" in his *Obra crítica*, ed. Emma Susana Speratti Piñero, prologue by Jorge Luis Borges. Mexico, Fondo de Cultura Económica, 1960, pp. 331–444.

Historia de la cultura en la América Hispánica. Mexico, Fondo de Cultura Económica, 1964 [1947].

Hentschel, Cedric. "Zur Synthese von Literatur und Naturwissenschaft beim Alexander von Humboldt" in *Alexander von Humboldt: Werk und Weltgeltung*, ed. Heinrich Pfeiffer. Munich, Piper, 1969, pp. 31–95.

Heredia Herrera, Antonia M. "Los cedularios de oficio y de partes del Consejo de Indias: sus tipos documentales, s. XVII," *Anuario de Estudios Americanos* (Seville), 29 (1972), pp. 1–60.

"Las cartas de los virreyes de Nueva España a la corona española, en el siglo XVI. Características diplomáticas, índices cronológicos y de materias," *Anuario de Estudios Americanos* (Seville), 31 (1974), pp. 441–596.

"La carta como tipo diplomático indiano," *Anuario de Estudios Americanos* (Seville), 34 (1977), pp. 65–95.

Herman, Susan. "The *Conquista y descubrimiento del Nuevo Reino de Granada*. Otherwise Known as *El Carnero*: the *corónica*, the *historia*, and the *novela*," Doctoral dissertation, Yale University, 1978.

Hernández, Max and Fernando Saba. "Garcilaso Inca de la Vega, historia de un patronímico" in *Perú: identidad nacional*. Lima, Centro de Estudios para el Desarrollo y la Participación, 1979, pp. 109–21.

Herrera y Tordesillas, Antonio de. *Historia general de los hechos de los castellanos en las islas i tierra firme del mar Océano*. Madrid, Imprenta Real–Juan Flamenco, 1601.

Herrero, Javier. "The Great Icons of the *Lazarillo*: the Bull, the Wine, the Sausage and the Turnip," *Ideologies and Literatures*, 1, no. 5 (1978), pp. 3–18.

Hilton, Ronald. "The Significance of Travel Literature With Special Reference to the Spanish and Portuguese Speaking World," *Hispania* (AATSP), 49 (1966), pp. 836–45.

Humboldt, Alexander von. *Voyage aux régions équinoxiales du Nouveau Continent, fait en 1799, 1800, 1801, 1802, 1803 et 1804, par Al. de Humbold et A. Bonpland*. Paris, Librairie Grecque–Latine–Allemande, 1816.

Iglesia, Ramón. *Vida del Almirante don Cristóbal Colón escrita por su hijo don Hernando*, edited with a prologue and note by Ramón Iglesia. Mexico: Fondo de Cultura Económica, 1947.

Ilgen, William D. "La configuración mítica de la historia en los *Comentarios reales* del Inca Garcilaso de la Vega," *Estudios de literatura hispanoamericana en honor de José J. Arrom*, eds. Andrew P. Debicki and Enrique Pupo-Walker. Chapel Hill: North Carolina Studies in the Romance Languages and Literatures, 1974, pp. 37–46.

Irby, James E. "Borges and the Idea of Utopia," *Books Abroad*, 45, no. 3 (1971), pp. 411–19.

Johnson, Julie Greer. *The Book in the Americas: The Role of Books and Printing in the Development of Culture and Society in Colonial Latin America*. Providence, The John Carter Brown Library, 1988.

Kagan, Richard L. *Students and Society in Early Modern Spain*. Baltimore, The Johns Hopkins University Press, 1974.

Karsen, Sonja, "Charles Marie de la Condamine's Travels in Latin America," *Revista Interamericana de Bibliografía/Inter-American Review of Bibliography*, 36, no. 3 (1986), pp. 315–23.

Keniston, Hayward. *Francisco de los Cobos: Secretary of the Emperor Charles V.* University of Pittsburgh Press, 1958.

Klinkenborg, Verlyn. "Introduction" to *Sir Francis Drake and the Age of Discovery*. New York, The Pierpont Morgan Library, 1988.

Koenigsberger, H. G. *The Practice of Empire: Emended Edition of The Government of Sicily under Philip II of Spain*. Ithaca, Cornell University Press, 1969.

Kristal, Efraín. *The Andes Viewed from the City: Literary and Political Discourse on the Indian in Peru 1848–1930*. New York, Peter Lang, 1987.

Kubler, George. "The Neo-Inca State (1537–1572)," *Hispanic American Historical Review*, 27, no. 2 (1947), pp. 189–203.

Lévi-Strauss, Claude. *Tristes tropiques*, tr. John and Doreen Weightman. New York, Atheneum, 1974 [1955].

Lezama Lima, José. *Las eras imaginarias*. Madrid, Fundamentos, 1971.

Oppiano Licario. Havana, Editorial Arte y Literatura, 1977.

López-Baralt, Mercedes. "*Cien años de soledad*: cultura e historia latinoamericanas replanteadas en el idioma del parentesco," *Revista de Estudios Hispánicos* (San Juan de Puerto Rico), Year 6 (1979), pp. 153–75.

Lovejoy, Arthur O. *The Great Chain of Being*. Cambridge, Mass., Harvard University Press, 1936.

Luis, William. *Literary Bondage: Slavery in Cuban Narrative*. Austin, University of Texas Press, 1990.

Luján Muñoz, Jorge. "La literatura notarial en España e Hispanoamérica, 1500–1820," *Anuario de Estudios Americanos* (Seville), 18 (1981), pp. 101–16.

Lukács, Georg. *The Theory of the Novel: A Historico-Philosophical Essay on the Forms of Great Epic Literature*, tr. Anna Bostock. Cambridge, The MIT Press, 1971 [original German publication, 1920].

Malagón Barceló, Javier. *El distrito de la audiencia de Santo Domingo en los siglos XVI a XIX*. Santo Domingo, Editora Montalvo, 1942.

"The Role of the *Letrado* in the Colonization of America," *The Americas*, 18, no. 1 (1961), pp. 1–7.

Márquez Villanueva, Francisco. "Letrados, consejeros y justicias (artículo–reseña)" *Hispanic Review*, 53 (1985), pp. 201–27.

Martin, Claire. "Alejo Carpentier y las crónicas de Indias: orígenes de una escritura americana," unpublished Ph.D. dissertation, Yale University, 1988.

Martz, John D. *Acción democrática: Evolution of a Modern Political Party in Venezuela*. Princeton University Press, 1966, pp. 49–106.

Mena, Lucila I. "La huelga de la compañía bananera como expresión de 'lo real maravilloso' americano en *Cien años de soledad*," *Bulletin Hispanique*, 74 (1972), pp. 379–405.

Méndez Rodenas, Adriana. "A Journey to the (Literary) Source: The Invention of Origins in Merlin's *Viaje a La Habana*," Unpublished manuscript.

Menéndez Pidal, Ramón. "Idea Imperial de Carlos V" in his *Mis páginas preferidas. Estudios lingüísticos e históricos*. Madrid, Gredos, 1957, pp. 232–53.

México ilustrado por Europa del Renacimiento al Romanticismo. Catalogue of an exhibition presented at the Palacio de Iturbide, Mexico City, from 24 March to 30 June 1983.

Miller, Christopher L. *Blank Darkness: Africanist Discourse in French*. University of Chicago Press, 1985.

"Theories of Africans: The Question of Literary Anthropology," *Critical Inquiry*, 13, no. 1 (1986), pp. 120–39.

Mohanty, S. P. "Us and Them: On the Philosophical Bases of Political Criticism," *The Yale Journal of Criticism*, 2, no. 2 (1989), pp. 1–31.

Mohler, Stephen C. "Publishing in Colonial Spanish America; An Overview," *Revista Interamericana de Bibliografía/Inter-American Review of Bibliography*, 28 (1978), pp. 259–73.

Molinari, Diego Luis. "Naturalidad y connaturalización en el derecho de Indias," *Revista Jurídica y de Ciencias Sociales* (Buenos Aires), Year 32 (1915), pp. 698–714.

Montero Díaz, Santiago. "La doctrina de la historia en los tratadistas españoles del Siglo de Oro," *Hispania. Revista Española de Historia* (Madrid), 4 (1941), pp. 3–39.

Morales Padrón, Francisco, ed. "Capitulaciones de Santa Fe," *Teoría y leyes de la Conquista*. Madrid, Ediciones Cultura Hispánica, 1979.

Moreno Fraginals, Manuel. Review of *Biografía de un cimarrón* in *Casa de las Américas*, no. 40 (1967), p. 132.

El ingenio: complejo económico-social del azúcar, 2nd edn. Havana, Editorial de Ciencias Sociales, 1978; *The Sugarmill*, tr. Cedric Belfrage. New York, Monthly Press, 1976.

Morse, Richard M. "Political Foundations" in *Man, State and Society in Latin American History*, eds. Sheldon B. Liss and Peggy K. Liss. New York, Praeger Publishers, 1972, pp. 72–8.

Motolinía, Fray Toribio de. *Historia de los indios de la nueva España*, ed. Georges Baudot. Madrid, Castalia, 1985.

Muro Orejón, Antonio, ed. *Pleitos colombinos*. Seville, Escuela de Estudios Hispanoamericanos, 1964.

Núñez Cabeza de Vaca, Alvar. *Naufragios*, ed. Enrique Pupo-Walker, Madrid, Editorial Castalia, 1990.

Núñez Lagos, Rafael. *El documento medieval y Rolandino (notas de historia)*. Madrid, Imprenta Góngora, 1951.

Núñez, Luján, Jorge. *Los escribanos en las Indias Occidentales y en particular en el Reino de Guatemala*. Guatemala City, Instituto Guatemalteco de Derecho Notarial, 1977.

Ortiz, Fernando. "La Sociedad de Estudios Afrocubanos Contra Racismos. Advertencia, compresión y designio," *Estudios Afrocubanos* (Havana) 1, no. 1 (1937), pp. 3–6.

Hampa Afro-Cubana. Los negros brujos. Apuntes para un estudio de etnología criminal, ed. Alberto N. Pamies. Miami, Ediciones Universal, 1973 [1906].

Osorio Romero, Ignacio. ¯*Floresta de gramática, política y retórica en Nueva España (1521–1767)*. Mexico, Universidad Nacional Autónoma de México, 1980.

Ots Capdequí, J. M. *El estado español en las Indias*, 2nd edn. Mexico, Fondo de Cultura Económica, 1946 [1941].

Palop, Josefina. "El Brasil visto por los viajeros alemanes," *Revista de Indias*, Year 21, no. 83 (1961), pp. 107–27.

Pané, Ramón. *Relación acerca de las antigüedades de los indios: el primer tratado escrito en América*, in a new version with notes, map and appendices by José Juan Arrom. Mexico, Siglo XXI Editores, 1974.

Parry, J. H. *The Audiencia of New Galicia: A Study in Spanish Colonial Government*. Cambridge University Press, 1948.

The Spanish Theory of Empire in the Sixteenth Century. New York, Octagon Books, 1974 [1940].

Paso, Fernando del. *Noticias del Imperio*. Mexico, Editorial Diana, 1987.

Passaggeri, Rolandino. *Aurora, con las adiciones de Pedro de Unzola*, versión al castellano del Illmo. Señor Don Víctor Vicente Vela, y del Excmo Señor don Rafael Núñez Lagos. Madrid, Ilustre Colegio Notarial de Madrid–Imprenta Góngora, 1950.

Paz, Octavio. *Lévi-Strauss o el nuevo festín de Esopo*. Mexico, Mortiz, 1968.

Peña y Cámara, José María de la. *Archivo General de Indias de Sevilla. Guía del*

visitante. Valencia, Dirección General de Archivos y Bibliotecas–
Tipografía Moderna, 1958.

Phelan, John Leddy. "Authority and Flexibility in the Spanish Imperial
Bureaucracy," *Administrative Science Quarterly* (Cornell University), 5,
no. 1 (1960).

Picón Salas, Mariano. *A Cultural History of Spanish America: From Conquest to
Independence*, tr. Irving A. Leonard. Berkeley, University of California
Press, 1962 [1944].

Posner, Richard. *Law and Literature: A Misunderstood Relation*. Cambridge,
Mass., Harvard University Press, 1988.

Pratt, Mary Louise. "Scratches on the Face of the Country; What Mr.
Barrow Saw in the Land of the Bushmen," *Critical Inquiry*, 12, no. 1
(1985), pp. 119–43.

"Fieldwork in Common Places" in *Writing Culture: The Poetics and Politics
of Ethnography*, ed. James Clifford and George E. Marcus. Berkeley,
University of California Press, 1986, pp. 27–50.

Price, Richard. *Maroon Societies: Rebel Communities in the Americas*. New York,
Anchor Books, 1973.

Prieto, René. "The New American Idiom of Miguel Angel Asturias,"
Hispanic Review. 56 (1988), pp. 191–208.

Pupo-Walker, Enrique. *Historia, creación y profecía en los textos del Inca
Garcilaso de la Vega*. Madrid, José Porrúa Turanzas, 1982.

*La vocación literaria del pensamiento histórico en América. Desarrollo de la prosa
de ficción: siglos XVI, XVII, XVIII y XIX*. Madrid, Gredos, 1982.

Rachowiecki, Rob "The Lost World of Venezuela," *Américas* (OAS) 40,
no. 5 (1988), p. 44–9, 64–5.

Rama, Angel. *La ciudad letrada*. Hanover, New Hampshire, Ediciones del
Norte, 1984.

Rearick, Charles. *Pleasures of the Belle Epoque: Entertainment and Festivity in
Turn-of-the-Century France*. New Haven, Yale University Press, 1985.

Recopilación de las leyes de los reynos de las Indias. Madrid, Consejo de la
Hispanidad, 1943, 3 vols.

Ricard, Robert. *La Conquête spirituelle du Méxique. Essai sur l'apostolat et les
missionaires des Ordres Mendiants en Nouvelle-Espagne de 1523–24 à 1572*
(Paris, Institut d'Ethnologie, 1933). Translated as: *The Spiritual Con-
quest of Mexico: An Essay on the Apostolate and Evangelizing Methods of the
Mendicant Orders in New Spain: 1523–1572* by Lesley Byrd Sympson.
Berkeley, University of California Press, 1966 [1933].

Roa Bastos, Augusto. *Yo el Supremo*. Buenos Aires, Siglo XXI, Editores,
1974.

Rockinger, Ludwig, ed. *Briefsteller und Formelbucher des elften bis vierzehnten
Jahrhunderts*. New York, B. Franklin, 1961 [1863–64]. 2 vols.

Rodrigues, Selma Calasans. "*Cien años de soledad* y las crónicas de la conquista," *Revista de la Universidad de México*, 38, no. 23 (1983), pp. 13–16.

Rodríguez-Buckingham, Antonio. "The Establishment, Production and Equipment of the First Printing Press in South America," *Harvard Library Bulletin*, 26, no. 3 (1978), pp. 342–54.

Rodríguez Freyle, Juan. *El Carnero. Conquista y descubrimiento del Nuevo Reino de Granada de las Indias Occidentales del Mar Océano* .... Bogotá, Bolsilibros Bedout, 1973 [1636]; *The Conquest of New Granada*, tr. William C. Atkinson. London, Folio Society, 1961.

Rodríguez Monegal, Emir. *El Boom de la novela latinoamericana*. Caracas, Editorial Tiempo Nuevo, 1972.

"*One Hundred Years of Solitude*: The Last Three Pages," *Books Abroad*, 47 (1973), pp. 485–9.

"Borges and Politics," *Diacritics*, 8, no. 4 (1978), pp. 55–69.

ed. *The Borzoi Anthology of Latin American Literature*. New York, Alfred A. Knopf, 1977, 2 vols.

Rojas-Mix, Miguel. "Las ideas artístico-científicas de Humboldt y su influencia en los artistas naturalistas que pasan a América a mediados del siglo XIX" in *Nouveau monde et renouveau de l'histoire naturelle*, présentation M. C. Bénassy-Berling. Paris, Service des Publications Université de la Sorbonne Nouvelle, Paris III, 1986, pp. 85–114.

Romero de Castilla y Perosso, Francisco. *Apuntes históricos sobre el Archivo General de Simancas*. Madrid, Imprenta y Estereotipía de Aribau y Co., 1873.

Roth, Michael Palencia. "Los pergaminos de Aureliano Babilonia," *Revista Iberoamericana*, nos. 123–4 (1983), pp. 403–17.

Rowe, John Howland. "The Incas Under Spanish Colonial Institutions," *Hispanic American Historical Review*, 37, no. 2 (1957), pp. 155–99.

Sahlins, Marshall. *Islands of History*. University of Chicago Press, 1985.

Said, Edward W. *Orientalism*. New York, Vintage Books, 1979.

"Representing the Colonized: Anthropology's Interlocutors," *Critical Inquiry*, 15, no. 2 (1989), pp. 205–25.

Salvadorini, Vittorio. "Las 'relaciones' de Hernán Cortés," *Thesaurus (Boletín del Instituto Caro y Cuervo)*, 18, no. 1 (1963), pp. 77–97.

Sanziti, Gary. "A Humanist Historian and His Documents: Giovanni Simonetta, Secretary to the Sforzas," *Renaissance Quarterly* 34, no. 4 (1981), pp. 491–516.

Sarduy, Severo. *Cobra*. Buenos Aires, Sudamericana, 1972.

Sarfatti, Magali. *Spanish Bureaucratic Patrimonialism in America*. Berkeley, Institute of International Studies, 1966.

Sarmiento, Domingo F. *Conflicto y armonías de las razas en América*. Buenos Aires, "La Cultura Argentina," 1915.

Facundo o civilización y barbarie en las pampas argentinas, text established with prologue and appendices by Moglia, xylographs by Nicasio. Buenos Aires, Ediciones Peuser, 1955; *Life in the Argentine Republic in the Days of the Tyrants; or Civilization and Barbarism.* First American edition based on the third Spanish edition, New York, 1868 [Reprint 1960 Hafner Library of Classics].

Schafer, Ernst. *El Consejo Real y Supremo de las Indias. Su historia, organización y labor administrativa hasta la terminación de la Casa de Austria.* Seville, Publicaciones del Centro de Estudios de Historia de América, 1933–47.

Schatzberg, Walter, Ronald A. Waite, and Jonathan K. Johnson, eds. *The Relations of Literature and Science: An Annotated Bibliography of Scholarship, 1880–1980.* New York, The Modern Language Association of America, 1987.

Schomburgk, Moritz Richard. *Reisen in Britisch-Guiana in den jahren 1840–1844.* Leipzig, J. J. Wever, 1847–8.

Schwartz Lerner, Lía. "El letrado en la sátira de Quevedo," *Hispanic Review,* 54 (1986), pp. 27–46.

Seigel, Jerrold E. *Rhetoric and Philosophy in Renaissance Humanism: The Union of Eloquence and Wisdom, Petrarch to Valla.* Princeton University Press, 1968.

Shattuck, Roger. *The Banquet Years: The Origins of the Avant-Garde in France, 1885 to World War I,* revised edn. New York, Vintage Books, 1968.

Shaw, Donald. "Towards a Description of the Post-Boom," *Bulletin of Hispanic Studies,* 66 (1989), pp. 87–94.

Sieber, Harry. *Language and Society in La vida de Lazarillo de Tormes.* Baltimore, The Johns Hopkins University Press, 1978.

Silva Herzog, Jesús. *Breve historia de la Revolución Mexicana.* 2nd edn. Mexico, Fondo de Cultura Económica, 1962.

Simpson, George Gaylord. *Splendid Isolation: The Curious History of South American Mammals.* New Haven, Yale University Press, 1980.

Discoverers of the Lost World: An Account of Some of Those Who Brought Back to Life South American Mammals Long Buried in the Abyss of Time. New Haven, Yale University Press, 1984.

Simpson, Lesley Byrd. *The Encomienda in New Spain: The Beginnings of Spanish Mexico.* Berkeley, University of California Press, 1966 [1929].

Stabb, Martin S. "El continente enfermo y sus diagnosticadores" in his *América Latina en busca de una identidad.* Caracas, Monte Avila, 1969.

Stafford, Barbara. "Rude Sublime: The Taste for Nature's Colossi ..." *Gazette des Beaux Arts* (April 1976), pp. 113–26.

Steele, Arthur Robert. *Flowers for the King: The Expedition of Ruiz and Pavón and the Flora of Peru.* Durham, Duke University Press, 1964.

Stepan, Nancy. *Beginnings of Brazilian Science: Oswaldo Cruz, Medical Research and Policy, 1890–1920.* New York, Science History Publications, 1976.

The Idea of Race in Science: Great Britain 1800–1960. New Haven, Archon Books, 1982.

Stocking, George W., Jr. *Victorian Anthropology*. New York, The Free Press, 1987.

Stolley, Karen Anne. "*El Lazarillo de ciegos caminantes*: un itinerario crítico," Ph.D. dissertation, Yale University, 1985.

Taussing, Michael. *Shamanism: A Study in Colonialism, and Terror and the Wild Man Healing*. University of Chicago Press, 1987.

Tobin, Patricia. *Time and the Novel: The Genealogical Imperative*. Princeton University Press, 1978.

Todorov, Tzevetan. *Michaïl Bakhtine. Le principe dialogique*, followed by Ecrits du Cercle de Bakhtine. Paris, Editions du Seuil, 1981.

Torre Revello, José. *Los artistas pintores de la expedición Malaspina*. Buenos Aires, Universidad de Buenos Aires – Instituto de Investigaciones Históricas de la Facultad de Filosofía y Letras, 1944.

"Las cartillas para enseñar a leer a los niños en América española," *Thesaurus*, 15 (1960), pp. 214–34.

"La enseñanza de las lenguas a los naturales de América," *Thesaurus*, 17, no. 3 (1962), pp. 501–26.

Trifilo, Samuel. "Nineteenth-century English Travel Books on Argentina: A Revival in Spanish Translation," *Hispania* (AATSP), 41 (1958), pp. 491–6.

van Acker, Gertrui. "The Creed in a Nahuatl Schoolbook of 1569," *LIAS. Sources and Documents Relating to the Early Modern History of Ideas* (Amsterdam), 11, no. 1 (1984), pp. 117–36.

Vargas Llosa, Mario. *García Márquez: historia de un deicidio*. Barcelona, Barral Editores, 1971.

El hablador. Barcelona, Seix Barral, 1987.

Varner, John Grier. *El Inca: The Life and Times of Garcilaso de la Vega*. Austin, University of Texas Press, 1968.

Vega, Garcilaso de la. *Obras completas del Inca Garcilaso de la Vega*. Edited with an introduction by P. Carmelo Sáenz de Santa María, S.I., Madrid, Biblioteca de Autores Españoles, 1963, 4 vols; *Royal Commentaries of the Incas and General History of Peru*, tr. with an introduction by Harold V. Livermore, foreword by Arnold J. Toynbee. Austin, University of Texas Press, 1966, 2 vols.

The Florida of the Inca, tr. John Grier Varner and Jeannette Johnson Varner. Austin, University of Texas Press, 1980.

Véliz, Claudio. *The Centralist Tradition of Latin America*. Princeton University Press, 1980.

Weber, Max. "Bureaucracy" in *From Max Weber*, tr. H. H. Gerth and C. Wright Mills (New York, Oxford University Press, 1946), pp. 196–244.

Welch, Thomas L. and Myriam Figueras. *Travel Accounts and Descriptions of Latin America and the Caribbean, 1800–1920: A Selective Bibliography*, with a foreword by Val T. McComie. Washington, D.C., Organization of American States, 1982.

Wilgus, A. Curtis. "Viajeros del siglo XIX: Henry Marie Brackenridge," *Americas* (OAS), vol. 24, no. 4 (1972), pp. 31–6.

Zamora, Margarita. "Language and Authority in the *Comentarios reales*," *Modern Language Quarterly*, 43 (1982), pp. 228–41.

Language, Authority, and Indigenous History in the Comentarios reales de los incas. Cambridge University Press, 1988.

Zárate, Agustín de. *Historia del descubrimiento y conquista de la provincia del Peru, y de las guerras, y cosas señaladas en ella, acaecidas hasta el vencimiento de Gonzalo Pizarro, y de sus sequaces, que en ella se rebelaron, contra su Magestad,* in *Historiadores primitivos de las Indias Occidentales*, que juntó, tradujo en parte, y sacó a la luz, ilustrados con eruditas notas, y copiosos indices, el ilustrisimo señor D. Andrés González Barcia. Madrid, Imprenta de Francisco Martínez Abad, 1749.

Zárate, Armando. *Facundo Quiroga, Barranca Yaco: juicios y testimonios.* Buenos Aires, Editorial Plus Ultra, 1985.

Zavala, Iris M. "*Cien años de soledad*, crónica de Indias," *Insula*, no. 286 (1970), pp. 3, 11.

Zavala, Silvio. *Las instituciones jurídicas en la Conquista de América.* 2nd edn. Mexico, Porrúa, 1971 [1935].

Index

Roberto González Echevarría is Sterling Professor of Hispanic
and Comparative Literatures at Yale University.

Library of Congress Cataloging-in-Publication Data

González Echevarría, Roberto.
Myth and archive : a theory of Latin American narrative / Roberto
González Echevarría.
p.   cm.
Includes bibliographical references and index.
ISBN 0-8223-2194-7 (alk. paper)
1. Latin American fiction—History and criticism—Theory, etc.
2. Narration (Rhetoric)   3. Myth in literature.   4. Literature and
history.   I. Title.
PQ7082.N7G68   1998
863.009'98—dc21   97-32274